Barcode in Back-

MW01518907

Girls Behind Bars

Girls Behind Bars

Reclaiming
Education in Transformative Spaces

Suniti Sharma

B L O O M S B U R Y
NEW YORK · LONDON · NEW DELHI · SYDNEY

Bloomsbury Academic

An imprint of Bloomsbury Publishing Plc

175 Fifth Avenue	50 Bedford Square
New York	London
NY 10010	WC1B 3DP
USA	UK

www.bloomsbury.com

First published 2013

Library of Congress Cataloging-in-Publication Data
Sharma, Suniti.
Girls behind bars : reclaiming education in transformative spaces / Suniti Sharma.
p. cm.
Includes bibliographical references and index.
ISBN 978-1-4411-5232-9 (hardcover : alk. paper) 1. Female juvenile
delinquents–Education–United States. 2. Education–United States–Biographical
methods. 3. Juvenile detention–United States. I. Title.
HV9081.S53 2012
365'.666–dc23

2012020235

ISBN: HB: 978-1-4411-5232-9
PDF: 978-1-4411-1124-1
ePub: 978-1-4411-8675-1

Typeset by Newgen Imaging System Pvt Ltd, Chennai, India
Printed and bound in the United States of America

Contents

Foreword

Training Cages: Young Women Trapped

Prisons have sprung up like weeds in every corner of the American landscape. Aggressive, hearty, resilient, and resistant, a carceral system powered by its own self-justifying internal logic and mechanisms, mass incarceration and a vast prison-industrial complex has become the fundamental feature of contemporary US society. There are more African-American men in prison, on probation or parole than were enslaved in 1850; there are more women, men and children—over six million—under correctional supervision than were in Stalin's *Gulag*; more than 50,000 men are held in isolation every day. And now, suffer the children: the US sentences 2,500 children to life without possibility of parole—or to die in prison with no opportunity for review—and is the only country in the world to use that sentence for youth, a stark violation of international human rights law. This is our predicament: prisons are an engulfing and transforming unnatural disaster, choking us to death, destroying our collective futures, limiting our sense of hope and possibility. And it starts with the young, and our fear of our own children.

Suniti Sharma, newly arrived from her native India, plunged into the American *Gulag* years ago when she accepted a position teaching English in a detention center for young women in the heartland of the country. Her experiences as teacher, student, participant-observer, sage, philosopher, mother and grandmother, oral historian, ethnographer, and personal essayist became an odyssey of unforeseen challenges and obstacles, of discovery and surprise, and finally of some triumph and transformation. Trying to make sense of the overwhelming world she entered then, she offers now a breath-taking journey into the ineffable.

For girls who are detained prior to trial, the complexities of analysis lead us back to a longing for narrative and meaning-making. Girls who are arrested for an offense committed under the age of 18 overwhelmingly enter the juvenile justice system for minor and petty offenses. Fully a quarter of girls are arrested for what is known as *status offenses* (an act that would not be a crime if it were committed by an adult, such as running away, being *unruly*, truancy, smoking, or drinking). Another quarter of girls are arrested for shoplifting (or larceny). Among those charged with offenses like battery or assault, most are for family or school altercations where no one is seriously injured.

Yet once girls enter the justice system, it is difficult for them to emerge. This is in part because these young women come to the attention of law enforcement for reasons the justice system does not acknowledge: poverty; racism and ethnic discrimination; family violence, sexual assault, and extreme trauma. Their underlying needs are never addressed, and they are released under conditions that make it likely that they will violate their probation. They are not recognized and rarely heard from except in remarkable pockets where they have organized to advocate after release.

But enter Suniti Sharma, diving into the wreckage with eyes wide open, confronting the contradiction of education under detention with courage and clarity. Education stands on the twin pillars of enlightenment and liberation, while detention rests dully on the demands of obedience and conformity. Education is unpredictable, unruly, noisy, and disobedient, and it is about opening doors, enlarging possibilities, opening minds; prison is all high walls and barbed wire. While educators aim to unleash the human spirit and liberate the body, mind, and soul, the cage is designed to restrain and smash, suppress and crush. Sharma finds herself at the crux of the conflict: a teacher powered by an ethic of care and a vision of freedom, and simultaneously a cog in a vast, entangling mechanism of confinement and control.

Stop a moment here: if we are honest with ourselves, we must note that Suniti Sharma's conflict is the contradiction in one form or another of every teacher in any school. Teachers often feel themselves shackled, bound, and gagged, and while many teachers and students long for schooling as something transcendent and powerful, we find ourselves too-often locked in institutions that reduce learning to a mindless and irrelevant routine of drill and skill, and teaching to a kind of glorified clerking, passing along a curriculum of received wisdom and predigested (and often false) bits of information. Classrooms for obedience and conformity are characterized by passivity and fatalism, and infused with anti-intellectualism and irrelevance. They turn on the little (and in prisons, extra-large) technologies for control and normalization—the elaborate schemes for managing the crowd, the knotted system of rules and discipline, the exhaustive machinery of schedules and clocks, the laborious programs of sorting the crowd into winners and losers through testing and punishing, grading, assessing, and judging, all of it adding up to a familiar cave, an intricately constructed hierarchy—everyone in a designated place and a place for everyone. In too many schools, finding and accepting one's pigeonhole on the towering and barren cliff becomes the only lesson one really needs.

If we hope to contribute to rescuing education from the tangle of its discontents, we must rearticulate and reignite—and try to live out in our daily lives—the basic proposition that all human beings are of incalculable value, and that life in a just and democratic society is geared toward and powered by a profoundly radical idea: the fullest development of all human beings is the necessary condition for the full development of each person; and, conversely, the fullest development of each is necessary for the full development of all. This is the engine powering the teaching we experience here.

The challenging intellectual work of teaching pivots on our ability to see the world as it is and simultaneously to see our students as three-dimensional creatures—human beings much like ourselves—with hopes and dreams, aspirations, skills, and capacities; with minds and hearts and spirits; with embodied experiences, histories, and stories to tell of a past and a possible future; with families, neighborhoods, cultural surrounds, and language communities all interacting, dynamic, and entangled. This knotty, complicated challenge calls forth an open heart and an inquiring mind since every judgment is contingent, every view partial, and each conclusion tentative.

Suniti Sharma offers unblinking attention and communicates a deep regard for students' lives, a respect for both their integrity and their vulnerability. She begins with a belief that each student—whatever she brings to the classroom—is unique, each the one and only who will ever trod the earth, each worthy of a certain reverence. Regard extends, importantly, to an insistence that students have access to the tools with which to negotiate and then to transform the world.

Those of us who work with young people whose humanity is routinely tossed aside or disregarded see dehumanization as both policy and practice, and yet we desperately want for our young people the miracles and the transformations, the hard efforts, the enduring hope, the generous investment. This is the territory of our battle for a more humane and human world. We work in ways that might allow them to become seekers after their own questions, authors of their own scripts rather than bit players in stories already written for them by others, actors in their own dramas rather than merely walk-ons in an oft-performed B-movie, artists and composers of their own lives.

Suniti Sharma's interviews with girls behind bars are always at bottom dialogues, depending on relationship more than technique. These interviews are not interrogations or intrusions or designed therapeutic moments; they are rather commonplace teacher/student moments: openings of narrative spaces that these young, incarcerated women may choose to enter or not. For the teacher/interviewer listening actively and attentively is the main idea; learning from the stories of a range of participants is the payoff. For the story teller, the conversation is another occasion to perform an account of events and experiences for an audience, a chance to reveal meanings and in the process to discover something valuable and possibly new.

Here is the poetry of the everyday, the literature of subjective experiences and personal perspectives—not a substitute but an essential piece of any accurate record of human events. Suniti Sharma is a teacher who chooses hope, as we all might. She recognizes that hope is a choice, not to minimize the horror, but as an antidote to cynicism and despair. Hope is the capacity to notice or invent alternatives, and then to do something, to get busy in projects of repair. Whatever is the case stands side-by-side with what *could* be or *should* be the case. Because the future is unknown, optimism is simply dreaming, pessimism merely a dreary turn of mind. Hopefulness, on the other hand, holds out the possibility of change, it is an opportunity to see life as infused with the capacity to cherish happiness, to respect evidence and argument and reason, to uphold integrity, and to imagine a world more loving, more peaceful, and more just than the one we were given. Of course we live in dark times, and some of us inhabit even darker places—prisons, detention centers, and war zones—and, yes, we act mostly in the dark. But we are never freer as teachers and students, citizens, residents, activists, and thinkers than when we refuse to see the situation or the world before us as the absolute end of the matter. With this brilliant Indian English teacher, we might choose life; choose possibility; choose action.

William Ayers and Bernadine Dohrn

William Ayers, Distinguished Professor of Education at the University of Illinois at Chicago (retired), has written extensively about social justice and education. His books include *Teaching toward Freedom*; *To Teach: The Journey, in Comics*; and *A Kind and Just Parent: The Children of Juvenile Court*.

Bernardine Dohrn, activist, academic and child advocate, is Clinical Associate Professor at the School of Law at Northwestern University. She teaches and lectures on women, children, gender, and human rights, children in conflict with the law, incarceration and torture, and international human rights. She is coauthor with William Ayers of *Race Course: Against White Supremacy*, and author and coeditor of *A Century of Juvenile Justice* and *Resisting Zero Tolerance: A Handbook for Parents, Teachers and Students*.

Acknowledgments

It has been almost ten years since I first began working on this project. I am grateful to several students, teachers, scholars, colleagues, friends, and family members for their support, inspiration, and ideas during this journey.

I will always be indebted to my students at the detention facility for sharing their life-stories with me; opening my perceptions to a world I would have otherwise never known; resisting prisons in numerous physical and symbolic ways; evidencing testimony that every life is worth fighting for and can be lived with hope and humor; and for their passionate involvement in the writing of this book. I think of the time spent with students every day and their life-stories continue to shape who I am both in and outside the classroom.

At the detention facility, I met some amazing and dedicated people. I am thankful to the detention facility Director J. Harmon for permission to research students' life-stories, and Director of Operations, R. Vance for taking the risk of ignoring the fact that I could neither remember nor follow the hundreds of rules and regulations of the facility, and which made this book possible. A number of very committed teachers at the facility, M. Stevens, E. Keys, R. Baird, and W. Brown, a warm thank you to them for introducing me to the working ways of US public schools, keeping me informed about the social and cultural norms, and, more than anything else, believing in educational change.

Two special friends and colleagues, Erik Malewski and Victoria Moore have been my closest allies in the writing process from conceptualizing the book to editing the proofs. I am grateful to Erik for being an exceptional mentor, always believing that my work at the detention facility was meaningful, insisting that life-stories of girls behind bars must be told, for all the discussions, disagreements, and for his passionate energy that went into thinking through this book, never failing to remind me that the future holds many possibilities, yet to come. I am grateful to Victoria for her continued enthusiasm for all my academic and non-academic projects, for reading and reviewing my work multiple times, for taking my calls at odd hours and keeping me company through many a Long Island Iced Tea, and being my unofficial editor, for without her keen eye and sharp critiques, this book would not be the same.

Works of several scholars have helped me think through the process of asking critical questions, interrogating texts, and connecting complex theoretical issues to everyday teaching and learning processes taking place inside marginalized spaces such as detention. Specifically, I would like to thank Bernadette Baker for her brilliant deconstruction of "What is a child?" which guided me in framing and exploring my own question, "What is a girl behind bars?" I am also indebted to Erica Meiners for her scholarship on prisons, particularly, *Right to be Hostile*, which helped me to connect policy, prisons, and education and recognize that change at the policy level is crucial to how we envision curriculum change.

For recognizing the political significance of life-stories of girls behind bars that run counter to contemporary discursive trends of a standards-based one-size-fits-all education, I owe a very big thank you to David Barker at Continuum; his insight and vision made this book a published reality.

Finally, a very special thank you to my husband, Hemant, for his unconditional support in going along with my at-times risky pursuits of personal and political change and my children, Abhinav and Nikhil, who keep me believing in the future.

1

Mapping the Journey

Introduction

In the spring of 2003, I accepted a teaching position in a detention school for young women in the United States. While searching for a new position in New Delhi, India through an employment agency online, a series of communication gaps resulted in a phone interview with the detention facility in the United States searching for an English teacher. In a bizarre conversation with the Director of the detention facility, I misunderstood the American accented English on the phone, so when the Director said he was based in Indiana, I assumed he said India. Oddly, when I said I was in Delhi, he later told me he assumed I was from Delhi, a small town in Texas, familiar to him. I had not applied for an overseas assignment; therefore, I was not thinking outside India at all. The next day the employment agency clarified the mistake to both of us; however, the Director of the facility made a job offer. I accepted.

The move, thousands of miles away from home in India, created major ripples within my personal and professional life. You could call this move a mid life crisis—empty nest syndrome, placid domesticity, or intellectual boredom; perhaps it was a combination of all three. I had been teaching English in India for 15 years. Surely I could teach anywhere in the world—that is, the western world. Like many middle class English-speaking women in India, I was part of the colonial hangover: well-schooled in western philosophy, literature, and the arts—one could call me an anglophile. That was 10 years ago. As I map this journey, I realize I can no longer specify the locations from where I speak—a woman, an Indian woman, a feminist, a teacher, a mother, a writer, an immigrant, a researcher, an autoethnographer—, and a recovering anglophile. What follows is my journey into unlearning what it means to be a teacher, of undoing what it means to be a woman, an autoethnography of my lived experiences teaching girls behind bars.

This book maps a seven-year journey into my experience teaching girls behind bars. What interests me is the intersection of my life history, the lived educational experiences of girls behind bars, and the search for curriculum change. Within the eight chapters, I explore the following questions in relation to teaching in a detention classroom for girls behind bars: What is a young girl behind bars? How do historical apriori conditions constitute certain groups of girls as objects to make detention possible? How might the notion of a multiply constituted subject of discourse contest historical apriori conditions that predicate detention? How does my teaching and learning intersect with the life stories of students? How do girls behind bars create transformative spaces for reclaiming education? What are the implications of such curriculum transformations for educational change? In this chapter, *Mapping the Journey*, I position the study within a historical, social, educational, and cultural context—mine, as well as my students'—to explore the above questions.

What is juvenile detention?

What is a detention school for girls, one might ask. Who is a young girl behind bars? How is she framed differently from other young girls? A detention school in the United States specifically for young girls is part of a detention facility, a place of temporary care for young girls in custody of the juvenile justice system. Young girls aged 7 to 21 who are in custody of the juvenile justice system for "criminal acts" such as arson, robbery, drug and alcohol abuse, and sex offenses are placed in detention (Chesney-Lind 2001). Other young girls enter the juvenile justice system for noncriminal offenses such as running away, truancy, not going to school, incorrigibility, promiscuity, prostitution, and behaviors at school deemed out of control (Brunson and Miller 2001). A number of young girls enter the juvenile justice system for being victims of various forms of sexual violence and physical and mental abuse (Krisberg 2005). An unexpected number of young girls are placed in detention, as they have nowhere else to go. Families, schools, and law enforcement agencies have the authority to place children and youth in custody of the juvenile justice system (Meiners 2007). Additionally, girls behind bars are also referred to as juvenile offenders, juvenile detainees, juvenile delinquents, and even inmates and prisoners.

According to Office of Juvenile Detention and Delinquency Prevention (OJDDP), an official wing of the US Department of Justice, the number of girls in the juvenile justice system has increased dramatically despite a drop in the overall juvenile crime rates (see Snyder and Sickmund 2006). Young women are the fastest growing segment in the juvenile justice population with a national rate increase by 83 percent between 1988 and 1997 and reported to further increase exponentially in the next decade (see American Bar Association and the National Bar Association 2001). Within this fast growing population, is a sub-group of "young people who are disproportionately minority, undereducated, and female" (Fine and McClelland 2006, p. 303), indicating the fast-tracking of school-to-prison pipeline for many minority women. By 2003, 61 percent of all juveniles in custody were minority youth. Among young women in custody, 35 percent are African American, 15 percent Hispanic, and the rest distributed among other minority groups (American Civil Liberties Union 2006).

All detention facilities, including those that are privately owned, are required by the US Department of Justice to abide by the rules and regulations specified by their respective state departments of corrections. For example, all detention facilities in the state of Indiana are required to follow the policies mandated by the Indiana Department of Corrections. In accordance, the explicit goals of the detention facility where I worked were threefold. The first goal was to discipline girls behind bars; the second was to ensure that the disciplinary measures facilitated rehabilitation; and the third was to assist all the young girls at the facility with their education. The above statistics on juvenile crime, what is labeled as juvenile delinquency, who is labeled as a juvenile offender, and the social, educational, legal, and institutional response to juvenile crime suggest an urgent need for studies on how and why young minority women are locked up in disproportionate numbers and what this means in terms of social justice practiced within institutions such as the juvenile justice and the school system.

The geography of the facility

As soon as I first arrived, getting familiar with the location of the facility, the layout of the building, and the unique architecture was foundational to understanding the aim and process of education in detention. The facility was situated on the main street of a small rural town surrounded by cornfields. The street to the facility had a very small sign indicating the facility's presence, almost hidden between some trees. The building was located at the end of a paved street with tall trees at the back of its chain-linked perimeters. The wired fencing and the cameras all along the perimeter were intrusive and recorded all arrivals and departures from the building. The oblong shaped parking lot circled back upon itself on the lower portion of a sloping acreage to serve its panoptic purpose.

As I stepped on the concrete sidewalk, I noticed the entrance door with large glass windows where black-backgrounded crayon drawings showed brilliant displays of etched out pictures. These approximately 7″ by 8″ pictures of rainbows and greetings covered each window, giving a welcome, sunny first impression that contrasted sharply with the signboard. The single signboard proclaimed the status of the facility—*Correctional Juvenile Facility for Girls*. The facility housed 88 young girls aged 10 to 21. This was a privately owned for-profit facility. Private facilities in the United States make up 60 percent of all residential detention facilities and account for 80 percent of facilities that hold 10 or fewer residents (Snyder and Sickmund 2006).

The main door to the building and thereafter all doors were securely locked and operated through a buzzer that connected to the main control office. Entry into a rectangle shaped area inside the first door is obtained by responding to the buzzer's voice request for information. Inside is a second waiting area where a view of a long hall can be glimpsed. At this checkpoint, every employee must swipe a card and pass an identification check while visitors' IDs are thoroughly scrutinized by security guards before they are escorted elsewhere in the building. At all times, security guards accompanied students wherever they went and student movement was in a straight line, single file, face forward, hands folded across the chest. The entire process from the parking lot, through the heavy doors, and inside the waiting area felt like a prison, the kind often portrayed in the media.

The students wore a uniform—blue shorts and white t-shirts—and at night they wore the same t-shirts with a different pair of shorts, which was strictly enforced by the security guards. They were not allowed any personal belongings, and all personal items, including underwear, was provided by the facility. I also learned that every item of clothing went into a collective pool and a fresh, clean set was handed to students each morning, regardless of who wore them the previous day. I was afraid that these were ways to strip students of all rights including that of owning their own clothes. Having studied in a boarding school since I was 4 years old, I was familiar with school uniforms and dress codes. What I was not familiar with was the depersonalizing of students who were not allowed to take ownership of anything that would individualize them.

Policies of the detention facility

Did this rigorous prison-like routine come as a shock to me? Yes, many things shocked me because this concerned children and youth. This was no media image but a real juvenile detention facility that housed (imprisoned?) young girls considered delinquent. I was most horrified at the blanket rule that students were not allowed to speak to one another, and had no activities, extra-curricular activities, or books to read besides self-help books and the Bible in every part of the building and the classroom was no exception. Students had to raise their hands and request permission to speak, move, or walk in the classroom. I wondered how students were expected to be socialized back into life outside under the restrictions and the deprivations of a detention classroom.

As a new teacher, I was expected to attend 120 hours of intensive training before I stepped into the classroom. Subsequently, every year I had to complete 40 hours of training. The first part of my training was learning the organizational and institutional policies and procedures of juvenile detention. Through lectures, simulation, role-play, and drill, followed by tests, I was initiated into the policies of teaching in a detention classroom. I was informed my overarching concern at all times must be the safety and security of students. The daily schedule was structured and timed with clockwork precision by the facility's administrators. There were no bells to mark the transition from one activity to another. Students were not allowed any contact with their family and friends, nor were they allowed to go out of the building. Every exterior door was locked and could only be opened by remote from a central keyboard at the control center. The center monitored and recorded what transpired in every classroom at all times. There were security cameras and guards inside and outside every classroom. This kind of omnipresent surveillance was unnerving because it felt invasive in a forbidding manner. I was being monitored too.

The policies of the facility were explained through terminology specific to detention. I learned that the control center in the reception area is simply called "control," from where cameras digitally monitor and record every corner of the facility, except the rest rooms and the shower. I had to learn crisis prevention intervention (CPI), a physical intervention, which meant "restraining" a student down onto the ground and immobilizing her until help arrived. A "lockdown" was when security officers at the facility ordered all movement to come to a standstill in the event of an impending threat. For example, if a staff member lost a bunch of keys, the building went into lockdown as each student was "strip searched" for the keys—a full body search minus the clothes. Every employee had to carry a radio transmitter and stay in constant touch with "control."

Inside the classroom, I was to make sure students did not speak with each other, walk around, or carry any pencil or paper out of the class. I wondered how I was going to teach without interacting with the students. Surely, I could work around this rule, I thought. I was naive enough to ask why students were not allowed to speak and was told, "These girls are prisoners, they think like prisoners, so we have to monitor them like prisoners. Our first rule is to keep them locked up, theirs is to escape" (personal communication). My desk was to be routinely locked. I was told that the locking of desks was necessary, as the students were capable of abusing themselves with objects and destroying property as a way of escape. In the classroom, there were only desks and chairs, the teacher's desk and chair, and a blackboard. Students stayed in the school area from 7:30 a.m. to 4 p.m., after which they ate dinner and moved to the dorms, where they were expected to sit in silence until bedtime at 8:30 p.m.

The rationale for education in detention

While the technicalities of my training might sound quite textured, a sense of the structured and controlled everyday life in detention is necessary for understanding the second part of my training. The second part of training focused on education and entailed learning the officially sanctioned psychological and educational theories used to rationalize education in detention. The juvenile justice system was created in nineteenth century America to correct juvenile delinquent behavior. It was informed by the social theory that by virtue of social conditions, such as poverty and bad parenting, some children are deviant from the norm and therefore exhibit antisocial behaviors and commit criminal acts (DuBois & Karcher 2005). Hence, it was considered necessary to correct such deviancy through discipline and punishment of youth who did not conform to the norm (Bleschman & Bopp 2005). I was hopeful that time-tested theories on learning and behaviors would equip me to understand my role as a teacher in a detention classroom.

In order to establish rigorous discipline in the classroom, I had to observe strict codes and rules. For example, no teacher was allowed to exchange personal information with students, give rewards to students, and have any conversations with students other than school work. In accordance with psychological theories of correcting juvenile behaviors, the relation between teachers and students was expected to be based on rationality and objectivity. I was informed that detention, based on the principle of discipline and correction, had no room for building sustained relationships. I saw this as compromising the rehabilitative goals of detention because I felt it would be impossible to make an impact on students' behaviors if I was not emotionally connected.

With the emergence of psychology and the study of human behavior, the juvenile justice system added the "rehabilitative ideal" approach to reforming deviant behavior of youth (Blechman & Bopp 2005). The rehabilitative school of thought focused primarily on addressing deviancy by controlling deviant minds and behaviors. The rationale for the rehabilitative ideal was based on claims from evidence-based research that youth differ from adults and need to be treated differently; their behaviors could be scientifically observed, clinically diagnosed, and effectively treated; and prescriptive plans would address youth offenders' rehabilitation by altering and modifying undesirable behaviors (Rhodes 2001). Relying on empirical studies of human behavior that suggest the focus should be on the offender rather than offense, the rehabilitative ideal aimed at transforming character, habits, and attitudes of youth. Here the aim was to prevent recidivism (relapse into deviant behavior) and enable readjustment into family, school, and community.

In keeping with the institutional goals of detention, my first and foremost goal was to focus on rehabilitation of students. A combination of the social theory of deviance and a psychological approach to rehabilitation pave the way for the cognitive development theory (Piaget 1947) of education in detention. Piaget's cognitive development theory plays an important role in the application of cognition to deviant and criminal behavior in youth. According to Piaget, cognition is a normal development in youth, but this ability may be damaged in some children and youth due to harmful social experiences or physical trauma, making them deficit in cognitive capacities. The deficit explained deviancy, which was measured from the norms of behavior, attitude, and ability. As a deficit model, Piaget's and Vygotsky's theories were critical to explaining deviancy control, especially in juvenile detention, and opened the possibility for education as an intervention or a tool for addressing cognitive deficiencies or deviancies (see Daniels 2007). Therefore, learning was seen as key to the rehabilitative process of detention.

As a teacher, I was expected to address specific cognitive defects, deficiencies, and deviancies by focusing on teaching girls behind bars how to think, develop decision-making skills, and make correct choices. Thus, the goal of education was to retrain behaviorally deviant and cognitively deficit students to conform to the norm. I was also expected to develop a curriculum that would combine the rehabilitative goal of detention with the educational reforms of the NCLB Act (2001). Finally, I was given a valuable and trusted resource—the "golden" tool that was supposed to guide my practices as a teacher: *Reasoning and Rehabilitation: A Handbook for Teaching Cognitive Skills to Female Juvenile Offenders* (compiled by the detention facility). This handbook, I was told, would help smooth the transition from a teacher-outsider to a teacher inside a detention classroom.

The entire process of my training was punctuated with detainee stories, detention lore, prison and prisoner myths and stories, the dos and don'ts of detention, and a shared sisterhood of the "secrets of surviving" among staff members in a detention facility. In fact, we were forbidden from discussing the facility's happenings outside the premises. Breaking any of the rules was taken seriously, and employees at the facility were fired on a weekly basis for going against the rules.

What did I think?

My training at the facility and the discussions that followed introduced me to the American penal system, prison culture, and the language of prisons. Prison-talk concerning adult prisoners did not overwhelm me. I was familiar with prisoner stories. In the 1970s and 1980s, while most young women in India my age were raising children, decorating, and redecorating their homes, I was busy on a typewriter or a telex machine deciphering prison stories told by members of the then banned African National Congress of South Africa (ANC). This was my ANC phase, when I was 21 and drunk on the idea of freedom and democracy—I believed in the fight for the release of Nelson Mandela and free elections in South Africa. In fact, I spent some of the most exhilarating years of my life working with banned ANC members who had been sent to prison in South Africa, escaped from prison, or were fugitives. Detention, prison, and prisoners, therefore, shocked me less than what one might think. What shocked me was the use of language that constructed children under 21 under terms describing adult prisoners.

While I was prepared for the prison stories, what I was not prepared for was how to teach high school girls behind bars. My extensive training at the facility was a form of indoctrination into the structures and conditions meant to inform my teaching and shape students' rehabilitation. Therefore, the facility considered it important that as a teacher I should learn the institutional and structural relationship among teaching, disciplining, detainee, detention, rational thinking, and conformity. Naively I thought that the cognitive model of education would be effective in helping students return to society rehabilitated, and my teaching abilities would do the rest.

In my classroom

In accordance with psychological theories of correcting juvenile behaviors, classroom relations between teachers and students was expected to be based on rationality and objectivity. Although the number of students at the facility changed on a weekly basis as students would arrive or leave the facility as mandated by the court system, when I began my teaching assignment in 2003, there were 44 African American students, 36 Caucasian, 2 Native American, 2 Latino, 1 Asian, and 3 students of African American and Caucasian parents.

According to the detention facility's records, all 88 students were victims of physical, sexual, or/and emotional abuse. National statistics show that 85 percent of girls behind bars have experienced sexual or emotional abuse before being labeled as juvenile offenders (Chesney-Lind 2001). Added to the racialized and gendered experiences, most of the students had a history of school failure as well. Thus, students came to my classroom carrying official labels given them by the public schools they had previously attended, such as reading disabled, dyslexic, academically challenged, slow learners, at-risk, incorrigible, emotionally disturbed, behaviorally challenged, promiscuous, deviant, abnormal, different, and delinquent.

For students, their life stories—whether mediated through the sorting and labeling process of schooling, the dislocations caused by the juvenile justice system, the rise of social movements such as feminism, institutional representation, or resistance to authority—represented a world with few secure psychological or academic markers. How then were girls behind bars making meaning from their lived experiences? Were they living out their racial or/and gendered marginality through various forms of resistance and creating multiple spaces for resistance to reposition themselves within the social, cultural, and educational worlds? What unfolds in this introductory chapter is my entry into the lives of girls behind bars; lives that run counter to the institutional authority of the juvenile justice and school system, which has implications for teaching in detention classrooms.

After my training, I was the official English teacher for all 88 students at the facility and soon became popular with students who seemed to be appreciative of my cultural background and the differences I brought into the classroom. Most of the students came to my classroom carrying labels given them by the public schools they had previously attended, such as reading disabled, dyslexic, emotionally disturbed, and behaviorally challenged. The students came from different ethnicities, but the majority of them were Caucasian or African American. African Americans made up 13 percent of the national juvenile population (Snyder & Sickmund 2006), however, they represented 44 percent of the population at this particular detention facility. While the Caucasian students were mostly from rural areas, the African American students were all inner city residents. Very few students in the 7 years that I taught at the facility had attended public school on a regular basis. Often I groped blindly in my attempts to teach students with wide gaps in their schooling.

Each day I arrived at 7 a.m. and left at 4 p.m., 11 months of the year, taking the month of December for my annual visit to India. I taught English and American literature, writing and composition, and reading courses to students from grade six to twelve. I also helped eleventh and twelfth grade students prepare for their GED, SATs, and for college. In support I established a system whereby students ready to graduate were allowed to apply for college admissions, started a library on a minimal scale through book donations from the neighborhood and town libraries, and organized drama and literary clubs that met twice a week after school. The students were very excited with these additions; the administrators supported my ideas but were doubtful any of my schemes would last very long.

Furthermore, I spent time with students outside class to listen to their complaints, suggestions, and their plans for the future and decided to call the meeting "Student Council Affairs," in case the administration disallowed our meetings. These meetings were informal and meant to give students space to vent feelings and thoughts that they were normally not permitted to express. The meetings also gave them an opportunity to speak freely about some of the ideas that we could use in planning class and extracurricular activities. The meetings were successful; however, there were many instances when I struggled to understand and act within the context of the facility's rules, as I found myself more supportive of giving students freedom to express themselves in opposition to the facility's disciplinary tactics.

I spent a lot of time wondering about students' backgrounds, their previous experiences, public schooling, and their psychological state of mind. What, I wondered, were the effects of sexual abuse, physical abuse, neglect, and violence on their ability to recompose their lives and to be able to trust adults after their traumatic experiences? If criminal and delinquent behavior is natural, as some scientists and psychologists believe, what does it mean for students for whom violence and abuse have designated them "delinquent?" There was a sense of socialization into violence or at least conversations on violence and abuse that was routine at the facility. I felt that it might be safer for my own emotions to distance myself from students' experiences, especially when I encountered stories of violence each day. My horror at the desensitization to violence against children and teens was given a reprieve each day when I left school for home. However, the students did not get to go home and, although considered physically safe within the walls of the facility, their previous experiences with violence and abuse was an underlying presence. At times, students enacted disturbed behaviors manifested in terms of self-harming, cursing, destroying school property, and refusing to follow the rules. Although considered normal in detention, such behaviors unsettled my own life and were major obstacles to teaching.

For students, context and contingency—whether mediated through the media or through the dislocations caused by the juvenile justice system, exclusions within the school system, the rise of social movements such as feminism, or the crisis of representation—situates them as girls behind bars. Were students living on the margins or creating multiple meanings to reposition themselves and reclaim their social, cultural, and educational worlds? What unfolds in the following section is the world of girls behind bars through my introduction to Chris, a young woman brought into the facility as a juvenile offender.

Experiencing students' life stories

Chris' life stories

For me Chris' story began on July 13, 2003, a few months after I had first arrived at the detention facility. Chris was a 16-year-old African American student assigned to the detention facility on charges of drug abuse, running away, and treatment for sexual abuse. This was the first time I was called to "do an intake." A new student brought into detention is an "intake," the disembodied process of normalizing a student into detention policy and procedure is "doing an intake," and the student's life compressed into a legal "case sheet." Chris' case sheet was brief:

July 13, 2003

New Intake: 16-year-old black female. Detention on and off for 7 years. Lives with father and stepmother. One child, father unknown. Intake does not have custody of child. Child with protection services. Intake is on the run since March 2003. Sexually abused by father. Intake to complete program, drug and alcohol group, domestic violence group. Inform medical and case manager. No visitation or contact with father until court hearing. No action until further notice.

DOC [Department of Corrections]

I was required to fill in for security personnel, as there was no female staff on hand. I stared at the new intake. Nothing in all my training had prepared me for the young woman before me—a beautiful young female, calm and composed, and hands and feet in shackles. Where was the dirty, struggling, and foul-mouthed woman of the myths and stories I had heard during training? Or the student who, according to the facility's myths and stories, is brought in with a glazed eye and has to be propped up?

In my confusion, I forgot the strict procedures I was supposed to follow. To my surprise, Chris led me through the rituals of intake like a pro. She walked herself through the entire two-hour process of standing against the wall with her hands up and feet apart, and getting a body and hair search for any hidden object or substance. She knew the entire protocol—strip search, three-minute bath, hair treatment for lice, change into a uniform, go through the daily schedule, and read the detention rules twenty times. Each time I looked around nervously, Chris informed me with a matter-of-fact ease that we were both on camera so I needed to check mark all the steps, and finish the intake without getting us into "trouble."

I felt this was not my intake but that Chris was intaking me—leading me through the process I was to be guiding her through. At the time, I wanted to ask Chris about her experiences growing up and her family. Why was she brought here? Later, I learned from Chris' case manager, the facility official in charge of taking care of Chris' treatment and counseling program while in detention, that Chris was "into" drugs, irregular at school, and occasionally prostituted for a living. Further, I learned from Chris' essays in class that she had a drunken father, a mother who was nowhere to be found, and five siblings she loved dearly. When she came to my classroom, I learned she was an avid reader of *chicken soup* stories, wrote well, and was a math whiz. Now in eleventh grade, she excelled in reading and math in spite of being expelled from school in ninth grade. After being expelled, she walked the streets by day as a prostitute and became familiar with the struggles and uncertainties that come with gang and street life.

Chris never talked openly about these things; however, I composed Chris from snippets of what I heard from others, her essays in the English class, her input in class discussions, and my experience with her. One might say I created a montage of Chris' life taken from various sources and put together over time. In class, I was often tempted to talk to Chris about her family, her friends, her school. I wanted to ask about her siblings. But this did not happen. Institutional rules forbade me from speaking to Chris about her personal life. Or telling her about mine.

Six months later, when it was time for Chris' release from detention, I wanted to ask how she planned to navigate her life. When I learned she was not going back to her family because of court orders, I knew she would be devastated. I wanted to tell her that I wished her life had been simpler, happier, or that I wish I could change it for her, make it better. I wanted to tell her to call me for help with schoolwork, to get through school and put her talents to work. I wanted to tell her to stay in touch. However, I did not. When Chris came to say goodbye, she had the same calm exterior she walked into the building with. This time I was less nervous than sad. I will never forget her last words to me. As if she felt she should comfort me, let me know I mattered, she said she would never forget the teacher who taught "Indian English." I wanted to say, I would never forget the half woman-half child who I know as Chris. However, the words did not come to my lips. I just smiled and remained silent. Now, almost 3 years later, I am compelled to speak, to tell Chris' story—one could say, I am trying to share now what I was unable to share with Chris back then.

Sharonika's life stories

I give multiple life stories of Sharonika, a young woman in detention, to reveal the disconnect between institutional discourses that define girls behind bars and their lived educational experiences. Other people's stories, previously filtered through violent media images on the evening news and crime shows, were becoming an inescapable reality in my classroom. In the summer of 2005, a security guard escorted Sharonika, a new "intake" into my class. The school principal at the detention facility told me I was now "a well-trained detention educator" (School Principal, pers. comm.). In reality, I was learning the hard way to put faces and names to official statistics on rape, abuse, and neglect. Other people's stories previously filtered through violent media images on the evening news and crime shows were an inescapable reality in my classroom. I had also won some minor battles—I refused to carry a radio into class to stay in touch with "control," refused to teach with a security guard in my room, and openly allowed conversations and group discussions in the class.

The students began to tell me they loved coming to my classroom. Perhaps, it was the Indian stories I told, or the shared feeling of difference, of not quite fitting in that brought them each day to my room. Perhaps, the students had noticed my acts of defiance against some of the rules and the deliberate indifference to some of the policies, which placed us both in opposition to the facility. Innumerable variables perhaps, but the students' words and nonverbal communication slowly over time began to shift. One example of this change—Sharonika commented she was going to love my class, as she liked the faint perfume of body lotion that lingered around me. It reminded Sharonika of her grandmother. It also made her feel safe, she said. We bonded instantly.

Sharonika was a 16-year-old African American student diagnosed as a "self-harmer." I was new to the term, meant for persons who cut and bruise themselves for a number of reasons. Sharonika's body was scarred with self-inflicted injuries. Some of the scars looked like intricate tattoos that must have taken many painful hours in the making. She informed me there were reasons for her self-harming. According to Sharonika, sometimes she wanted to punish herself, get an adrenaline rush, get attention, or simply die. According to her case manager, Sharonika was a drug user, with a history of sexual abuse, and given to violent outbursts. She was sent into detention for joining a group of friends and setting fire to cars and buildings.

It was distressing to see a young woman like Sharonika engage in destructive practices toward herself and others. I was confused because, in the classroom Sharonika showed no signs of violence and was enthusiastic about school. She worked hard in my class, which contrasted with what her case manager claimed. For me it was hard to imagine that she had so many dimensions to her personality that might be contradictory. I was unwilling to deal with anything that spelled uncertainty and did not want any further complications than what I was experiencing.

Two years into teaching at the detention school, I began to have serious doubts about the application of cognitive theories in my English class. I was equally doubtful of the simple cause and effect explanations for detention provided by social theories of deviance (Newburn and Shiner 2005). However, I clung to the rehabilitative ideal and wanted my students to succeed academically. More than anything else, I wanted them to feel safe in my class. Not safety and security as the institution understood it, but differently, as I understood it given their lived histories and who I knew them to be. I wanted students to trust me when speaking their minds.

I think by the second year I had stopped being an English teacher in a detention classroom as defined by the facility's handbook and became in part resistant to the rules and regulations of the facility, and in part more involved in understanding what the students were experiencing as opposed to keeping an objective distance from students. I no longer focused on standardized tests and scores as a priority. Even though I had relegated such forms of teacher and student accountability measured by test scores to the back of my mind and let go of some of the rules of the facility, they remained in my thoughts, with a lingering sense of discomfort about my lack of focus on standardization and rehabilitation as defined by the facility. I tried to live from moment to moment—if students could feel safe and happy in my classroom, I was glad to let them read, write, and talk, with no grand lesson plan unfolding. Somewhere along this journey, my feelings had gotten in the way of my neutrality.

Looking back, I think I was overwhelmed with the growing chasm between my students' lives and the pressures of meeting with institutional requirements. I found that as I became more attentive to students' lives, I became less attentive to my structured syllabus or the facility's agenda of discipline and rehabilitate. I broke the rules of being an objective, rational teacher in a detention classroom that was the core focus of the facility's handbook. Instead, I turned into a mother, a grandmother, an aunt to my students—I needed to make personal connections for my own sanity.

As one of many curriculum experiments, I tried to connect with students through poetry. The experience, like many of my teaching experiments at the facility, was not a success nor was it a failure. The experience of writing poetry on some days was exhilarating and on other days left me confused and depressed. I could never get complacent with regard to my success as a teacher because moments of success were punctuated regularly with breakdowns. One such example is my experience with Sharonika. Here is a poem that Sharonika wrote as an English assignment:

> *Live or Die*
> I don't want to live
> I don't want to die
> But for now I'm saying goodbye
> I grab the pills
> And take them one by one
> Then I stop and think
> "What have I done?"
> I'm lying on the floor
> As everything slowly turns black
> I scream "Please . . . God, bring me back."

I told Sharonika her poem was beautiful, slipped it into my folder, and made a mental note to speak with her about it. The next minute a scream jerked me back from the false sense of security that I had built for all of us in the classroom. Sharonika was on the floor in a fetal position near the door, in a pool of blood. I had no radio transmitter or security guard in the room so could not call for help. In a few seconds, there were screaming students everywhere, and more blood than I had ever seen in my life. Sharonika had tried to jab her throat with a pair of scissors. I looked at her face and she stared at me blankly. I had failed to connect with her. I had failed to notice the flatness of her tone or the expressionless look she had given me during class.

I never saw Sharonika again, as she was moved to a mental hospital for children the next day. All the policies of the facility, the rehabilitative ideal, various learning theories, and my teaching experience—nothing came to my rescue in the face of Sharonika's attempt at self-murder. Is there a handbook for understanding breakdowns or dealing with the numbness that follows? I tried to forget the incident, in vain. I have replayed those terrifying moments many times, but somehow the sequence of events breaks down before I can get to the end. One could say—it was the day I plummeted to the lowest point in my teaching.

Sharonika's story is important because it signified to me that students like Sharonika played out life and death battles for survival each day. However, the everyday acts of such violence normalized into the daily routine of detention leaves educators ill-equipped to process or address the lives really at stake. When educators are not trained to address Sharonika's lived experience, her resistance, her call for help, or her self-destruction, there is a reinscribing of institutional oppression. When institutions that represent social justice view violence in detention as the norm or when detention is offered as treatment or as the only option, there is a double injustice done to students like Sharonika—first they are discriminated for being different, then they are normalized into detention. Looking back, I was overwhelmed with the growing chasm between my students' racialized and gendered experiences and the pressures of meeting with institutional requirements. The conflict between the goals of education and rehabilitation aimed at assimilation of students like Sharonika into mainstream cultural norms through discipline and punishment and the limitations of disciplinary forms of knowledge in the face of students' counter-stories provided the impetus for this autoethnographic study.

April's life stories

In 2006, I was introduced to April, a 19-year-old Caucasian student who was brought into the facility because she was "on the run" from juvenile custody. After being raped in a hospital where she was being treated for psychiatric problems, April fled the hospital and literally lived on the run for a year before she was found and subsequently brought into the detention facility. In academics, April was on top of her class and scored well on standardized tests. She wanted to go to college and informed me that she expected me to help her with filling out the necessary college and financial aid forms. It excited me to know that she wanted to go to college. This is because most students in detention are not college-bound nor do they have the luxury of thinking about college for a number of reasons. Spending a lifetime privileging college education, at the facility I tried my best not to make this obvious. In detention, speaking about college education seems like another form of violence when most students are negotiating life-threatening situations. However, many of the students loved sitting with me to hear about college admission, courses they might take, and prospects that college might open for them. In fact, talking about college was April's favorite conversation.

It was my fourth year teaching in a detention classroom and I had witnessed many girls behind bars. I had also witnessed many certified teachers come and go. Some teachers left because they found the challenge of teaching girls behind bars overwhelming; others were asked to leave because they did not abide by the rules of the facility. I imagine the reason I was not asked to leave was that no one seemed to understand the legal implications of hiring or firing an overseas teacher. Another reason might have been my outsider status of being non-American, hence, already outside the familiar norms that the administrators at the facility were used to. Although the rehabilitative ideal as defined by the facility had lost its meaning, I was unwilling to give up, or let go, and was still in search for answers that would make teaching and learning work for my students and me. However, nothing had prepared me for the starkness of April's thoughts and experiences. April would not speak about herself but wrote her life story:

My Life-Story
1988 – born, parents divorced
1999 – first seen my dad
2002 – taken away from mom, into foster care
2003 – foster dad beat and jumped me
2004 – drugs, alcohol, sex, kicked out of school
2004 – tried to kill myself with 75 pills
2005 – raped in hospital, ran away
2006 – locked up

April had not only voiced her experiences but the matter-of-fact way she noted her experiences contrasted with the horrors of her life. At 19, April seemed accustomed to downplaying the discontinuities of her life or the conventions of family, womanhood, schooling, therapy, and history. Reading April's understated autobiography that gave the stark facts of her life, I struggled for some form and continuity to her life story, so much a part of my cultivated sense of order that wished to tie up loose ends, and bring every piece of writing to a satisfying conclusion. It was one thing to speak about the silences imposed on Chris' life or the darkness of Sharonika's world. It was quite another to come face-to-face with April's life story. What could I say without trivializing what she had written? What was there to say?

Unlike Sharonika, April completed the program in detention and went on to live on her own, but under supervision of the juvenile court. However, by naming unspeakable forms of physical and mental violence inflicted upon her, April made it difficult for me to continue to think, act, and teach as I had done in the past. In other words, April's life story made it impossible for me to carry on in a recognizable form. Unknowingly, like Chris and Sharonika, April had unsettled my practice as a teacher of English. In the middle of the disruptions and uncertainties of a detention classroom, I had clung to English literature for dear life. However, I was beginning to feel that literature had a habit of turning everything into fiction, and like detention and rehabilitation theories, left too many questions unanswered.

I desperately wanted education for rehabilitation to work for my students, to provide answers, to provide options to students who all too often were offered none in the past. I strongly desired that they experience success at school to have that feeling of a job well done. I also wanted to make sense of this not-knowing-feeling-experiencing self that I was confronting, this stranger that was myself. Who was I becoming? One could say—I was losing my grip on the schooled, rational, thinking self.

Searching for answers

So far, I have given the institutional rationale for detention, rehabilitation, and education. I have also given a glimpse into the lived histories of girls behind bars and my own lived experience of teaching in a detention classroom. The growing disconnect between the powerful authority of the juvenile justice and school system, and lived histories of students' as I knew them, was disquieting. Increasingly, the tension challenged many of my teaching assumptions and practices. In the light of my difficulties and challenges, I went beyond the detention school and conventional wisdom of teaching at-risk young women to other sources for help. I looked toward professional training in becoming a mentor, attended workshops on teaching girls behind bars, and enrolled for professional development courses at graduate school. The desire for understanding teaching in detention eventually led to professional development course work at a mid-Western university. During the professional development, I was introduced to the autobiographical theory of curriculum (Pinar 1998); postfeminist poststructural readings (Patti Lather 2000b; Britzman 1989); and various forms of autoethnography (Ellis 2004; Spry 2001). My curriculum search convinced me that the following question remained unexplored and under theorized: How do institutional structures and theories affect the lived experience of teaching and learning in a detention classroom?

Institutional structures such as the juvenile justice, the school systems, and their practices are informed by theories derived from evidence-based research, developmental psychology, and cognitive learning. Many of these theories stem from the European Enlightenment's notion of rationality as the basis of all knowledge that placed man as the center of the Universe. Accordingly, rationality was privileged over emotions and synonymous with the pursuit of objective knowledge. The rise of rationality as a major organizing principle for the success of institutions and individuals is critical to understanding the construction of goals, interactions, and practices of detention (Arrigo 1999).

First, philosophies such as that of Locke, Descartes, and Hume privileged reason over emotion and paved the way for empirical science and developmental psychology (Russell 1945). Second, developmental psychology validated cognition and learning that placed greater emphasis on rational decision-making skills and analytical techniques in schools (Meiners 2007). Third, privileging the rational over the emotional led to the subordination of personal narratives, lived histories, and emotional expressions as subjective feelings considered as interference with the search for objective knowledge (Sanchez 1999). This privileged position assigned to reason and objective knowledge is foundational to a detention classroom and exemplified in the catchwords of current teaching and learning in detention classrooms—cognition, problem solving, decision making, intelligence tests, and psychological evaluation.

In many ways, the institutional normalization of detention and the pedagogic function of education in detention derive meaning from the privilege given to rational thinking which positions minority groups in the school-to-prison pipeline. Viewed from this perspective, one can see how education translates into processing girls behind bars into expected behaviors and attitudes through disciplining, testing, and grading. The success of my teaching was to be measured by test scores, which in turn would index the rate of recidivism in behavior patterns and attitudes. Education in detention is by no means an objective, neutral contract between an institution and its stakeholders. Rather, detention is a regimented institution based on calculated control exercised on students considered deviant or delinquent. As a teacher, I was expected to honor this contract, not challenge it.

Contrary to my training at the facility, I spent a lot of time listening to my students and reaching out to them, thus, crossing the institutional line between the personal and the professional. When students claimed me as a mother, a grandmother, an aunt, and embraced me as their "Indian English" teacher, my students were reformulating the scripted relation between a teacher and students in detention. In spite of the unsettling and shifting contexts of our lives, the students and I were, in our own way, refusing to be imprisoned within an institutional logic of rules and regulations. In trying to redefine our teacher-student relationship, we were creating new modes of thought, rather than fulfilling predetermined roles. Within the network of detention, rehabilitation, education, knowledge, rationality, and objectivity was emerging a different kind of understanding—a space for understanding breakdowns, discontinuities, inconsistencies, excesses, and for feeling, yearning, remembering, imagining, and awakening. Counter-stories of students like Sharonika contest the racialized and gendered institutional discourse of the juvenile justice and the school system on a daily basis. Students' counter-stories are troubling, but more importantly, they draw attention to the structural issues and institutional relations that shape and prepare some students for detention, thereby creating, recreating, and sustaining experiences similar to Sharonika's.

From autobiographical to autoethnography

Desperate for some answers to resolve my tensions at the detention school, I began recalling my experiences of teaching girls behind bars to fellow graduate students during a course in foundations of curriculum. We discussed various philosophical traditions in education that alienated certain groups of students. The discussion moved to the politics of knowledge, what is said in classrooms and what is not, whose knowledge is valued and whose is not, and how such inclusions and exclusions structure the educational possibilities of students. In the process of discussing *Understanding Curriculum: An Introduction to the Study of Historical and Contemporary Curriculum Discourses,* I saw the significance of autobiography as a tool for understanding the educational lived experience of students (Pinar et al. 2004*)*.

Perhaps a class project for writing autobiographies might give me a partial understanding of the lived histories of girls behind bars in ways that did not fit into any academic framework I knew. I had been looking for a way or ways to address the dichotomy between the disciplinary controls of institutional life and the educational needs of the girls behind bars as I knew them. Pinar's scholarship gave me the intellectual space to organize not only a class project, but a larger research project aimed at writing and exploring life stories of girls behind bars. This was the beginning of what later grew into a critical autoethnographic study. Pinar's scholarship prompted me to ask fundamental questions about the construction and marginalization of girls behind bars as the "other," questioning assumptions and values that define detention, rehabilitation, and education and investigating inclusions and exclusions that shape the educational experience of students. In emphasizing the social, historical, cultural, and political embeddedness of all personal and academic knowledge, Pinar implicated educators in the production of school knowledge. Therefore, any attempt at telling the lived histories of girls behind bars not only brings into question how knowledge about girls behind bars is produced but who is telling these lived histories and the process of telling itself.

To ask questions about girls behind bars meant asking questions about disjunctures and breakdowns in students' lives and in my teaching, which indicated that my telling of lived histories of girls behind bars was more than traditional autobiographical understandings. It was about shifting knowledge from a stable and knowing self to a self that is multiple, complex, and contingent. My focus had shifted to searching for a nontraditional methodology wherein I would first study the concept of detention historically, before studying the life stories of students, or my own life stories.

The kind of questions I was asking also created a space for me to explore the discontinuous histories of students and time specific conditions that made the experience of detention possible for them. In order to do this, it was important that I study the history of the concept of detention and the social, cultural, and historical conditions under which juvenile detention was constructed. This meant going back into historical documents to study the discourses that influenced key frameworks, practices, and assumptions of detention and rehabilitation as I saw it enacted in the present context. I considered it necessary to deconstruct the effects of how discourses such as detention and rehabilitation were established as truths and to unearth the layers of meaning and associations that have gone into their construction. Subsequently, I studied the life stories of girls behind bars, the mutually constitutive discourses that have made the experience of their detention possible, and the subject positions that enable students to be understood different from the historical script that defines them.

As a teacher bound within official institutional regulations, how might I write about the life stories of girls behind bars without creating new forms of inclusion and exclusion? Entering the doctoral program introduced me to educational inquiry, theory, and practice focusing my attention on studying the lived educational experiences of girls behind bars and their attempts at reclaiming education. What methodologies would enable me to write about the disjunctive life stories of girls behind bars yet allow me to resist the institutional conditions in which those stories are intricately embedded? I turned my questions inward to ask myself how retelling autobiographies is structured by my subjectivity, and how much of my understanding is structured by institutional discourse. The choice of methodologies within my study would frame my experiences to make meaning of the life stories of girls behind bars without reinscribing the institutional discourse of detention.

Extending my experience with teaching girls behind bars into another 3 years of research, this book stems from my lived experience of the unique realities and every day breakdowns that confront teachers and students in a detention classroom. My lived experience, the research project, and the telling of this book are interwoven, as I was very much a subjective participant in this process. Unlike traditional ethnography, which favors an objective researcher looking at a culture from the outside, I was not a distant, removed researcher. Rather, my encounters with students had left their mark on me, a mark that deepened with every subsequent experience at the detention facility. I remained fully engaged in the day-to-day lived experiences of my students blurring the line between being an English teacher and a researcher moving toward autoethnography.

Outline of the book

Chapter 2, *Foucault's Conditions Without a Subject*, develops and considers how the conditions for the possibility of detention are constructed as a historical apriori that constitute the subject of detention as object of discourse to make entrance into the juvenile justice system contingent for certain groups of young girls. Using Foucauldian genealogy and poststructural practice of deconstruction, the first part of the chapter investigates the historical, social, legal, scientific, and institutional origins of the conditions that make detention for certain groups of youth, possible. In particular, the chapter evidences that from *Discipline and Punish* to *The History of Sexuality*, Foucault offers a departure from and argues against professional expertise such as science, psychology, and medicine for their role in producing and legitimizing certain discourses that in turn construct the subject of detention, therapy, and treatment—a construct that is intimately connected with other academic disciplines such as education. This construction of the subject and production of science, psychology, medicine, detention, and education consolidates power, authority, and privilege within an exclusive group of professional experts. Therefore, a critique of the processes and practices of education and incarceration and their relation to the instrumental use of professional knowledge that serves to dominate and exclude certain groups of youth from schools and society is repositioned.

Chapter 3, *Making, Unmaking, and Resituating the Subject,* validates that in spite of historical apriori conditions that make possible common, everyday, naturalized, institutional practices of detention, the subject of detention becomes constituted and compels us to address its existence. In this chapter, the discussion on Foucauldian notions of the subject of historical discourse is advanced to illustrate how the subject of detention is a modernist philosophical construct. As a construct, the subject is neither static nor universal. This is key to understanding the poststructural decentering of the modernist subject—that is, the subject is constructed as a historical apriori positioned for detention. However, the chapter argues that the embodied subject is also capable of desubjectification by offering critical resistance to educational and social practices. The displacement and resituating of the modernist subject offering pluralist understandings of difference is explored through a series of readings. Some of these scholars and their concepts are Baker's deconstruction of the modernist construction of the child, Butler's notion of the body as the locus of performative possibilities, Britzman's language for gender, desire, and sexuality as multiple and always in the process of becoming, and Lather's autoethnographic telling as the transformative space for rethinking educational inquiry, policy, and practice.

Chapter 4, *Qualitative Methodology, Critical Autoethnography, and Self-Reflexivity,* frames this ten year autoethnographic educational inquiry. Central to this chapter are key methodology issues such as how to "do" autoethnography, what makes autoethnography "critical," and why consider ethical and self-reflexive issues in qualitative research. Ellis (2004) and Spry's (2001) autoethnographic works, Scheper-Hughes' (1992) disruption of traditional ethnography, Lather's (2000) troubling of the objective researcher, and Britzman's (1989) self-reflexive readings of other people's stories provide the ground for a discussion on autoethnography and the relevance of ethics to critical inquiry. This chapter discusses the ethical responsibility of deconstructing dominant forms of educational knowledge, disrupting the status quo in education; unsettling notions of objectivity in research by bringing into focus the hidden dynamics of power and privilege, and acknowledging researcher-subjectivity in the research process. The importance of ethics and self-reflexivity to a study that researches possibilities for changing how we understand evidence and knowledge in educational inquiry, policy, and practice is highlighted in this chapter.

Chapter 5, *Embodied Life-stories and Counter-stories* is the "doing" of critical autoethnography by offering an interpretive reading of the autobiographies of young girls behind bars. The common thread of this section argues against the notion of a modernist self and a fixed humanist identity. Using the body as the locus or space for struggle and change, life stories are interpreted to show young girls as subjects constituted by discursive practices on the one hand, and as embodied subjects who constitute themselves through changing subject positions on the other. In opposition to Cartesian binaries, hierarchies, and categories central to normative constructions of identity, the focus of this chapter is on the body as a contested and transformative space for creating and negotiating knowledge and engenders possibilities for curriculum change.

Chapter 6, *Guilty Readings of Other People's Stories*, unfolds self-portraits of young girls behind bars painted on canvas. The chapter interprets and analyzes dramatic enactments of gender, desire, and sexuality to unpack the complexities and intersectionalities that shape the lives of young girls behind bars. What is illustrated in this chapter is how young girls behind bars enact gender as performative to contest the historical apriori script and create transformative spaces for reclaiming education. The term theatrical epistemology is deliberate as it is a construct that evokes theater and life stories in order to bring attention to the forbidden or disowned conversations in education and the urgency and immediacy of attending to differences among young girls. Deconstructing gender as a category of analysis, the chapter fleshes out the female subject of incarceration to bring into discussion gender, desire, and sexuality, critical issues that are absent in dominant educational discourse.

Moving to Chapter 7, *Agents of Change, Not Subjects or Objects of Discourse*, draws together educators, educational reformers, curriculum developers, policy makers, and communities of practice as agents of change in the struggle for social justice. Revisiting Foucault's genealogy, the chapter engages educators in ongoing discussion and reflection about dominant discourses of knowledge production to reposition young girls not as subjects or objects of discourse, but agents of change. Returning to feminist deconstruction, this chapter argues for the usefulness of critical autoethnography as a methodological space for thinking through simplistic understandings of cultural difference. Reexamining differences among, between, and within young girls enables the opening of epistemological and methodological spaces for the production of embodied knowledge, agency, and action as recourse for students, educators, and policy makers to reclaim education in transformative spaces.

Chapter 8, *Girls Behind Bars Reclaiming Education in Transformative Spaces*, opens autoethnographical readings to show how young girls behind bars reclaim education in transformative spaces. This chapter is getting to the work of autoethnographic telling by speaking from the author's multiply split voices of researcher, educator, student, and author. The chapter uses seven classroom moments as the springboard for speaking about the author's lived educational experiences, and the impact of stories and counter-stories of the lives of young girls behind bars. The author reflects on how each young girl behind bars gives a unique view of education as a contested space for historical and situated knowledge in the struggle for reclaiming education in transformative spaces.

2

Foucault's Conditions without a Subject

Introduction

Before I begin to speak about the life stories of girls behind bars, I consider it necessary to understand how the concept of detention came about, and to investigate the historical conditions that make the experience of detention possible. In this chapter, I use Foucauldian concepts to examine the historical conditions that make detention possible. The title of this chapter is taken from Foucault's critique of the philosophical foundations of knowledge wherein he speaks of the "conditions necessary for the appearance of an object of discourse" (Foucault 1972a, p. 44). Unsettling 2000 years of Western philosophy based on the Enlightenment humanist vision, Foucault deconstructs the principles of universal reason, absolute truth, and continuity of human progress. He posits that historical apriori conditions predetermine experience, not onto-epistemological claims to truth. In other works, Foucault traces the birth of the clinic (1973), madness, (1965), and prisons (1977) to challenge the continuity of history and its unquestioned coherence.

Aligning with Foucault's notion of discourse, I examine the history of the concept of detention and the dramatic shifts in thought that make it an unstable category. Rather than a fixed concept, I analyze the historical construction of detention as a series of shifting discourses with their own rules of formation. In examining the discourses constitutive of detention, I also investigate how educational discourse is constitutive of the conditions that predetermine the experience of detention. The overarching purpose of the study is to understand the educational experience of my students, and in order to do this, I begin with the historical apriori conditions that make detention possible.

The Enlightenment emphasized two interrelated themes: the subject/object dualism and faith in universal reason. The subject/object dualism was based on the belief that man is the center of all knowledge and was reflected in the Kantian subject as the object of all knowledge, the Cartesian rational subject, Husserl's transcendental being who makes his own meaning, and Heidegger's being-in-the-making. Man's faith in himself was based on the belief that absolute truth derived from empirical science and was the key to progress and the prosperity of humankind (Cusset 2008). The two themes converged to celebrate human history as a grand narrative of the human subject founded on the principles of universal reason, objective truth, and scientific progress. Foucault's work challenges each of the taken-for-granted truth claims of the Enlightenment's failed humanist ideals (Shrift 2006). Instead, he offers a rereading and rethinking of this grand narrative of human history.

According to Foucault (1972a), to reread history is to read the history of concepts. For example, how did a concept such as madness come about, how was it constructed, what were the rules for its construction, how was it organized, how was it articulated, and how was it transformed from an assumption or a belief, into an established truth, assuming a taken-for-grantedness in the practice of daily life. In other words, to study human history is to study the history of concepts; to study the history of a concept is to study the conditions necessary to make the concept possible. The task of studying the conditions of possibility is to study the historical conditions prior to the emergence of the subject, that is, to study the historical apriori conditions without a subject that will make the subject possible. If I purport to examine historical knowledge to address the absence of lived histories of girls behind bars, how do I begin to speak about the conditions of possibility without speaking of the subject of detention? Besides, if I am complicit in the conditions that create and continue to sustain the practice of detention, then how do I claim to question the very foundation on which I stand?

In what follows, I take up this task, using Foucault among other poststructural scholars, to investigate not the history of detention but the history of the concept of detention—the historical apriori conditions that made detention possible. The driving force for the study is to address the divide between the institutional framing of girls behind bars and their lived experiences. It stems from the troubling awareness that lived histories of girls behind bars is neither acknowledged nor condoned in detention or education, the very institutions that speak of transformation, empowerment, and ownership. It also stems from knowing that my understanding of the scholarly construction of knowledge is intertwined with the politics of my own colonized and internalized forms of Western knowledge deeply embedded in all I say, do, and write. I admit my research is not an innocent academic endeavor; it is a political practice that stems from multiple meanings and motivations. I see my research as emerging from a space where my Indian cultural knowledge, my western education, and the institutional power of being a teacher and a woman unwilling to give up the ideals of humanism all combined. This research is also a space where I am a feminist intensely aware of the personal, political, cultural, and historical context of othering and being othered, and on occasions both at the same time.

Beginning with an outline, this chapter is divided into three sections. In the first section, I use Baker's (2001) question "What is a child?" (p. 1) to ask, "What is detention?" By way of investigating the origins and evolution of the concept of detention, I present three excerpts from different periods in history aimed to show that detention is not a natural condition that existed waiting to be discovered. Rather, what is highlighted are the discontinuities in the concept of detention indicating detention is an unstable and invented category constituted by social, cultural, and contingent forces and interests. In addition, western philosophical epistemology has created categories, binaries, and hierarchies that shape and structure our understanding of difference, hence, our experiences need reexamination and retheorization.

In the next section, I examine various forms of discourse constitutive of detention, making it a precondition of possibility for defining experience. I analyze the social and institutional rationale for the conditions as the historical apriori for the emergence of detention. I also study the rules of formation, the networks of meaning, the hidden assumptions, the implicit values, the social practices, the setting of limits, what is said, what is not said, what can be said, and what is not to be said that are constituted before experience. The aim here is to use Foucault's (1972a) notion of rules of formation produced by specific discourses to illustrate their constructed nature.

In the final section, I consider how the conditions created by social, institutional, and professional forms of knowledge constitute the conditions that shape the horizon of possibility for the educational experience of detention. I relate the conditions for detention to the categories formed by assessment and testing practices of schooling and education that reinforce exclusion of difference. Moreover, I wish to illustrate that education itself becomes a condition for the possibility of detention. Finally, the chapter concludes with a discussion on the philosophical and epistemological foundations of detention and their impact on present day detention practices, assumptions, and policies that have consequences for girls behind bars.

Changing concept of detention

What is detention?

In studying the history of any concept, Foucault (1972a) writes that one is not led to the origins of the concept in a linear unending tracing of how the idea came about. Rather, one encounters a new type of discourse and its various effects that indicate a displacement, discontinuity, and transformations of the original concept. Foucault suggests studying the history of a concept by revisiting old documents and "questioning of the *document*" (ibid., p. 6). Accordingly, I present three excerpts to show the discontinuities and changes made visible in rereading the history of the concept of detention. The excerpts underline the complexity of answering the question, "What is detention?"

Excerpt one: 1913

The first excerpt is taken from the progressive era when saving the child was viewed as a collective problem of the entire community. One of the earliest saviors of children of the late nineteenth and early twentiethth century, Ernest Coulter (1913) notes that children and youth who ran into the law were mostly victims of circumstance and that unruly behavior was either due to parental neglect or a byproduct of the environment worsened by immigration, industrialization, and urban poverty. Below is one of the many contexts in which some of the earliest conditions, such as poverty and city overcrowding, were being associated with the term detention:

> In the Children's Courts appear most clearly all the wrongs and inequalities whereby organized society, selfish and therefore ignorant, warps, thwarts and denies the future citizen. If the child is not to grow up to become a public charge, to fill the charitable institutions, the hospitals, the prisons, he must have light and air and space. Every crowded, ill-ventilated tenement is a tax upon the future. Each too, is a breeding ground of parental as well as juvenile delinquency; for each the community is responsible. It has the right, the privilege, the power to correct these evils, but it has not been attending to the conduct of its own affairs. These matters, the massing of the population, the regulation of immigration, the hygienic conditions of the tenements, rents and wages have been left in the hand of those, who profiting by congestion and extortion, have been blind to the rights of our neighbor and his child. (ibid., xvi)

By bringing attention to conditions such as poverty, Coulter and fellow Child Savers, as they were known at the time, succeeded in attempts to locate a social base for their humanitarian cause and provided the impetus for the first juvenile justice system. The juvenile justice system was part of the social movement to reform youth and was considered to have revolutionized the way society viewed poverty and overcrowding—as undesirable social conditions in need of reform. Their efforts resulted in the first juvenile court system in Chicago in 1899 that inadvertently linked social conditions to reform, reform to youth in poor social conditions, and all of these to legal intervention.

Excerpt two: 1951

An excerpt in *The Journal of Criminal Law, Criminology, and Police Science* gives a view that raises the problem of defining detentions in opposition to the presumed norm (Stullken 1956, p. 833). The author cites the *Illinois Review Statute of 1951* stating the legal conditions for identifying detention:

> Any male child who while under the age of 17 or any female child who while under the age of 18 violates any law of this state; or is incorrigible, or knowingly associates with thieves, vicious or immoral persons; or without just cause and without consents of its parents, guardian, or custodian absents itself from its home or place of abode, or is growing up in idleness or crime; or know-kingly frequents a house of ill-repute; or knowingly frequents any policy shop or place where any gaming device is operated; or frequents any saloon or dram shop where intoxicating liquors are sold; or patronizes or visits any public pool room or bucket shop; or wanders about the streets in the night without being on any lawful business, or lawful occupation; or habitually wanders about any railroad yards or tracks or jumps or attempts to jump onto any moving train; or enters any car or engine without lawful authority; or uses vile, obscene, vulgar, profane or indecent language in any public place or about any school house; or is guilty of indecent or lascivious conduct. (*Illinois Review Statute* 1951, 190–221, cited in Stullken 1956, 833)

In contrast to the first excerpt, the emphasis has shifted dramatically from youth as victims of parental neglect to delinquent youth as morally responsible for making poor choices. Although the conditions described above practically implicate a large population of youth as delinquent, new conditions of age, gender, morality, habits, and behaviors such as loitering, profanity, and incorrigibility have been added to the possibilities for the emergence and identification of detention, of one who is guilty and in need of correction.

Excerpt three: 2009

Today, conditions necessary for the experience of detention are more than social and legal—medical and clinical conditions are being constituted on a daily basis, as are surveillance techniques. Below is the mission statement of the detention facility for girls where I worked as a teacher:

> At the Juvenile Academy the treatment process for examination, monitoring, and treatment begins upon arrival. Progress is noted constantly. We agree with Mr. Robert Ressler, former head of the FBI Behavioral Sciences Unit, and Dr. Stanton Samenow, chief psychologist for the federal St. Elizabeth's Hospital in Washington, DC, that many youth lack appropriate morals and ideals and develop ways of thinking and behaving detrimental to themselves and society. The treatment at Juvenile Academy focuses on providing good role models and high ideals for delinquent youth while simultaneously helping them correct the thinking errors, which plague them and prevent them from reaching their goals. When pre- and post-treatment scores on the MMPI-A are compared we find that students consistently show a significant decrease in anger, depression, and suspiciousness, and also show clear increases in self-esteem and moral direction. Thus, both clinical impressions and clinical testing indicate the value of the treatment experience at Juvenile Academy. (Juvenile Facility webpage, 2009)

Discontinuities and displacements

The above excerpts illustrate that the history of detention is not about linear development and progress; rather, the history of detention indicates many breaks and reversals. The first excerpt is a discourse from 1913 that explicitly identifies youth as victims of circumstance. Youth are identified, their behaviors considered a direct effect of parental neglect compounded by community indifference. While holding parents responsible for child neglect is taken for granted in most situations, what is noteworthy is that the community is also held accountable for child neglect and other "social" ills. In the second excerpt from 1951, there is a profusion of conditions identified—idleness, loitering, profanity, and lasciviousness—conditions that point not to any empirical or scientific knowledge. Instead, the conditions reflect the development of a social and moral sensibility eager to delineate categories of sameness and difference for dividing people, places, and actions. However, as the discourse indicates, community is no longer held accountable, marking a major disruption in the move from community responsibility to domestic/parental care or neglect.

As is evident from the difference in the excerpts, the notion that children and youth were victims ended abruptly, to be replaced by various categories of offenses classified and ranked by degrees of deviant behaviors. What was viewed in 1913 as parental neglect changed to societal neglect, and by 2009, youth once considered neglected are seen as criminals. The classifications of a range of behaviors designated as normal or offending are now taken for granted when in fact they are invented categories and labels that speak the language and practice of normalization, inclusion, and exclusion.

In the last excerpt from 2009, there is a marked shift from social categories that exclude and include youth behaviors, to a new level of objectification, that of institutional and disciplinary techniques of observation, examination, and normalization. Today, the conditions of possibility for detention are measurable, predictable, and controllable by institutional surveillance and professional systems of knowledge such as medical, clinical, and statistical. A parent is no longer blamed, nor is the community held responsible. Rather, the discourse has shifted to constitute the individual as object of observation, medicalization, and criminalization before being subjected to rehabilitation, normalization, and socialization.

The conditions that make detention possible today are not based on empirical evidence or objective truth; they are an amalgam of historical and social practices that have constructed categories confirming the possibility of power for those who dominate over the dominated. Such discourses create the spaces for subject-positions such that categories can be formed and boundaries drawn between what can be included and what can be excluded. The theme of discontinuity is set in contrast with the continuous history of juvenile detention. The social forces and cultural sensibilities that produce dramatic shifts in thought point to a system of categorization and classification taking shape through various forms of discourse.

What is evident is not the unfolding of a grand narrative of development and progress but a dramatic dislocation of thought, "*displacements and transformations*" (Foucault 1972a, p. 4) of old conditions and formation of new ones where both continuity and discontinuity might be located. In the last century, the changing concept of detention has constituted penal justice, rehabilitative ideal, and restorative justice. The discourses on penal, rehabilitation, and restorative justice are distinct discourses, yet they retain traces of previous discourses and are organized within a network of discourses that constitute the conditions for the possibility of detention. The changing history of detention reveals a "proliferation of discontinuities in the history of ideas" (ibid., p. 7) that challenges all attempts at creating totalities.

In summary, the history of detention reveals that in the last hundred years, the concept of detention has undergone many changes indicating that there is no single idea, ideology, policy, or practice that can define detention with any certitude. The conditions that create detention are contingent upon context, not upon objectivity, and therefore cannot be represented or generalized across time and space. The assumptions and beliefs that inform the practice of detention cannot be located within any form of empirical science or transcendental condition; rather, they are a product of cultural practices and historical forces. The inclusion and exclusion of what constitutes detention is an arbitrary system that cannot be pinned either to the principle of absolute truth, universal reason, or human progress.

In the next section, I examine the historical conditions for detention formed and articulated through discursive practices. I illustrate how different discourses relate to one another to form a network of discursive practices and the rules of their formation.

Historical apriori conditions

In this section, I use a Foucauldian reading of the historical apriori conditions that make detention possible. In order to understand the lived experience of students, it became important to examine the history of detention. To examine the history of detention as it has been documented is not enough; I needed to examine the history of the concept of detention. The historical conditions I elaborate upon are social, judicial, scientific, and institutional beginning at the end of the nineteenth century. In a Foucauldian reading of history, historical concepts are not rooted in origins or traditions but are formed by discursive practices. Discursive practices abide by historical, cultural, and linguistic rules of formation for selecting, organizing, producing, and distributing forms of knowledge and creating the conditions that allow certain statements and relations among statements to be made (Foucault 1972a). I also deconstruct the "rules of formation" (ibid., p. 52) to understand how discursive practices are constituted. According to Foucault, the rules of formation are the production of objects, enunciative modalities, constitution of the concept, and strategic possibilities.

In reading historical documents through a Foucauldian lens, I illustrate the shift in discourses that have created detention as it currently exists. Specifically, my focus is on the discourse of parental neglect in raising children that shifts to societal responsibility for not taking care of children neglected by parents. The latter discourse shifts once again to blame youth for their behaviors and lifestyles leading to the discourse on criminalization of youth. The purpose of reading historical conditions as emerging from a set of discursive practices is to demystify history from the claims to truth, absolute knowledge, and universal reason. Alternately, it is to see historical contingencies, reversals, and discontinuities that push the limits beyond what has been said or thought.

I will use the three excerpts given in the previous section to make a Foucauldian analysis of the historical conditions that created detention highlighting the various forms of discourse. What conditions made detention possible over a 100 years ago? The following questions guide the analysis: How did one particular discourse become privileged over another? How have science, society, and the law chosen detention as the object of discourse and deployed it as a system of knowledge with its own rules, regulations, limits, and histories?

Many historical forces can be traced to the constitution of detention over the past 110 years. The formation of the concept of detention occurred in conjunction with other practices of social exclusion, imprisonment of nonnormative persons, kinds of hospitalizations, and judicial laws—factors that provide the conditions for the normalization of social exclusion in everyday life. The origin of a concept or emergence of the object cannot be situated within a single field of knowledge. There is a relation between statements even when they emerge from different fields of knowledge (Baker 2002). Statements include all forms of implicit knowledge (everyday conversations), formal knowledge (academic theories and disciplines), and everything that is said about the concept. The link between statements is the referent, as "statements different in form, and dispersed in time, form a group if they refer to one and the same object" (Foucault 1972a, p. 32). Hence, a concept such as detention emerges as the object of multiple discourses from diverse fields such as judicial, legal, and medical.

The three excerpts in the previous section reveal that a set of conditions was put into place whereby the objects of detention were constituted and the rules made operative. The location of particular conditions such as poverty, misery, and vice, or incorrigibility, indecency, and profanity provide the rationalization for identifying the object for those conditions. The conditions defined in the excerpts differentiate, limit, and objectify detention in spite of its nonexistence to make the object "manifest, nameable, and describable" as a social problem (ibid., p. 41).

Social apriori conditions

By the end of the nineteenth century, social welfare, the child saving movement, education, science, and the law saw a convergence of beliefs and practices that made detention possible. During this time, social conditions saw many changes such as industrialization, urbanization, and immigration that created new classes of people such as the urban poor and the labor class, displacing communities and creating homelessness and destitution (Stullken 1956). Social researchers report that poverty, overcrowding, poor health conditions, and increases in disease and crime were seen as interrelated social ills that needed philanthropic and government intervention. In keeping with the humanist ideals, social welfare organizations focused on how to solve the problems of homelessness, poor hygiene, loitering, inadequate health, child neglect, housing problems, and struggling parents.

As the first excerpt reveals, by 1913, "the massing of population, the regulation of immigration, the hygienic conditions of the tenements, rents, and wages" became a focus—the dividing line between groups of people was easily drawn. Through a system of identification, the emergence of the concept of detention began to take shape—inventing a social problem that needed attention. Private social welfare organizations constituted by philanthropists, such as Child Savers, focused their attention on rescuing children and youth from conditions triggered by immigration, industrialization, and urbanization. What occurs is making the social problem visible and linking it to other conditions that will form a matrix of conditions necessary for the production of detention. Urbanization, immigration, and overpopulation are directly linked to charitable institutions, the hospitals, and the prisons (Addams 1925).

Legal and judicial apriori conditions

Articulating a new discourse that called for humanist responses to social problems, Child Savers succeeded in making the condition of children and youth as victims visible to the public eye as well as in the eyes of the law (Platt 1969). While they condemned the family of youth who were neglected and saw poverty and other related conditions as harmful, they started a social discourse that organized and grouped youth according to the help they needed. They made humanitarian appeals to the public to come forward in rescuing children and youth from the poverty-stricken conditions that denied youth the right to basic living conditions. The Child Savers also felt the community was responsible, and petitioned the law to legitimize their appeals in order to elicit a generous public response. In their view, the social system had failed youth and the legal system needed to intervene.

Although Child Savers formally requested the establishment of a Children's Court to assist children and youth, the children's court soon transformed into the first juvenile justice court in 1899 (Krisberg 2005). The Child Savers implicated the community and the legal system through their humanist discourse of helping children and youth. More importantly, the humanist discourse indicates an organized and systematic order by which groups of people could be sorted and selected based on the social conditions of their day-to-day existence. The intervention of the law transformed the social discourse into a legal one through a series of writs and statutes aimed at helping youth considered neglected. However, the legal condition also produced and imposed a set of rules for caregivers who were required to take care of children along legal guidelines for parenting (Baker and Macguire 2005). A law-abiding family would now be responsible for raising children in a specific way and within specified regulations. Legislation was in place for protecting youth and children from parental neglect, and other legislation was introduced for dealing with errant parents (ibid. 2005). It was not long before the Chicago juvenile justice system was replicated in other states, setting in motion not only the juvenile justice system but a host of other related services such as child protection laws, juvenile detention homes, and correctional facilities for children and neglected youth.

If the aim of Child Savers in 1913 was to care for youth who were victims, by 1951—as the second excerpt shows—the emphasis is on behavior identified as delinquent and ways to identify and monitor forms of delinquency (Dubois and Karcher 2005). This transformation in the language indicates the history of detention is not one of continuity and progress; rather, it is marked by discontinuity and displacement of thought. The discourse has shifted from parental and societal neglect to criminalization of youth. A noticeable emphasis is on the moral imperative as a condition that enabled the dividing practice of sorting groups of people into categories.

Whereas youth are considered victims in 1913, by 1951 they are considered responsible for their own conduct. For example, in 1951 new conditions linked to the formation of detention are constituted such as running away from home, being idle, incorrigible, and immoral. Conditions that were signs of delinquent behavior were not new to the social order but are now given a new meaning under a legal and judicial framework. The shift is to modify undesirable behaviors of youth who are held responsible for their decisions. Thus within each of these conditions are networks of meaning that define, for example, what is normativity, what is criminal, what is deviancy.

In spite of the historical break in thought, traces of the old conditions are visible in the creation of new conditions. For example, in 1913 society had the "power" and "privilege" to right social ills; however, by 1951 the law assumes this power and speaks in terms of "lawful business" and "lawful occupation." When traces of the old conditions are reconstituted as new conditions, they are contextual. Taken out of context, the foundation on which the law stands is constructed on assumed authority. When the historical apriori conditions for detention are proven unstable, they also indicate possibilities for future change.

Social reformers, scientists, and law enforcement, while not necessarily working together, simultaneously define the conditions necessary for detention. In the field of empirical science, youth behavior was studied in terms of binaries such as normativity and deviancy, and by 2009, similar lines of exclusions and inclusions were drawn by the medical profession in the language of infection, immunization, and treatment (Baker 2002). Professionals such as psychologists, therapists, doctors, counselors, educators, probation officers, lawyers, and judges assume important roles in the constitution of the conditions that made detention possible. Different agencies and groups decide what the problem is, who constitutes the problem, how to view the problem, how to speak about the problem, and how to treat the problem. This is the professionalization and institutionalization of the conditions necessary for the existence of detention and its subsequent naming, describing, and treating.

Scientific apriori conditions

Originating from the biological sciences, social Darwinism gave credence to the belief that social problems were caused by innate criminal tendencies, stating that biological defects caused criminal behavior and was a natural occurrence in certain groups of people (Baker 2002). Dr I. N. Kerlin (1890) of the Pennsylvania Institute of Feeble-Minded Children conducted a study on "feeble-mindedness" as a condition for criminal behavior in children and notes:

> . . . if there existed a class of little children whose heredity and aberrations are such as to make them predestined inmates of our insane hospitals and jails, what an advance we would make in the diminution of crime and lunacy by a methodized registration and training of such children, or these failing, by their early and entire withdrawal from the community . . . that he shall not scathe our common stock with permanent taint in blood and morale. (PNCCC 1890, 244–50)

On a similar note, Galton's (1881) eugenics claimed that biological conditions divided the human race into superior and inferior races, a division that reinforces categories of inclusion and exclusion in the name of scientific practice. Lombroso (1893), a giant figure in criminology in the nineteenth century, conducted experimental research to conclude that physical features are a condition for degenerative behavior. Lombroso advocated that instead of the law identifying conditions for detention, science should be left to identify, observe, and treat the conditions, adding "The criminal by nature is lazy, debauched, cowardly, not susceptible to remorse, without foresight. . . . As the born criminal is without remedy, he must be continually confined, and allowed no provisional mercy or liberty . . ." (ibid., pp. 44–5). With the increasing empirical and scientific research on human behavior, certain behaviors or physical features were considered abnormal and later became conditions for objectification through observation and treatment (see Gould 1895; see also Winfield 2007). Clinical observation, medical examinations, and psychological evaluations, continue to create many conditions for normalization and socialization of behaviors.

Discursive and nondiscursive conditions

As the third excerpt indicates, another transformation occurs by 2009, one based on constituting scientific and disciplinary techniques for identifying the conditions for detention. According to the excerpt, conditions can now be scientifically observed and diagnostically treated through "clinical impressions and clinical testing." The convergence of several discourses such as social, legal, medical, therapeutic, biological, as well as moral are regulated through their own systems of knowledge as well as mediated by institutional discourse (see Baker 2002; see also Winfield 2007). Today all these discourses coexist even as they are produced in different contexts. Social, legal, scientific, medical, therapeutic, and moral discourses are not permanent givens; rather, they exist by themselves, coexist with each other, displace one another, and influence one another.

The dispersion and displacement of discursive formations indicates that their lines of interiority and exteriority are not fixed and are, therefore, subject to change. As an example, Foucault describes how in the eighteenth century the medical question addressed to the patient changed from, "What is the matter with you?" to "Where does it hurt?" (Foucault 1973, p. xviii). The difference in the doctor's question denotes a shift from seeing the person/patient to examining a medical "case" or a "condition," a move that shifts the focus from the human subject to the object of scientific examination. Foucault calls this shift from the subject to the object a shift in discursive practices that create the conditions for a denial of the human subject.

The process of objectification continues through a constant reformation of discursive and nondiscursive relations to constitute new versions of detention. For example, detention as correctional or penal shifted to rehabilitative in the 1930s only to shift once again to a combination of the penal and rehabilitative (Platt 1969). Significantly, in present day practices detention is constantly being reordered through discursive as well as nondiscursive practices. Nondiscursive practices are closely related to the discursive practices. For example, the relation between institutions such as the judiciary and detention are also linked through nondiscursive relations such as monitoring devices, cameras, and other disciplinary machines required by detention. Nondiscursive practices can be located in business practices that continue to reconstitute detention through surveillance machinery or medical diagnostics that create clinical conditions for sorting out abnormalities.

So far, I have deconstructed the historical conditions that constitute the present history of detention. I have drawn from a Foucauldian reading of history to show that the concept of detention is constituted by cultural and historical conditions. Hence, detention cannot be explained on humanist, transcendental, metaphysical, or rational grounds. The purpose of my analysis is not to reconstruct what detention is, but to show the relationship between heterogeneous discourses and the conditions for detention. Evidence to my claims is not limited to the documents I study and can be traced to other historical documents that study and record the sociology, politics, and context of crime such as *Journal of*

Criminal Law; Criminology and Police Science; Annals of the American Academy of Political and Social Science; American Sociological Review; National Probation and Parole Association Yearbook; and *Proceedings of the National Conference of Charities and Correction (PNCCC)* (see Platt 1969).

Studying the contexts that influence the production of knowledge about detention shows the constitutive role these contexts play in the creation and validation of detention knowledge. Foucault (1972a) speaks of a set of "laws of possibility, rules of existence for the objects that are names, designated, or described within it, and for the relations that are affirmed or denied in it" (p. 91)—historical apriori that determines the object before it appears. The discursive practices that construct detention exist prior to understanding how detention is positioned as object. Discursive practices that constitute detention offer a different view of history and an interpretation of how knowledge about detention is always produced from a specific position, inscribed within particular interests, values, and beliefs.

Principles of categories, normative rules, and institutional regulations are all interrelated although not universalized, and their homogenous unity cannot be accepted without question (Baker 2002). They have not arisen out of nothing and are constructs whose rationale must be examined. The conditions that legitimize such forms of knowledge must be questioned for their structure and purpose. The lack of origins or foundations for the conditions of detention or the decontextualization of statements that emerge, disappear, or reappear has to do with the purpose of detention. As Baker (2001) suggests, isolated statements held together by virtue of a set of relations are unstable and subject to change. Thus, discursive practices constitute the concept of detention and predetermine the conditions for its emergence, and also offer a way out of the circuit by suggesting possibilities for existence rather than predetermining one possibility by shutting out multiplicities.

What rules of formation structure the privileging of certain discourses over others? By referring to the same object, statements from several contexts form networks of meaning that maintain a thematic consistency and validity of an interrelated "corpus of knowledge" (Foucault 1972a, p. 33). The set of relations between different discourses "define these objects without reference to the *ground*, the *foundation* of things, but by relating them to the body of rules that enable them to form objects of a discourse and thus constitute the conditions of their historical appearance" (ibid., pp. 47–8). According to the rules of formation, detention as a discourse within the justice system that intersects with other discourses is formed through the linking of discourses that speak of the same object. Whether social, legal, or scientific, a series of discourses that give detention a specific identity are "constituted by the functioning of the *field of use* in which it is placed" (ibid., p. 104). The discursive links in a discursive field form the object of discourse and operate as discursive practices that reconstitute, order, and reorder the conditions for detention.

In summary, the constitution of the conditions of possibility for the experience of detention emerged in relation to two interrelated interventions: child saving and the juvenile justice system. The Child Savers initiated the discourse on helping children and youth who were victims of parental neglect. During the time, public demand for action to protect children and youth led to the establishment of the Children's Court, which eventually became the first juvenile court in Chicago. The subsequent creation of juvenile detention emerged from the juvenile court system. Such interventions, whether child saving, Children's court, juvenile justice system, or juvenile detention, were based on a set of rules and regulations that are now common assumptions of detention. Some of the taken-for-granted regulations include categorization of normal and offending behaviors; classification of offending behaviors under the label of status or criminal acts; and stratification within classifications to form hierarchies and systems. The construction of conditions indicates that the subject is not only objectified, but the conditions for its experience are laid out as historical apriori constituted by various discourses.

Thus, the construction of detention does not indicate a continuous history of progress and development; rather it is marked by dramatic shifts and breaks that continue to constitute and reconstitute what detention is or should be. The constitution of the historical conditions for the emergence of detention has undergone multiple transformations, making it impossible to trace its origins, its limits, or its definition. The above Foucauldian analysis is positioned against the ontological foundations for a universal subject of detention, or an essential detainee. It is also a challenge to the scientific and empirical claims to rationality or the will to truth and knowledge that are the epistemological foundations of detention. Predetermining the possibility for the experience of detention is the very point at which detention becomes an impossibility. Within this impossibility is the opening of strategic possibilities for change—a field that is open to the unthought, the unintelligible, and the unknowable.

In the next section, I turn to practices in schooling that categorize conditions for detention. I offer examples of classroom-based constructed categories that constitute the historical apriori conditions for detention. I analyze some of these categories to show how educational discourse intersects with multiple discourses that continue to create and recreate detention.

Educational discourses and detention

Educational discourse

Knowledge about detention is produced from specific discourses, inscribed within particular interests, values, and beliefs. In this section, my interest is to trace particular effects of educational discourses, particularly through a poststructural analytics of the effects of power or the circulation of power as being effects that are both productive and repressive (Foucault 1972a). I attempt to trace how categorical differences such as gender and sexuality are the products of developmental science and to see not only how such categories were formed but also their implications for the education of detainees. What are the effects of power/knowledge when such categories are normalized and universalized through educational and theoretical practices? What I illustrate is the web of discourses from philosophy, history, and education that make detention as it is known possible.

Detention is a concept within a discursive field that draws attention to the formation of categories, binaries, and hierarchies as well as the ruptures and displacements that have been suppressed in the reporting of history (Foucault 1977). Foucauldian ideas and terms are important for conceptualizing how education in detention has been constituted and for reconceptualizing new ways of thinking. Foucault (1972a) conceives a concept as an "effect" (p. 193) or a process of discursive formation that is continuous and discontinuous as it combines with many other processes to make up a discursive practice. A discursive practice is neither corporeal nor physical but exists in a discursive relationship to other discursive practices. Education in detention functions through a series of processes, in what Foucault calls discursive practices, operating within a discursive field. These practices function with other practices such as bodies, identities, subjectivities, time, and space. Such practices also function as "prohibitions, exclusions, limitations, values, freedoms, and transgressions" and are linked directly to the ethical (ibid., p. 193).

What discursivity enables is a field of power relations in which the embodied have a capacity to be affected by discursive effects that have no link to the referent.

Such discursive practices need to be examined as they legitimate domination by constructing a reality and the conditions for the experience of subjugation. In the light of Foucault's analysis, I examine the categorical frameworks driven by empiricist and positivist reasoning that informs classroom practices in detention. The philosophy of the individual self who makes the right decisions in order to succeed academically is predicated upon claims to rationality and truth (Braidotti 1993). This hierarchical privilege bestowed on rationality over embodiment is a condition for school success evidenced in the categories and binaries that constitute the labeling practices of schooling. Foucault (1977) calls labels dividing practices.

Labeling through IQ tests, psychological evaluations, medical tests, and standardized tests are some of the more obvious forms of conditions constituted by philosophy, psychology, and science and sustained by educational and detention discourses. Low IQ, learning disabled, slow learners, retarded, academically challenged, ADHD, and LD, are some of the school labels that indicate some form of learning or behavioral disorder. The labels do not follow any systematic process of selection as physical, mental, neurological, social, or psychological disorders are indiscriminately used to differentiate between students who can be predicted to succeed and those who are slated to fail (Baker 2002). In spite of the bell curve phenomena, social research shows that IQ and IQ tests do not explain educational achievement and test scores, and nor is educational ability genetically determined as claimed by Galton and social Darwinists (Winfield 2007). Rather, educational achievement as measured through tracking and testing reveal that when categories are constituted they are designed for giving some students greater exposure to knowledge while other students suffer reduced exposure to knowledge and low expectations from teachers letting the latter group of students fall through the cracks (Apple 2004). Therefore, deconstructing concepts and practices in the educational system such as special education reveal the discursive dividing processes by which education simultaneously constitutes privilege for some students while disempowering others.

I will give four examples of this discursive division as conditions necessary for the domination of certain forms of practices that differentiate in the context of schools.

Intervention in detention: One particular example of an intervention is rehabilitation. Rehabilitation as a prime site for the production and legitimizing of categorical distinctions underlies the discourse on education for rehabilitation. The literature on education for rehabilitation has been primarily atheoretical and totalizing, with an underlying tendency to view interventions as unproblematic (Newburn and Shiner 2005). In examining closely, it becomes clear that interventions constitute a perceived danger to the social order produced through dividing practices that claim moral authority. For example, the discourse on poverty as seen from the 1911 excerpt reveals that interventions deployed in the name of rehabilitation are dividing practices that gain legitimacy through their links with other discourses such as gender and schooling, and these are constituted as threats or disruption to the normative sense of order and controlled through categories of deviance and normalcy. As noted in this example, interventions in education are not constituted or reproduced in an objective field but emerge within conceptual categories of deviance and normalcy.

The social and empirical ordering of behaviors and objectifying of institutional knowledge is integral to rehabilitation. Rehabilitation is an enactment of the social normative order and a testimonial to the constitutive conceptualization of detention and its practices (Platt 1969). Education for rehabilitation is questionable when it is based on the concept of detention whose meaning and form are marked by discontinuity and change. Viewed from this perspective, detention is not an unchanging, permanent continuity but shaped by the meaning that is attributed to it. Hence, when detention is an interpretive practice, so are concepts such as education and rehabilitation.

Tests: The third excerpt, taken from a detention facility in 2009, shows the centrality of monitoring, testing, and measuring especially pervasive in justifying the need for creating "scientific" categories to contain differences. Testing, standardized, IQ, English proficiency, psychological evaluation, medical examination, and clinical tests to name a few, are ways of drawing distinctions between different types of students with the assumption that tests are an objective marker of abilities and deficiencies through classifying practices. What Baker calls "problem populations" or the "production and the hunt for different forms of disability, unreadiness, at-risk-city" (Baker 2002, p. 5). Rather than engage with difference, conditions constitutive of subjects for ADHD, English proficiency, and LD classrooms are created. The justification for conditions without a subject, in the context of testing, comes from emphasizing that scientific methods and procedures have been followed at every step of the process of labeling and classifying.

Special Education: Various testing measures are instrumental in creating subcategories such as special education. Education categories in detention, such as special education, are not only constituted by discourse but function to hide inequalities in the language of absence. Psychometric tests used to define intelligence or mismeasure intelligence in order to explain the achievement gap as a cognitive deficiency are the rationale for categorizing students as "learning disabled," "remedial learner," and "slow learner," thereby segregating some students from the rest of the student population (ibid. 2002).

Embedded in the practice of testing is the assumption that rational and objective scientific methods can solve the challenges of schooling when in fact scientific methods provide the conditions for categories that are oppressive (Grumet 2006). School practices such as testing and tracking become representative of institutional structures, and their ongoing existence depends upon their continued reconstruction in everyday discourses. Once a particular discourse dominates all others, it is kept alive discursively as an established truth. Thus, the interconnected discourses of scientific methods, empirical science, and education construct differential categories to produce inequality that is legitimized through institutional power such as schools and prisons and sustained through an institutional set of connections.

Gender: The constructed nature of empirical science and its claims to objective knowledge is evident in the categories of man and woman that universalize and exclude differences within categories (Braidotti 1993). Therefore, to break categories down to their conceptual level is to uncover how they are constructed by discourse and to challenge their constitutive reality. Key to categorical differentiation between the sexes is the belief that girls need to be treated differently from boys as sexuality and motherhood call for gendered tracking of girl's bodies (Chesney-Lind 2001). This is reflected in formal instructional programs designed as interventions in detention classrooms. For example, as seen from the 2009 excerpt, there was a general assumption that in contrast to boys, all girls were to be protected from early sexual activity and be given preemptive moral counseling (see Feld 1999).

The biological conceptualization of girls as the weaker sex hides the underlying values and the sociohistorical contexts in which ideas are created, shaped, and deployed. Under the discourse of girls needing protection is a more insidious power relation that places girls in an inferior, weaker position than boys. Curricula that advocates gendering of education restricts the right to vital information such as sexuality, choice and consent, sexual freedom, sexual violence, health care, and parenting. The concept of gendered differentiation locates the problem not with social and cultural discursively related practices, but with the biological and is constitutive of the production of gendered identities in the name of science.

Thus, the creation of categories to be studied, diagnosed, and treated is part of the discourse on the school practice of labeling and "hunting" for disabilities/ aberrations. One context where difference is constantly under surveillance is in the context of education. The terms "normal behavior" and "offending behavior" refer to how everyday usage of terms, policies, practices, and discourses constitute what is considered as normal and how a person who is normal should be, behave, and become, indicating that normalcy is a construct of discourse and that which destabilizes the discourse must be contained (Foucault 1965). Implicit in defining or constructing normativity is the tracking of deviancy. Complicit in the defining of a normal student is the defining of a deviant one. While rehabilitation becomes the road to bringing deviancy back to normativity, the treatments for being different are constituted prior to detention. Expressed differently, if students are labeled as different, then the aim of rehabilitation shifts to "correcting" difference into sameness.

The new discourse in education in the form of school reforms such as the NCLB Act (2001) does not exclude certain groups from mainstream schooling per se but has conceptualized and reframed categories that define, exclude, marginalize, and set apart for treatment, therapy, and correction—exceptional, gifted, regular, remedial, disabled, deviant, criminal, and so on and so forth (Pinar 2004). The relationship in debates around what is considered inclusive schooling, who falls into the mainstream dominant culture of schooling, and who must be excluded are in place prior to the student's arrival.

Detention deploys a categorization system that provides, on multiple levels, for the specific conditions of possibility for social and institutional control. Whether the conditions mark students for failure or success, according to Baker, "all forms of schooling teleologically seek to govern, discipline, and engineer students' being toward some named ideal" (Baker 2002, p. 7). In spite of the above categories, detention is a development within civilized societies and is seen as a sign of progress.

The question then is, is this categorization and exclusion aimed at prevention, remedy, or protection of those who are labeled able and normative? Whatever the answer to the question, public schools and detention classrooms are two sides of the same objective—one creates conditions for educating the normative and promising, the other creates conditions for weeding out difference. On the surface, the normalizing and humanist goals of rehabilitation leaves no room for questioning those goals, which has implications for detention as a system of normalization as well as a policy for controlling difference.

The "production and hunt for different forms of disability" from the 1911 and 1951 excerpts the first section of this chapter, combined with the developmental theories of adolescent behavior as seen in the 2009 excerpt, create their own set of educational problems, each problem calling for specific diagnosis, study, and remedy. Baker's analyses of disability suggest that the move from penal justice to restorative justice discourse illustrates the new phase in rehabilitation even in the context of schools is at best another discourse on the hunt for deviancy. While restorative justice as an intervention seems new, it is viewed as dealing with the old discourse on deviancy.

Rehabilitative practices aimed at altering deviancy of mind and body contain unchallenged assumptions of what is right and what is considered wrong, implying freedom of choice, and that wrong choices have culminated in detention. By establishing the conditions for offensive behavior and how to normalize offensive behaviors through "responsibility" and "selfhood," the school system absolves itself of responsibilities. Instead the conditions authorize schools, teachers, therapists, psychologists, and doctors the power to evaluate behaviors, define problems, and decide upon the remedies, which leaves the basis for deviance unexamined or unquestioned.

While the concept of rehabilitation is not new, it takes on contemporary forms of the power/knowledge nexus that go beyond Foucauldian analysis to a nondiscursive technology-mediated reality of everyday life in detention. For example, detention did not remain unaffected with the coming of technology that put into place electronic and digital monitoring devices that changed the rules of rehabilitation due to a change in surveillance techniques. The shift from self-discipline of the individual to cameras, video recording, and computer systems has also modified the rules of rehabilitation and changed all the other fields such as medical, educational, and therapeutic in relation to detention. As technologies of power, detention can be viewed as a vehicle and object of power constituting the experience of social deviancy, psychological disorders, physiological abnormality, and educational disabilities (Foucault 1977).

Education, like rehabilitation discourse, is oriented toward defining conditions for normativity but, unlike the dominant rehabilitation discourse, conceives the relationship between detention and morality in significantly different ways. While the dominant discourse on rehabilitation, derived from developmental psychology, attempts to correct behaviors by focusing on the prevention of negative behaviors, educational aims in detention are put into practice by speaking to student responsibility and choice (Goodstein 2001). Intervention, therefore, is not to prevent behaviors that are undesirable but to manage and control behaviors that are considered abnormal, deviant, and offensive.

Rehabilitation is a set of conditions necessary for education in detention and is enacted in a detention space operating within the discourse of psychology, therapy, education, and other normative value systems. As a discursive formation, detention cannot be frozen in time, nor can the object of detention be represented as a fixed image rooted in place, a movement across time periods, places, events, concepts, transformations, mutations. The complex flows between different discourses such as the excerpts dated 1911 and 2009 are evidenced by the process of rehabilitation as well as the degree to which rehabilitation is used to regulate and control difference at this time.

In the last hundred years, there has been an increase in categories of differences used to mark students who do not fall within the norms defined by educational standards and developmental psychology (Newburn and Shiner 2005). Studies reveal that students labeled different from the norm have higher dropout rates, emotional difficulties, and behavioral problems. The problem is manifested in school interventions under labels such as ADHD (attention deficit hyperactivity disorder), ESL, ELL, LD (learning disabled), and BD (behavior disorder), to name a few. Although interventions are meant to help students to reach higher levels of educational achievement, studies show that such labels that track students have a negative impact on students (ibid. 2005). At the same time, the interventions show that the discourse on rehabilitation has moved from a moral one to a medical one. Labeling differences through medical, empirical, or educational testing is part of school policies reinforcing marginalization (Fine and McClelland 2006) through, for example, tracking or school reform such as the NCLB Act that promote categories based on academic disability aimed at homogenization of heterogeneous groups.

The construction of difference at the beginning of the twenty-first century is framed within social and cultural contexts as well as medical and scientific diagnosis and produces norms of behaviors and attitudes. Psychologists, therapists, and educators do not agree on the nature of deviancy, its various manifestations, its treatment or even what constitutes the norm from which deviancy is measured (Meiners 2007). Nevertheless, in the interweaving of the different discourses on detention, deviancy, and rehabilitation, or the moral and medical rationale for prevention and cures for deviancy, is the ever-changing construction of detention. When the constitution of detention is connected to discursive practices that are historically unstable, then the category of detention is an unstable category challenging all the different ways its stability is presented and represented. Therefore, to see detention as neither stable nor universal is to occupy a different position in the formulation of what counts as knowledge about detention.

These multiple levels of professional expertise indicate conditions constituted through medical, educational, and many other discourses. Foucault refers to these systems as technologies or "methods of power and knowledge assumed responsibility for the life processes and undertook to control and modify them" in an attempt to normalize and homogenize all social groups including children (Foucault 1977, pp. 142–4). Foucault's work is a reminder that detention, rehabilitation, and education have become technologies of power as part of the discourse to control and regulate the mind, body, and emotions functioning through disciplinary supervision, psychological testing, physical monitoring—technologies of power—organized around sameness and difference.

Discussion

Every discourse contributes to the meanings of terms and practices that constitute identities as objects of discourse. Discourse has significant consequences as it predicates the appearance as well as the objectification of difference. The production of meaning within the discourse is embedded in local, cultural, social, and political contexts. The meaning of each discourse is significant only in the specific historical context of its production, within the context of its articulation. For example, take rehabilitation. Rehabilitation can be traced over time to identify its main articulations as moments with special historically embedded discourses.

In 1951, it could be the penalization of youth where youth were punished and corrected or it could be articulated within a reform discourse where rehabilitation was considered a restorative process. As context changes discourse changes, as production of meaning changes it calls for change in the deployment of knowledge by social and institutional systems. Discourse is contingent and cannot be fixed or constituted as the foundation applicable to the entire field of differences and multiplicities. There is never any total interiority or exteriority of any space, discursive or nondiscursive—the conditions necessary are always constitutive; identity cannot be generalized or totalized (Butler 1990). Any form of centrality can be subverted within a discursive field that is discontinuous.

For example, detention is a recent historical development dating to the end of the nineteenth century. Yet laws, policies, and discourses about detention have imprinted our collective cultural memory to believe that detention has always existed and must therefore continue to exist to protect the public and correct the offender. What is forgotten is that detention is a construct that confers and reduces the value placed upon the life of those who are detained mostly for being different from mainstream definitions of the normative.

The point at which detention fulfils the rehabilitation program is also the point at which it offends the very principle of rehabilitation—the production of subservience. How detention comes to be seen as possessing certain inherent or natural attributes such as deviancy or immorality is intricately related to the acontextual and ahistorical representation of detention. The history of detention cannot be written outside the discursive networks of criminal justice, school, and medical epistemology. The workings of the justice system enable us to view the importance assumed by detention as a political problematic. The process of pathologizing difference entails observing, dissecting, classifying, labeling, excluding, normalizing, correcting—discursive practices that turn into a mechanics of power. To turn young women's nonconforming behaviors into pathological problems or medical problems that can be treated, to construct young women who are different as defective are the disastrous consequences of assuming the truth claims of positivist and scientific methods.

There is disagreement in literature, whether looked at historically or in contemporary terms, on how to define or map a concept such as detention. However, according to the literature, there is general agreement on some of the conditions for detention. This is understood within educational literature on detention as advocating for developmental, psychological, therapeutic, child saving, and social welfare discourses that promote the belief that empirical evidence proves children can be classified according to their behavior patterns and characteristics, with the assumption that a diagnosis would effect a cure. As a social condition, it comes under the scrutiny of Child Savers who conceive its emergence as a discovery of an object already present, not an object constituted by its discovery.

The historical conditions from which detention arises as well as the networks that came before it do not indicate a point of origin or a linear continuity (see Foucault 1977). Rather, as Foucault argues, there is no historical preexistence of its object, nor do the concerned agencies such as the justice system or welfare groups such as the Child Savers, possess knowledge of an independently existing object. Once detention is suspended of tradition, continuity, or unity, it is a free concept understood as a discursive process or field. The authorized subject is absent, as the discursive practice forms the object of which it speaks. Occupying a discursive space, no condition is completely fixed and every discourse contains elements of uncertainty and displacements (Foucault 1972a). The displacement of discourse shows the impossibility of pinning any form of difference or sameness—the points at which the conditions for detention become possible are also the space for its impossibility. Therefore, the conditions that make detention possible are the very conditions that open multiple possibilities for existence. Furthermore, historical apriori conditions that constitute detention reveal that the historical subject is too important to be subsumed under the weight of denial, repression, or silence.

The history of detention cannot be read as the unfolding of a progressive continuity, nor can the subject remain as the center of all knowledge. The disagreement over policies and rationale for the policies reveal a rejection of universal norms over what and who constitutes the subject or object of detention. Investigating discursive practices that constitute detention without a subject does not imply asking, "How can a free subject penetrate the substance of things and give it meaning?" Rather, the question to ask is "How, under what conditions and in what forms can something like a subject appear in the order of discourse? What place can it occupy in each type of discourse, what functions can it assume, and by obeying what rules?" (Foucault 1984a, p. 118). The above questions are key to understanding the condition that makes detention possible. It is impossible to fix the space detention occupies at a particular time and space, literal, symbolic, or discursive, as no one discourse can stand a fixed place in time. The conditions that predicate detention's existence are faced with ambiguity, contradictions, and possibilities emerging from an unstable and contested space.

3

Making, Unmaking, and
Resituating the Subject

Introduction

In studying the history of the concept of detention, the question that comes to mind is the role of the subject in relation to the conditions that make the experience of detention possible. Historically, discourses of detention oversimplify and therefore misunderstand the complex lived experiences of students, leaving underlying assumptions unquestioned. In creating a universal detention subject, detention, along with rehabilitation and education discourses, fixes the lived histories of students, making them static representations rather than historically and culturally constituted and constituting. Functioning as a transparent representation of a concept that already exists—the historical apriori conditions—detention, rehabilitation, and education discourses reify a stable identity that fails to recognize the changing contexts of students' lives. In so doing, detention overlooks the instability of identity and the contradictions and ambiguities that accompany contextual negotiations of lived experience in the making, unmaking, and resituating of the female educational subject—girls behind bars.

Any notion of an essentialized and fixed subject excludes possibilities for existence, resistance, and educational change. Therefore, in this chapter, what I suggest is an epistemological shift in the way the female educational subject of detention is articulated and understood, a shift that calls into question all forms of centeredness, essentialism, and universality that engender exclusion. Such a shift does not claim any epistemological or ontological primacy; rather, it offers transformative spaces for rethinking and reconceptualizing what is meant by the female educational subject and its relation to representation, knowledge, truth, and power.

This chapter examines how young girls behind bars are constituted as educational subjects of detention through a process of othering derived from a consensus of norms and values. The discourses on philosophy, history, and education are inscribed in normative practices to produce subjects that are universal. Detention presents an example of the workings of constructed norms in relation to the othering of the nonnormative. In constituting a particular kind of subject, in presenting a particular version of the subject normative or nonnormative, detention brings into question the philosophical concepts of the self, representation, knowledge, truth, and power. It also brings into question how the category of woman is constructed in relation to the body, sexuality, gender, and desire.

As noted in the previous chapter, the making of the scripted detention subject does not present an original; rather, it represents that which is always already constituted by historical apriori conditions without a subject. The already constituted subject combined with the humanist narrative of the universal subject call for an analysis of discourse on the making of the subject. What follows is the making of the detention subject as a false representation that fixes reality and represses a play of difference within and among subjects. Accordingly, this chapter investigates the absence, the silence, or the lack of awareness of the historicity of the educational subject of detention when it is philosophically misrepresented. The basis of this investigation is that the female educational subject of detention cannot be separated from the philosophical, historical, social, and educational discursive practices of exclusions and repression that constitute it; nor can the subject be denied the "psychic, corporeal, and consciousness formation which exists beyond the constraining ideologies of much feminist and indeed modernist thinking" (Kennedy 2000, p. 23).

In the first section of this chapter, "Making and unmaking the modernist subject," I examine the philosophical tradition of the subject and its influence on contemporary notions of the subject. Briefly tracing this tradition from Plato to Nietzsche, I use French poststructural thought to show how major philosophical tenets such as a fixed universal subject, binary thinking, and the pursuit of certainty and truth are now being questioned and problematized for their "epistemic failure" (Lather 2001, p. 203). Using Nietzsche as the intellectual rupture in Western philosophy, I focus on Foucault's decentering as a way of unmaking the modernist subject and the role of discourse in producing subjects as effects of power (Foucault 1972a). Foucault's unmaking of the subject is followed by Derrida's (1970) deconstruction of the subject as a play of multiple differences and Deleuze's (1977) deterritorial unmaking of the centered subject. The section concludes with Kristeva's (1984, 1987) provocative reconstruction of the female subject-in-the-making not totally produced by discursive practices but by psychic, contingent intersubjectivities and interpretive intertextualities.

Turning the spotlight on the decentered subject as it has been taken up in the field of education, "Resituating the educational subject," the second section of this chapter, attends to the work of three scholars. The first reading is Baker's (2001) *In Perpetual Motion*, a historicizing of the subject of education via the mapping of discursive shifts in the way educational categories and labels construct the child as the subject of education. The second is Butler's (1990) *Gender Trouble*, in which she theorizes the notion of gender, bodies, subjectivity, and critical agency. Butler uses a Foucauldian framework to challenge Freudian notions of the repressed and melancholic female subject, giving a renewed sense of agency through the performative body and desire. Lather and Smithies (1997) complicate Baker and Butler's deconstructive work to recreate a discursive field where the researcher is a subject in relation to research subjects in *Troubling the Angels: Women Working with HIV/AIDS*. The above postfeminist texts interrogate the constitution of the educational subject, question basic philosophical tenets, such as the universal subject and its representation, and problematize the subject to suggest decentered spaces for political action through new forms of inquiry.

The third section, "Making, unmaking, and resituating the female educational subject of detention," builds upon the themes developed by Baker, Butler, and Lather. Drawing from their work, I push discourse around the female educational subject of detention to question the constitution of the subject founded on Western philosophical assumptions such as categorical and binary thinking. Focusing on the female educational subject of detention, I suggest that detention is a critical site for raising questions of representation in history, culture, society, and education, and their relation to the discourse on the female body, sexuality, and desire. I examine how the context of detention is one of contesting and contested female educational subjects attempting to reclaim voice by accounting for and recounting the asymmetry and differences between their lived histories and backgrounds, and the policies and practices of detention. Here my aim is to explore how educational discourse in detention, rehabilitation, and education shape and take shape within the asymmetrical relations of sameness and difference to construct a desexed, disembodied, and denaturalized subject of detention.

Modernist subject

Making and unmaking the modernist subject

The making of the modernist subject implies introducing the human being, giving the human being a proper name, placing the human being within a network of relations, turning the human being into a universal that makes the human being recognizable confirming its new identity. It would also mean turning to the theoretical interpretive analysis that complicates this identity, indeed, which problematizes the present frames of existence of being viewed as the subject. The modernist subject is defined in terms of binary oppositions such as the knowing subject and its objective relationship to all knowledge, the construction of a fixed identity in opposition to difference, and the autonomous self in contrast to the "other" (Gilmore 1994). These notions of the subject, and its opposite, function within hierarchies that privilege mind over body, rationality over emotions, male over female, sameness over difference, and the self over the "other." Keeping this in mind, this section examines Foucault's (1965, 1977, 1978) discursive subject of knowledge, power, and sexuality, Derrida's (1970, 1981a, 1992, 1994) decentering the subject, Deleuze's (1990, 1994) nomadic subject, and Kristeva's (1980, 1984) female subject-in-the-making. Each of the scholars have in his or her own way called into question the making of the subject-centered epistemology of modernity, claiming in different ways that a fixed universal subject of history, society, or education is a silencing of the multiplicity of subject-positions and subjective lived experiences of cultural difference.

Western philosophical inquiry in the Platonic tradition is based on man's desire to know the human being in its totality, assuming the human subject could be defined and confined. Plato's theory of forms explains the world as made up of unchanging eternal forms of reality with changing representations of an essential existence of being or the essence of a universal subject existing as a permanent presence (Russell 1945). Following this lineage, Descartes' search for mathematical certitude and scientific explanations for the matter/spirit split established fundamental conceptual binaries such as mind/body, reason/emotion, and nature/nurture that are now taken for granted. Maintaining binaries and categories of sameness and difference that are regulated into a hierarchical order assumes a normative and foundational universal subject and constitutes conditions intolerant of different forms of difference (Derrida 1981a). Such structures, norms, practices, and assumptions that constitute historical apriori conditions are realized through discursive networks of language and power relations that normalize, differentiate, and discriminate (Foucault 1977).

The Cartesian *cogito ergo sum* as a frame of reference has established many contemporary assumptions of the modernist subject, chiefly, man as a rational subject who is the object of all knowledge, the all knowing subject, and categorical divisions of binaries and hierarchies to order, predict, and control (Emmanuel & Gould 2002; see also Hekman 1991). In the modernist tradition, the subject is important as the center of all knowledge, and the idea of rationality becomes the means through which subjects gain knowledge about who they are and their position in an uncertain world. For almost 2,000 years, Western philosophical inquiries in the modernist tradition have been a search for man's sense of self by appealing to rationality and the drive to know with certainty his position in the world.

In the late nineteenth century, Nietzsche was one of the first philosophers to disrupt Western philosophical notions of the modernist subject (Nietzsche 1967). He problematized the modernist privileging of certain forms of truth by contesting the value placed on certainty. According to Nietzsche, searching for certainty privileged one perspective as truth that created norms and an otherness attributed to those who are different by excluding all that did not conform to that particular claim to truth. Recognizing the subject's position as directly related to negotiating positions of difference, Nietzsche suggests the contingent and contextual nature of subjectivity. Rather than accept philosophical makings of the universal subject and a fixed reality, Nietzsche argues, "there is no 'being' behind doing, effecting, becoming 'the doer' is merely a fiction added to the deed" (ibid., p. 481). By constructing a fixed subject and negating difference, the subject is self-deceiving as it denies the contingency and uncertainty of human relations. Taking their cue from Nietzsche, in the 1960s, scholars in France turned their attention to the modernist notion of certainty, the role it plays in making the modernist subject, and implications for those who are different.

Against positions purported to give a fixed account of the workings of the subject, scholars instead engage in a revival of Nietzsche's warnings against modernist philosophy as a form of false representation and self-deception in the name of humanism and progress (1967, 2003). Following the Second World War, scholars began to reconsider this modernist mapping of certainty in the Enlightenment tradition in a much more critical light. For instance, scholars such as Foucault and Derrida refused to accept the assumptions of modernity and engaged in critical reading practices such as archaeology, genealogy, and deconstruction of received forms of knowledge to reread the values and purpose of the Enlightenment vision and its humanist framework.

The Enlightenment vision emphasized freedom, individuality, and rationality. However, poststructural scholars saw these claims as totalizing and dominating and challenged the constructed categories of Cartesian dualism, Kantian reason, and Hegelian dialectics as part of the failed Enlightenment vision (Shrift 2006). Joining theoretical positions with Nietzsche, poststructural scholars began to "unmake" the construction of the modernist subject (Peters 2001). Within the Enlightenment tradition, the modernist subject constituted the ideals of the transcendental subject of ontology, the universal subject of humanism, and the rational subject of epistemology.

Contesting the modernist subject, French poststructural thought is critical to understanding the making and unmaking of the subject in the present context for three reasons. The first is poststructural reading practices that critique the tenets of Western philosophy and their subsequent challenge to the modernist subject; second is a return to historicism to understand the present differently; and third is an engagement with difference that opens multiple spaces for interpretive frameworks for understanding difference (see Derrida 1982, 1988, 1995; see also Foucault 1972a).

I will begin with Saussure's antihumanist stand against the modernist subject. The main impetus of Saussure's structural argument was to replace the privileged human subject by a system of predetermined structures, oppositions, and differences. Explaining the structures and conventions of language as signs, signified and signifiers, Saussure claims that there is no independent reality other than in the minds and practices of those who create them. Hence, when we give meaning to a word, it is an arbitrary construction as there is nothing natural about the relationship (Saussure 1959, p. 67). When meaning is established, however, arbitrary, it becomes a convention, and convention is the only link between the subject and the meaning. To prove the linguistic sign as arbitrary is to challenge the relation between the subject and object and the ontological and epistemological status of the subject. Such a distinction has consequences for the value placed on the speaking subject or the way in which meaning is constructed for differentiating one word from another. Thus, difference or opposition becomes key to understanding, defining, and naming—"the linguistic mechanism is geared to differences and identities" making language and identity a function for creating the "other" within relational terms (ibid., p. 80). Language is, therefore, a system of conventions, and the value placed on any convention, including that of the universal or modernist subject and objective or timeless knowledge, is purely arbitrary and constructed, not natural or neutral.

This understanding of the constructed nature of the modernist subject paved the way for a new kind of subject, filtered through 'posts' calling for rereading of all that had gone before in philosophy, history, anthropology, art, and education articulated in a language now known as the postmodern language of fragmentation and hyperreality (Baudrillard 1983). The horrors of the Second World War, combined with the negative impact of capitalism, led postmodernists such as Jean-Francois Lyotard (1984) to see the modernist subject as a failure of the times. Lyotard is most closely associated with the new language of postmodernism to express structural and cultural decomposition, decentering, dispersal, fragmentation, and the beginning of the end of the grand singular narrative of the modernist subject. The new critical debates of postmodernism replaced the "human being" with the "subject as agent of discourse" and introduced the politics of reading and writing about cultural difference such as gender, ethnicity, race, and sexual orientation, and the connection between histories and subjectivities as challenges to some of the foundational tenets of modernist thought (Gilmore 1994, p. 3).

The response to the failure of humanist ideals and the representation of the modernist subject gained momentum as an intellectual commentary on twentieth-century Enlightenment vision. The Enlightenment vision built around modernist discourses of certainty, rationality, and the liberated self promoted a binary view of the modernist subject as the epitome of progress and anything outside the realm of the Western European, male, rational subject was viewed as the irrational "other" (Said 1978). The progress of mankind, triumph of capitalism, grand narrative of Western civilization, glory of imperialism, construction of the "other," suppression of histories and cultures of non-Western people, and the relation between knowledge and power became major themes for a postmodern questioning of the modernist subject (see Niranjana 1992).

The postmodern context in which poststructuralism, both as a reactionary term and an intellectual concept, took shape called for a rethinking of the dynamics by which the modernist subject was constituted (Peters 1998). Significant is Foucault's positing the modernist subject as discursively constituted in terms of sameness and difference. Rejecting essentialist notions of the true human being, Foucault analyzes how subjects are constituted as subjects of power, knowledge, sexuality, and ethics, as well as their own actions. The subject is central to Foucault's work. His archaeological and genealogical practices are linked to the deconstruction of classical systems of thought and the principle of dualism upon which marginalization and oppression of subjects are based. Hierarchies, binaries, silences, and other forms of violence are excavated in Foucault's discursive practices—poststructural tools to interpret the subject.

For Foucault, philosophy is an interrogative practice, a form of inquiry enabling questions rather than establishing truths. As a student, a teacher in philosophy, and as a philosopher himself, Foucault notes that "There is no sovereign philosophy. . . . The displacement and transformation of frameworks of thinking, the changing of received values, and all the work that has been done to think otherwise . . . is a way of interrogating ourselves" (1990, p. 330). For Foucault, this means displacement of the traditional philosophical subject of humanism, existentialism, and phenomenology. These challenges, combined with Nietzsche's suspicion of the Enlightenment, shaped the themes of Foucault's work.

Using Nietzsche's genealogy, Foucault (1978) analyzes the modernist subject from various positions to show how power determines the subject. In *The History of Sexuality*, Foucault examines the construction of sexuality in the west and sees it as a form of repression. Victorian society viewed sexuality as a silent topic not to be discussed in normal terms but under legal and judicial language, regulated by the law. Explaining how normative assumptions become legal and medical truths that pathologize difference with use of labels such as abnormal and perverse, Foucault says, "There is no question that the appearance in the nineteenth century psychiatry, jurisprudence, and literature of a whole series of discourses on the species and subspecies of homosexuality, inversion, pederasty, . . . made possible . . . this area of 'perversity'" (1978, p. 101). Foucault critiques the reading of silence around sexuality saying that repressive and violent regulation incited by psychology and legitimized by the law produce the discourse on homosexuality as perversion. For Foucault, the homosexual subject did not exist before the development of this discourse, revealing how knowledge is shaped and organized around certain forms of discourse. Thus, categories of subjects such as gay, lesbian, homosexual, and heterosexual explain how social identities are produced by social, legal, and medical discourse. Foucault finds that subjects internalize the claims made by science to monitor themselves in terms of popular morality. Foucault's analysis is critical in suggesting a discursive shift from the foundational modernist subject to a discursively produced subject as a challenge to exclusions and marginalizations emerging from foundational prediscursive claims.

Extending his unmaking of the modernist subject, in *Discipline and Punish*, a genealogical study of how institutions develop into technologies of disciplinary power, Foucault (1977) maps the history of crime, criminals, and criminality as a constructed category of the abnormal subject. The distinctive feature of this critique of the disciplinary system shows how the normal subject is created and what is arbitrarily judged as normal and abnormal. In the construction of such a notion of normalcy and its relation to deviancy as categories pervasive in society, Foucault sees a method of institutional control for knowledge and power. Disrupting traditional concepts of prisons and prisoners, Foucault argues that discipline and punishment is a discourse that enables categories that license the subjection of people. In this process of labeling and subjection, knowledge becomes an instrument of power—knowledge that cannot be separated from the deployment of power by those who construct subjects to be silenced and subjugated.

When discourses on power and knowledge create categories to privilege the modernist subject, resistant subject-positions produce a counter discourse to power. Foucault brings out the contradictory and ambiguous nature of the subject-position, pointing out the subject does not have a definitive or fixed identity. For example, social, medical, and scientific discourses regarding homosexuality have created the category of homosexuals; however, these discourses can only be recognized as determining identity up to a point. Foucault points out that the any category is sustained as much by those who create categories as subjects who identify themselves as homosexuals. According to Butler (1990), this is especially evident in discourses on individual rights where the very discourses used to exclude categories such as homosexual are subverted and sustained by subjects who fight for rights based on the very same category.

Foucault focuses on three interrelated issues—subject, power, and discourse—to underscore the exclusion of difference and the practices that label, classify, and subjugate individuals. His notion of the subject contests the "moral cages that the Enlightenment notion of freedom and emancipation through knowledge mistakenly offers" (Foucault 1984a, p. 71) in perpetuating a unified, stable, foundational, and normative subject. When the subject is represented as unified and history is relayed as "transcendental teleology," the singularity, immediacy, and the context is repressed "as humanity installs each of its violences in a system of rules and thus proceeds from domination to domination" (ibid., pp. 85–9). Under such questioning, Foucault (1972b, 1978, 1984b) argues that the rules by which we understand the subject of philosophy, science, institutions, governments, and society are ruled by regimes of truth, governmentality, power/knowledge, and biopower and need to be interrogated as technologies of control.

Deconstruction of the modernist subject's claims to truth, knowledge, and power is a continuous process of challenge to those who claim to know or hold truth, knowledge, and power (Derrida 1981b, 2001). By exposing the constructed nature of truth, Derrida resituates the fixed rational subject within a dispersed philosophical and sociohistorical context that is always subject to change. He rejects the ontological subject, as it does not account for difference leading to violence against groups of people who do not fall into the defined category. Speaking of the violence of universality, foundationalism, and essentialism, Derrida (1992) says that "No cultural identity presents itself as the opaque body of an untranslatable idiom, but always, on the contrary, as the irreplaceable inscription of the universal in the singular, the unique testimony to the human essence and to what is proper to man" (pp. 72–3).

Derrida (1972) refers to Saussure's concepts, confirming that "in language there are only differences *without positive terms* . . . these differences are themselves *effects*" (p. 11). Derrida tells us that if language is a system of difference based on opposition, or what something is not—*absence*, then his notion of *differance* is *presence* in spite of opposition; it is that which allows us to think in terms of possibilities. This is because as soon as something is articulated it "is" and it is no longer a lack of, which is why *differance* is a *presence* without opposition and important as a practice of constantly undoing conventions in order to generate possibilities for interpreting difference. It is not surprising that Derrida's language of possibility, uncertainty, and decentering poses a significant challenge to the fixed and universal subject as well as opens a space for rereading difference. In a sense, difference is indefinable, as meaning is always deferred, making *differance* a concept that looks forward to future possibility. At the same time, the practice of deconstructive reading is antifoundational, as it is always in deferment, meaning it is always being deferred rather than referred to some ontological subject or fixed truth.

Thus, according to Derrida, philosophy, history, and literature, cannot be separated from the cultural context in which they are produced, nor can the subject be removed from the cultural context that sustains its absence. Derrida's deconstructive readings subvert the modernist subject, exposing assumptions and values underneath the dogma of philosophy and science. Allowing multiple readings is a democratic practice that engages difference so that multiple forms of knowledge are created by multiple subject-positions. Binaries such as subjective and objective are part of interpretation, denoting we are constantly working within binary relations even as we try to overcome them (Derrida 1978, p. 293). The play between absence and presence has implications for the making of the marginalized subject, as it draws attention to the arbitrariness of hierarchies, binaries and the silences implicit in fixed philosophies and singular histories.

Deleuze's notion of the nomadic subject, rhizomatic thought, and lines of flight and intensities challenges fixed identities and absolute knowledge represented in educational thought. Deleuze (1994) suggests deterritorialization of all foundational knowledge, power, and identities. According to Kennedy (2000), Deleuze's notion of the nomadic subject powerfully expresses difference that is cross-cultural, intercultural, and multicultural, opening spaces or lines of flight to multiple cross-references and intertextual readings. For Deleuze, difference cannot be categorized under representation in negative terms such as a lack because the repetition of difference creates more difference different from itself and is perpetual; therefore, it cannot be negated. Like Foucault and Derrida, Deleuze (1977) critiques Hegel's dialectics, saying, "What I have detested more than anything was the Hegelianism and the Dialectic" (p. 12). This is not to say that Deleuze does not draw from philosophic tradition. Rather, Deleuze considers the practice of deconstruction as a reading of philosophy, which according to Butler (1992) goes beyond historical affirmation to positioning the modernist subject within the "permanent possibility of a certain resignifying process" (p. 13) of the very terms on which philosophy has constituted the subject.

Sharing the same intellectual time and place as other French poststructural scholars, Kristeva views feminism as a site of failed ideals. Kristeva critiques modernist subject-centered epistemology that fixes the subject-position, leaving no room for signifying the play of difference. Contesting the unitary modernist subject, Kristeva (1980) claims that the subject is plural, the mastery of the rational subject is a myth because the subject is a product of cultural, historical, and social discourses, and recreates female subjectivities as a displacement of the patriarchal subject. As Kristeva writes, "The subject never is. The subject is only the signifying process and he appears only as a signifying practice, that is, only when he is absent within the position out of which social, historical and signifying activity unfolds. There is no science of the subject" (1984, p. 215).

Thus Kristeva rejects the modernist subject, however, she reconstitutes the subject as always-in-the-making, saying, "But we are subjects in process, ceaselessly losing our identity, destabilized by fluctuations in our relations with the other" (1987, p. 9). She calls this female subject with the potential for political action, a "subject-in-the-making, a subject on trial" (Kristeva 1980, p. 167). Challenging Freud's oedipal theory as well as Lacan's mirror theory, Kristeva gives a new reading of the maternal body by locating the discourse prior to childbirth, saying that the semiotic comes before the symbolic. Using psychoanalysis to push the limits of possibility, Kristeva's poststructural analysis goes back to the subject as a kind of double displacement—to unsettle fundamentals of identity and produce new understandings of female intersubjectivity.

As a response to the crisis of representing the modernist subject, poststructural scholarship is an intellectual critique of the modernist subject as fixed, foundational, universal, and normative. This has implications for the subject and timeless knowledge claims implicit in the constituted subject of history, as no subject exists independent of the conditions in which it is constituted, acknowledged, or repressed. At the same time, this constituted nature of the subject indicates that knowledge claims based on scientific and empirical research take place within social, historical, cultural, and educational discursive conditions. These conditions are based on shifting values and unaccounted for variables, loosening fixed subject identities from their foundational stranglehold. According to poststructural arguments, any form of stability and foundationalism points to an unproblematic representation of the modernist subject.

Rejecting totalizing and universalizing narratives of the modernist subject, postmodernist scholars offer tools to reexamine educational metanarratives such as the Tyler rationale and the NCLB reform act. Lyotard's antihumanist subject, Derrida's decentered subject, Foucault's historicizing of the subject, Deleuze's nomadic subject, and Kristeva's rewriting of the maternal subject offer ways to think about the subject without the privilege of any one subject-centered philosophy. Derridean, Foucauldian, Deleuzean, and Kristevan deconstruction of the modernist subject as a product of sameness and difference problematizes the subject. Poststructuralism is concerned with the relationship between subject and power in order to disrupt the link between the two. As a move away from structural and foundational thought, poststructuralism interrogates, contests, and problematizes humanist notions of a rational, disembodied subject. On the other hand, a relational and situated subject indicates the impossibility of writing the fixed subject when subject formation is marked by discontinuity and displacement.

This has implications for education, especially under modernist conditions that privilege the structures of developmental theories, child psychology, and psychometrics grounded in quantification and examination that is totalizing and oppressive. Many scholars have challenged the so-called poststructural death of the subject. Derrida's response is critical. He affirms, "The subject is absolutely indispensable, I don't destroy the subject; I situate it. I believe that at a certain level both of experience and of philosophical and scientific discourse, one cannot get along without the notion of the subject. It is a question of knowing where it comes from and how it functions" (Derrida 1970, p. 271).

Educational subject

Resituating the educational subject

The problematic of the subject becomes a significant site for raising questions about the category of the student and its relation to philosophy, history, and education. Poststructural articulations allow viewing the educational subject from multiple perspectives of race, class, gender, and other forms of difference. This has ongoing significance for education as the stability of a fixed identity as a category of analysis is in question.

The making of the educational subject means introducing the student, giving the student a proper name, placing the student within a network of relations, turning to the literal and the symbolic relations, constructing the student as a universal subject that makes her/him recognizable, and confirming the new identity. It would also mean turning to the interpretive network that complicates this identity, indeed, which problematizes the present frames of school existence of the educational subject. Keeping this in mind, this section examines Baker's (2001) genealogy of the educational subject, Butler's (1990) deconstruction of a gendered subject, and Lather's (1992) politics of researcher as subject researching other subjects.

Mainstream education under the "modernist paradigm" (Pinar et al. 2004, p. 500) alienates minority groups who are culturally different. According to Pinar, the modernist paradigm is evident in Tyler and Bobbitt's approach to teaching as a predetermined, preplanned, sequential, rational activity that causes "a radical separation of objective and subjective realities" (ibid., p. 499), leaving no room for lived experiences. Poststructural thought as a set of critical practices for reading, writing, and research problematizes and unsettles these taken-for-granted modernist notions in educational theory and practice.

Deconstruction, genealogy, rhizomatics, and intertextuality as powerful critical practices reemerge in the work of Baker, Butler, and Lather to uncover binaries, hierarchies, and categories that have become normative in the formation of educational subjects. However, Baker, Butler, and Lather do not unproblematically reproduce and consolidate French poststructuralism as a set of monolithic theories. Rather, they mobilize textual reading practices by resituating the educational subject as a productive yet irreducibly complex continuing process. This is not to suggest common qualities in their writing but to show individual play of repositioning the educational subject vis-à-vis critical issues in education.

Connections between subject, power, and discourse are played out in Baker's *In Perpetual Motion*. Baker's analysis of the role of discourse in establishing what is an educational subject, the child as an educational subject, what counts as valid knowledge, what forms of discourse place power in a few hands or in institutions, and the ways in which discourse constitutes the subject show how concepts are linked to each other as a disciplinary network. Baker is not interested in establishing what is true or false, right or wrong in educational philosophy or theory. Rather, she analyzes how specific ideas, beliefs, values, events, actions, and practices have been regarded as truth, how they are deployed subsequently in making the subject and with what effects. Thus, discourse on "what is the child" consists not only of what is said in its construction but also of what is left unsaid, what could never have been said, and the historical, social, and educational conditions that shape what is said or silenced.

Similar to Foucault's medical or psychological or penal discourse that constitute the patient, the insane, or the prisoner, education can be viewed as a discourse that constructs the child in specific ways (Baker 2001). In this sense, the history of educational reform from the Tyler Rationale to the NCLB Act become effects of discursive practices closely linked to power and knowledge. For example, academic tracking, labeling, and schooling are effects of dominant discourses in school policy and reform that construct the student in specific ways have consequences for the way the educational subject is constituted. It also has consequences for the ways in which the construction of the normative or universal educational subject is disrupted.

Baker (2001, 2002) uses Foucauldian genealogy to disrupt commonsense beliefs and practices in education. Concentrating on specific historical conjunctures such as childhood, philosophy, science, and history that make the educational subject, her analysis provides wider applicability to many other areas and contexts such as schooling, parenting, and counseling of children. The philosophical, psychological, and educational history of the construction of the child takes on a new meaning in ways that problematize the essentialist, fixed image of the child to create a deeper level of critique of the modernist subject and how it has been constituted by philosophy, science, and education. Baker disrupts education as a system of ideas using a Foucauldian lens to contest the constructed nature of childhood, the child, and schooling.

In *Discipline and Punish*, Foucault (1977) uses his genealogical method to explore the social, medical, clinical, and penal mechanisms that create a prisoner, explaining the multiple processes that create technologies of power exercised by prisons, schools, and hospitals. If Foucault peels the foundations of knowledge to expose the pathologies of constructed criminality (1977), sexuality (1978), medicine (1973), and madness (1965), Baker's (2001) reading is the unmaking of the foundational frames of education to resituate the child as a construction of reason, power, and discourse. Baker's *In Perpetual Motion* contends that scientific and educational discourse lend concepts and ideas a foundation, universality, and a commonness that have simplified the child to a natural category that is acontextual and ahistorical.

In a brilliant and subversive argument, Baker reveals "progress of the child," "development of the child," and "success of the child" as effects of historical relativity and cultural specificity, reproduced in the language of other disciplines such as biology, anatomy, cognitive science, psychology, religion, and through many other forces and influences. Hence, from "development of the child" emerges a string of labels—at-risk, retardation, attention deficit, learning deficit, disabled, gifted, delinquency, slow learner, advanced learner—inscribed within different categories of intelligences or lack of it and development or lack of it. Seen from Baker's reading of the discourse on the child, the norms of speaking and writing about the child, or any other educational subject are displaced from the position of being defined as a timeless philosophical and educational constant. Instead, how we speak about the child are effects of discursive practices in particular contexts, time, and place.

In education—various philosophical discourses such as Locke's tabula rasa or Rousseau's division between ontology and epistemology, Herbart's moral being, or Hall's educational psychology that defines and differentiates—the lasting result is that many of the politics and practices of contemporary inequality in education can be seen as perpetual motion of competing definitions of the educational subject or the child. Baker's contribution to the history of educational philosophy and its relation to present day educational norms show how subject-positions are shaped, reshaped, and resituated by those who dominate as well as those who are subjugated but create their own forms of power and resistance through changing subject-positions.

Understanding subject-positions in a particular context, time, and place, and the effects of discursive practices in their historical context offers educators a critical lens to revise the construction of difference in formulating educational theories. The violence of a universal, normative, foundational subject of education as singular and timeless shuts down possibilities for engaging with difference. Baker deconstructs the educational subject to unsettle the purpose and process of education where there is a growing emphasis by institutions to fix principles and universal rules and generalize as well as homogenize. Baker questions centuries of violence hidden under layers of philosophy, psychology, and scientific knowledge that constitute the child under categories, binaries, and hierarchies.

Like Baker, Butler's subject is also a product of the discursive working of power; however, Butler offers the possibility for resituating the subject through critical agency by giving a more detailed account of subjectivity and subject-positions. Butler not only critiques the foundational assumptions about the modernist subject and its claims to rationality but expands her critique to include a fluid and changing notion of subjectivity. For Butler, subjectivity is inevitable, but it also has subversive agency, which can be operated on a political level. Butler calls this "performative subjectivity," arguing that performativity is a discursive process that allows subjects to recognize themselves and their own decentered subjectivities. Butler suggests that discursive production of subjectivity makes agency possible. In *Gender Trouble*, Butler (1990) claims that if the Enlightenment subject is based on knowledge, reason, and power, then her work on sexuality and gender is that of subverting and unmaking those very foundations of knowledge.

Butler expands Foucault's critique of the discourse on sexuality by challenging the oppression of women and the domination of their bodies in materialistic terms as property, or psychological terms of desire, or subjectification as biological bodies—again contingent constructs of domination and subjugation. Butler asserts that her work aims "to interrogate what the theoretical move that establishes foundations *authorizes*, and what precisely it excludes or forecloses" (1990, p. 7). According to Butler, any male or female body is so saturated with violence and aggression that heterosexual normative sexual roles of male and female is a co-opting by both sexes. Instead, Butler chooses to speak a different language as it were—one of gendered performativity that transgresses the circumscribed man-made constructs and parameters of sexual behaviors.

In recasting the gendered subject, Butler rejects the patriarchal gaze of domination but also questions feminist complicities in women's victimization. A challenge to Cartesian dualism and hierarchies, Hegelian dialectics, and Western notions of rational thought and objectivity, Butler resituates sexuality as a site for understanding discourse in a new context, giving it a performative meaning. She displaces the notion of feminine and masculine gender, or male and female sex, as categories of language that become frozen timeless constructs foreclosing possibilities of different forms of performative gender, sexuality, and desire.

Butler's deconstruction of gender, sexuality, and desire is a Foucauldian reading of the subject, but her emphasis goes beyond critique to a more productive and dynamic understanding of embodiment and performativity. In this, she is closer to Kristeva, calling for an analysis not only of the Foucauldian body/subject of power and resistance but arguing that the psyche is a site of resistance where the normative is reinforced and resisted by the body and psyche and that which is yet unnamable and unthinkable—limit-work—pushing the boundaries of thought to that which has been unthought or unarticulated. Kristeva uses the term semiotic in its multiple meaning to argue that the semiotics of language associates semiotic with woman, but only because language as a medium for making meaning is used as a medium for domination suppressing multiple interpretations. Kristeva suggests subversion of language and meaning making by introducing intertextuality or multiple texts and voices that disrupts the dominant narrative or text.

Through intertextual subversion, semiotics promotes possibility by becoming the locus of subversion through displacement. Going a step further, Butler uses displacement not only to disrupt but to construct a performative subject premised upon a problematic view of the relation among gender, sexuality, and desire. While Butler contests the universal subject, she also speaks of the proliferation of identities that offers a political space for collective political action against exclusions. In Butler's view, subjectivity is flexible and capable of subverting discourse as well as capable of "fluidity of identities that suggests an openness to resignification and recontextualization" (1990, p. 338). Conversely, any fixed identity of the educational subject—whether ontological or epistemological— would foreclose all other possibilities, thereby engendering exclusion in educational practice.

For Butler, the aim is "not to prescribe new gendered way of life that might serve as a model" (1990, p. viii), but rather to uncover the ways thinking about a gendered subject is shut down by conventional, therefore, violent practices against those who live on the sexual margins. Speaking of the influence of French poststructuralism on her work, Butler calls her writing of the gendered subject a "cultural translation" (ibid., pp. viii–ix) of abstract French theory to ask questions about the gendered subject that are politically and socially urgent in an American context. Contextual meaning is one of contesting the inequality and asymmetry of relations among subjects, the text, the language used to police subjects, and universality and representation in education. As a reply to critics of poststructuralism and as a critique of poststructural scholars who apply French theory without contextual meaning, Butler says her work is "at the site where cultural horizons meet, where the demand for translation is acute and its promise of success, uncertain" (ibid., p. ix).

Gender as a practice shapes, and is shaped within unequal relations of power that operate under educational discourses. What the problematic of the gendered subject reveals is not only the disciplinary machinery of society, but also the discourses in philosophy, history, psychology, and education, constructed through practices that connect power and knowledge to multiple sites and discourses. More importantly, when gender is seen as a given, knowledge of gender becomes an unmediated, transparent absolute. Gender as unproblematic thus produces categories of containment and repression.

Weaving intertextualities and intersubjectivities makes Lather's research an unconventional and powerful challenge to traditional articulation of the modernist subject. Working from multiple axes in, against, and through categorical absolutes in a dynamic, shifting relationship of alignment and displacement of the modernist subject, Lather (2000b) rereads her own text to unsettle how we write about the educational subject. Lather (2000b) reflects that *Troubling the Angels: Women Living with HIV/AIDS* emerged out of interviews she and her coauthor Smithies conducted from 1992–5 with women living with HIV/AIDS. Collaborating with her research subjects but letting them speak for themselves, Lather gives the reader a closer look at the lives of women living with HIV/AIDS, breaking the silence that shrouds their personal lives under official statistics on HIV/AIDS. As a challenge to traditional, scientific research that is disembodied and faceless, Lather and her coresearcher Smithies dramatically subvert the principle of objective research of subjects as objects of research by resituating the subject of educational research and letting the women speak for themselves.

In writing as a methodologist, Lather hoped to "use the ruins of feminist ethnography as the very site of possibility" (2000b, p. 285) to let the research subjects speak for themselves. Rather than produce a "comfort text" (ibid.), Lather describes the book as a "messy text" because she tries not to impose her meaning over the voices of the research subjects. The result is a complicated text written on multiple registers reflecting the complexity of issues involved in the research and writing process when day-to-day lived experience of the research subjects encounter the unpredictability of disease, trauma, and death on the one hand, and the silence and shame surrounding HIV on the other, on a daily basis.

For Lather, methodology is not a prescription but a discursive site for interrogating, provoking, and creating multiple understandings of the educational subject. Contesting the dominant narrative of traditional ethnographic research in education, Lather critiques assumptions, beliefs, and foundations of knowledge and advocates that researchers ask pertinent questions such as how and why certain forms of knowledge have become foundational. In arguing methodology in educational research as problematic, Lather unsettles the totalizing claims of metanarratives in educational research. In her mistrust of positivist objective research is the attempt to decenter knowledge along rhizomatic multiples marked by subjectivity of participants in research, the irreducibility of lived experience, and the researcher's self-reflexivity.

Troubling the Angels illustrates what it means to trouble foundational methodologies and knowledge production in education and has implications for how we "do" research on the educational subject. By highlighting the politics of research on subjects and the impossibility of writing simply, Lather reflects the problematic of language that gives authority to the author. Lather's textual strategies such as intertextuality that lets multiple voices speak into, against, and through the text, pose an alternative set of questions that disrupt "bodies of knowledge" in research practices, propose new ways of thinking about research subjects, create a new language for it, and remind us we are complicit in what we present, represent, or misrepresent in educational research. Countering research frameworks anchored in positivism that objectify participants in research and erase the subjectivity of researchers, Lather collapses the subject/object of the research in a move that makes her work reflexive, critical, and complex. The binary between researcher and participant, academic and personal work, rational and emotional is disrupted when research depends on testimony (Lather 2000b), prompting researchers to rethink issues of objectivity and generalization in research methods.

Poststructural thought shares with structuralism the notion of subject as a construct. However, Baker, Butler, and Lather make a strong argument that historians, philosophers, and educators do not make objective use of language. Rather, they are direct participants in the world they write about, making their intentionality in the construction and validation of knowledge a subjective one. Lather shows that every step of the writing process can be a site for the dispersal of knowledge that decenters the historically constructed subject—the arrangement of the book and textual strategies can be turned into discursive texts and subtexts, intertexts, across texts articulating multiple voices that deauthorize the power and knowledge of the author. Her textual strategies illustrate how discourse shapes society, culture, and education represented through hierarchies in gender, sex, and relationships. At the same time, Lather's strategies subvert the notion of the universal modernist subject in traditional research practices to offer possibilities for alternative voices and subjectivities.

What poststructural scholars Baker, Butler, and Lather reimagine is a field of possibilities for engagement with difference in a way that the French poststructuralists could not—to be suspicious of origins, traditions, and foundations of American education; contextual readings of knowledge, power, and language need to attend more closely to slippery concepts such as gender, sexuality, and desire because to suppress concepts is to silence the subject. Baker, Butler, and Lather engage these concepts to make powerful arguments that in educational inquiry, theory and practice modernist conditions of rationality are oppressive as they limit possibilities by curbing the ways we might think about the educational subject.

Female educational subject of detention

Making, unmaking, and resituating the female educational subject of detention

The making of the educational subject implies a universal subject and making monolithic assumptions about the subject, whereas subjectivity and agency cannot be explored by grouping subjects under a universal identity. The female educational subject of detention has been constructed as possessing certain attributes that must be acquired in order to be one and to be represented or self-represented as one. Within the network of discourses and practices that construct the female educational subject of detention, there are constitutive possibilities for agency through the formation of subjectivities.

In this section, I explore the construction of the female educational subject of detention in relation to identity, subjectivity, and agency. The discourse on the female educational subject is intimately tied to the discourse on the body, gender, sexuality, and desire. Inherent in exploring the discourse on the female body, gender, sexuality, and desire is engagement with the female educational subject's specific experiences with the repressed body, gendered sexuality, and unrecognized desires. Drawing from Baker's educational subject, Butler's gendered subject, and Lather's researcher-as-subject, the analysis examines traditional notions of the educational subject and investigates the silences and absences of specificities and subjectivities in the making, unmaking, and resituating of the educational subject of detention.

With the advent of the juvenile justice system at the end of the nineteenth century, the subject of detention became the object of social monitoring, institutional discipline, medical examination, psychological evaluation, and educational testing (Platt 1969). In the twenty-first century, law enforcement, doctors, psychologists, and educators continue to play an important role in the institutional network of forces that constitute the Foucauldian technologies of power sustaining manipulation of the subject making the educational subject part of the larger historical, medical, and legal forces.

Baker (2001) presents a genealogy across centuries of the educational subject as a discursively produced docile body by deconstructing the web of normative and foundational social, philosophical, scientific, and institutional discourses. The history Baker tells is not the development of Locke's tabula rasa or Rousseau's natural child. Rather, the modern subject of education emerges as effects of specific historical, social, and philosophical forms of power and knowledge. Baker's critique is aimed at the objectifying techniques of education deployed through the normalizing practices of social, professional, and institutional power relations. This is evident in the discourse of detention, rehabilitation, and education.

The making of the educational subject of detention requires specific knowledge in order to build the student as an objective case under consideration by the school and the juvenile justice system. At the detention facility, knowledge of the female subject's body is gained from surveillance and recorded as evidence through case sheets, legal documents, medical history, counseling logs, treatment records, and school reports. Documentation assists specialists such as child psychologists, school counselors, behavioral therapists, and law enforcement in the labeling process of tagging a specific identity onto the subject. What this indicates is objectification of the body, rationalized through a series of medical, legal, and educational manipulation that sanction the construction of labels useful in normalizing the process of exclusion and inclusion.

In detention, the process of examination is multilevel. From the moment the student arrives, disciplinary measures are put into action by removing all personal belongings or markers of differing identities of students. The student's name and lived history is replaced with a number on a case sheet; personal clothing is replaced with a uniform, and every hour is prescheduled with timed precision. The student goes through a physical security check and the body is strip-searched. This is followed by a thorough medical examination for sexually transmitted or any other diseases.

The next step is an evaluation of the student's mental health through a series of psychological tests. The psychological examination is to allow the student to confess to offending behavior and assign necessary therapeutic intervention. For example, a pregnant teen is expected to confess to sexual promiscuity and attend counseling for correcting deviant behaviors. Once the physical and mental health screening is accomplished, the student is handed to educators who conduct academic tests for diagnosing the student's reading and math grade levels. By the end of this procedure, the student is transformed from a young girl into an object that is pinned, examined, labeled, and objectified—the educational subject of detention.

Education in detention is based on the premise that students are unable to make rational decisions and, therefore, need to be normalized into becoming thinking subjects through a well-planned, rigorous curriculum. The purpose of education in detention is aligned with the correctional aim of rehabilitation. Accordingly, the nonnormative subject's character, behavior, attitude, time, and space are monitored and disciplined by controlling the body and the mind. Once the subject is disgnosed, medicalized, and pathologized as deviant, the goal of education is normalization of the deviant subject. When the student is stripped of all claims to identity or ownership, the body becomes the site for sanctioning of specific strategies for enforcing normalization.

Thus, in detention, the body is central to the making of the female educational subject. Through the discourse on rehabilitation, the body becomes the medium for disciplining sexuality and gendered differences. Disciplining the subject's body, through the power dynamics of normative regulations is another dimension of the complex web of exclusionary discourses that give meaning to the identity-bearing subject. Butler (1990) argues that the body is not a natural condition but culturally sanctioned and regulated through the subject's relationship with disciplinary norms of sexuality. This disciplining starts at birth, when having one or the other defining sexual characteristics conditions a life-process that determines multiple aspects of the subject's existence. Names, clothes, what students are taught at home, at school, or in detention are only a few examples that dictate and monitor the role of the body through culturally sanctioned norms. Quoting Nietzsche, Butler (1990) agrees there is no "doer behind the deed" but that "the doer" is constructed in and by the deed through established norms (p. 33).

Discussing the relation between the body and sexuality, Butler uses drag as an example of bodies that subvert the norms but are dependent on already accepted norms for the body's sexual identity. In fact, drag as a subversive act makes sense only within the field of established heterosexual discourse where the discourse on the body involves identifying with a set of norms that are and are not realizable. At the same time, Butler suggests drag is an example of critical agency that can be located in the regulated process of repetition and in creative and subversive variations of performative repetition. The notion of the performative is key to understanding how subjectivity is a form of creative resistance to established norms with possibilities for agency when the subject refuses normalization and chooses to perform through changing subject-positions rather than represent a fixed identity.

As Butler suggests, subversion makes sense within established normalizing discourses. Similarly, the performing subject is recognized and made meaningful through its relation to the existing social world and the discourses and terms that normalize the social world. These social terms such as "female" and "woman" are the very norms that provide the context for the nonnormative in detention such as "female offender" and "juvenile delinquent" indicating that the subject of detention is possible only within the social context from which it gains its constructed meaning. For example, a subject identified as "woman" has to accept the social roles and meet the social expectations and conventions that come with being a woman in a patriarchal social order—a daughter, mother, and homemaker. In other words, through the construction of these roles, the social world provides the context through which a woman can exist in society. To exist otherwise is to exist outside these norms or be identified as deviant or delinquent—promiscuous, nymphomaniac, and dyke are some of the more obvious examples of deviant identities exclusively used for describing nonnormative young girls and women.

In detention, the subject is not only labeled but prescribed medical and psychological treatment for being labeled as promiscuous, nymphomaniac, or a dyke. Assigning labels such as promiscuous, nymphomaniac, or dyke to personal choices indicating cultural differences between women, the medical system, the school system, and the juvenile justice system camouflage control and repression behind sexual labels. When the normalized body is constructed as woman and represented as heterosexual, all other differences among and between women are unrecognized except as deviancies. Thus, in detention, female identity, sexual identity, and gender identity are collapsed into a heterosexual development of the female subject as a naturalized condition. The discourse on the body is acknowledged as heteronormativity, so any other notion of the body, sexuality, gender, womanhood, sex, or desire exists as deviancy in relation to the normative.

The power of normalization sets the limits of acceptable norms by distinguishing what is normal and what is deviant, imposing heterosexuality on all subjects. At the same time, examination of the subject allows mapping sexual deviations in order to be able to correct what is classified as deviancy. For example, in detention, any show of lesbianism provides the professional counselor with specific knowledge about the subject to be able to intervene and correct the deviation. With enough knowledge of the subject, the counselor can point out that lesbianism is not natural and suggest ways to resist it and cultivate normal heterosexuality. The result is a fixing of identity inside a space from where the student internalizes external domination to become its own object. Thus, everyday practices in detention do not operate on neutral ground and create a series of restraints for disembodying, desexing, and denaturalizing the female educational subject.

Although feminization of the female body and pathologizing of deviation from this norm can be viewed as Foucauldian effects of power to regulate "compulsory heterosexuality," subjects do not passively accept socially and culturally assigned roles (Britzman 1998). The stability of sexual and gender frames create spaces from where to contest the technologies and frameworks that confine subjects, bodies, and identities. Bodily responses, impulses, and pleasures can be "the rallying point for the counterattack against the deployment of sexuality ought not to be sex-desire, but bodies and pleasures" (Foucault 1978, p. 157). As Butler (1990) says, the dynamics of the body cannot be a one-sided show of violence and force; rather, the body is a transformative site for disrupting and destabilizing Cartesian conventions such as feminine and masculine to show that sex, gender, or desire do not necessarily flow from the scripted body.

The subject's body is also at the center of the struggle between the institutional strategies to repress it and the subject's own understanding and articulation for reclaiming the body (Brereton 1998). Scholars have argued that theorizing about the repressed body or the gendered body in terms of biological, social, and cultural differences does not take into account desire, intimacies, and pleasures that are traditionally associated with the emotional realm (Britzman 1998; see McNay 1991). The female body, biological sex, female identity, and gendered subjectivities are intimately linked to various subjective forms of desire. For example, the notion of motherhood as a naturalized desire of women is contested by feminists who claim that some women desire the historical destiny written by patriarchy, others desire motherhood for asserting a female identity against patriarchy, still others opt out of motherhood, and a few are disrupted because of motherhood.

While it is important to recognize the role of the body in the formation of the female educational subject of detention—girls behind bars—an understanding of this formation cannot be reached by bodily engagement alone; rather, a complex network of social, medical, legal, and educational constructs must be taken into account. In the spaces between stable, normalized, and oppressive norms, lived experience struggles to find voice. Historically realized experiences and self-recognized desires of girls behind bars continually displace and undermine their socially prescribed female roles. In detention classrooms, observation, examination, and normalization of students is an ongoing project. Throughout day-to-day interactions with students, the specter of an ideal or a normal student—white, heterosexual, healthy, high scoring, docile, obedient—is always present along with the discourse on deviance. Conversely, the social, moral, and academic inferiority of girls behind bars is taken for granted and constantly monitored.

In the classroom, movement, habits, behaviors, and words are monitored in relation to high stakes testing as well as moral prohibition. Techniques of measurement such as standardized and class tests, IQ tests, and behavioral markers lead to unintended effects. In an attempt to draw a line between students who are defined as normal or labeled disabled learners, there is an entire range of classification such as dyslexic, ADHD, learning disabled, mentally challenged conveying an articulation of disorder that fixes nonconforming students' identities as inferior. Difference viewed as deviance and considered pathological turns nonconforming subjects into a medical or a psychological or an educational problem in need of professional intervention.

Historically, the female subject is bound to domination, subjugation, and violence that constitute, exclude, or include women. Rethinking the body means resituating the subjugated body in a discursive field of embodiment, sexuality, and desire. Subjectivity constitutes changing feelings, desires, wishes, and thoughts and implies problematization of identity. What is significant in the discourse on subjectivity is the transforming possibilities of the notion of changing subject-positions as validation of embodied lived experience and plurality of voices that recognize the voices of difference. Subjectivity becomes an important transformative site for girls behind bars taking into account history, culture, the temporal, the changing, and offering possibilities for social, historical, and educational changes.

Discussion

My lived experience with girls behind bars reveals that the subject is not a single autonomous rational knowing self but a plural changing discursive one. If subjects are products of discourse, they also create discourse, and they resist it as much as they form it. As the symbolic is representative of the male order of things, many women do not identify with the symbolic representation of patriarchy. Lived experiences of students disrupt the historical and cultural inscription of women as passive, inferior subjects contrasted with the male, rational, autonomous Cartesian subject. In detention, the subject is constantly-in-the-making, and capable of resistance and action within and against the discursive formations as well as the historical apriori conditions that constitute them. Every new making and unmaking of the subject critiques, reforms, deconstructs, makes meaning of the previous one, and transforms it.

The subject is critical to poststructural thought. Contrary to its critics, poststructural scholars did not erase the subject—they decentered the human subject to resituate it within its historical and cultural complexity. The subject is not the Cartesian, "I think, therefore I am" but "I am because I desire, and I will always be in the process of being because desire is always a process." Interpreting the human subject is an interpretation of desire, self, and the body. Butler's subject can be understood as the splitting subject where desire is always a lack of or an absence of something (Lacan 1977). Historical apriori conditions as well as multiple changing contexts of the present continue to constitute the subject at any given moment in time and place, making it impossible to predetermine or predict, opening possibilities for being different and thinking about difference differently. A decentered subject implies that spaces can be created between identities and subjectivities that transgress categories and boundaries.

I have used poststructural tools for troubling received, dominant forms of knowing, and disrupting the status quo in education. Postfeminist studies and poststructural scholarship enjoy a special relationship that enables their work to critique, disrupt, and reread the modernist subject of philosophy, history, sciences, anthropology, and education (St Pierre & Pillow 2000). The notion of the modernist subject universalizes, dehistoricizes, and decontextualizes students' experiences and ignores subjectivities; however, it is possible to unsettle the major tenets of a subject-centered epistemology of modernist education.

Unsettling static and fixed sets of beliefs, rhizomatics, and deterritorialization, Butler offers the possibility of nomadic readings of gender, sex, and desire. In Butler's writing, nomadic becomes a metaphor for gendered spaces as different from the Eurocentric idea of fixed category such as woman, man, normative, and deviant. The use of metaphors as a writing practice to challenge sameness, representation, closure of ideas is a linguistic subverting practice seen in Butler's powerful troubling of gender that connects the body to the production of visceral knowledge. Butler combines Kristeva's semiotic intertextual subjectivities and Derrida's dispersed subject to create educational space for conflicts and multiplicity of discourses without anchoring any form or content to any one single subject as universal.

Derrida, Foucault, Deleuze, and Kristeva indicate that freedom of ideas is inclusive and productive, and that monoculture perpetuates violence in the destruction of difference. Human interaction, behaviors, and situations are not objects by themselves and cannot always be read as texts that are changeable and unstable—destabilizing the subject of history or dislodging philosophy is to see girls behind bars as a human object without answering questions of human justice. It is to reduce students to the "other" or to a text or even a textual alterity. It is an acceptance of marginalization, deviance, and further "othering" of the "other." Hence, it is not enough to be oppositional in the struggle for social and educational change.

From a different perspective, Baker translates nomadic as multiply powerful readings against the singularity of the philosophical educational subject. The concept of deconstruction as a reading practice is exceeded in Baker's process of perpetual motion, an endless nomadic process of shifting contexts where there is no fixed subject, only difference, where there are no building blocks of meaning, only a multitude of meanings. Lather's self-reflexivity and intertextual conversations remind educators to be attentive to conflicts and their connection to other political struggles and deconstruct their own subject-positions. Instead of attempting to emancipate the "other," educators are the "other" in need of interrogation from their own implication. In Baker, Butler, and Lather's work, deconstruction is both provocative and creative. Together they explore transformative possibilities that emerge when the normative and the foundational subject no longer restrict the discourse on education.

While I draw generously from Baker, Butler, and Lather, my study does not make any claim to solving the dilemmas of detention, rehabilitation, and education. It does not propose yet another way of theorizing the subject to enable narrowing the gap between the lived experience of girls behind bars and institutional practices. Rather, it seeks to think through the gap, working through difference to examine the positioning of histories, experiences, and desires of girls behind bars, describing the discursive field within which the discourse on the female detention subject circulates. Paying attention to the gendered body can inform as well as disrupt traditional imposition of an essentialized identity on girls behind bars. In conceptualizing and treating the female body in stereotypical and desexed terms or classifying the body as deviant, detention reflects the social and institutional structures and policies aimed at controlling difference.

In the next chapter, I will explore the complexities of telling life-stories using autoethnography as a qualitative research methodology to attend to the crisis of representation, and "doing" autoethnography to engage in the epistemological paradox of testimonial knowledge that comes from knowing both too little and too much (Lather 2001).

4

Qualitative Methodology, Critical Autoethnography, and Self-reflexivity

Introduction

Qualitative methodology, critical autoethnography, and self-reflexivity frame this ten year autoethnographic educational inquiry. Drawing from autoethnography as a qualitative methodology that attends to the crisis of representation and problematizes the normative and foundational subject of history, culture, and education, this chapter delineates historical issues on autobiographical and ethnographic origins that generated different forms of autoethnography. Key methodological issues such as what is autoethnography, what makes autoethnography "critical," how to do autoethnography, how to attend to ethical issues when "doing" autoethnography, and why be self-reflexive when studying lived educational experience are discussed. Exploring critical questions about "doing" research, this chapter also discusses the subject of ethnographic research, insider/outsider status of the researcher, and notions of subjectivity, objectivity, and neutrality of the researcher in the research process. The chapter opens the discussion on ethical responsibilities of the autoethnographer as a qualitative research methodologist when deconstructing dominant forms of educational knowledge, disrupting the status quo in education, unsettling traditional notions of objectivity in research, acknowledging the significance of the researcher-subjectivity, and validating life stories of self and other for bringing social and educational change.

Viewing the personal as political, autoethnography engages how we understand the self in relation to "other" within social, historical, cultural, and educational contexts. Working at the intersection of feminist, postmodern, and poststructural thought, autoethnographic work engages how we think about knowledge, the politics of disciplinary knowledge, the construction of personal knowledge, and the possibilities in educational theory and practice for self-reflexive inquiry. Self-reflexive readings of other people's stories present examples of autoethnography and the relevance of ethics to critical inquiry as seen in the works of Lather's (2000b) troubling of the objective ethnographer, Britzman's (2000) questioning of traditional autobiography, Ellis' (2004) analytical autobiographical narrative, Spry's (2011) performative self, and Scheper-Hughes' (1992) disruption of traditional ethnography. The importance of ethics and self-reflexivity is positioned to be critical to any understanding of the construction of knowledge in educational inquiry, policy, and practice.

Ethnographic, autobiographic, and poststructural origins of autoethnography

Implicit in understanding the place of autoethnography within qualitative research methodology and its epistemological significance is an engagement with its ethnographic, autobiographic, and poststructural origins. Twentieth century history of qualitative research methodology in North America is described by Denzin and Lincoln (2005) in *The Sage Handbook of Qualitative Research*, as representing eight moments beginning with the traditional period from the 1900s to the 1940s. While ethnography is situated within this traditional moment, as a research methodology, it has undergone many changes in design and continues to be a method of choice for many qualitative researchers. Like much of qualitative research from this period, early ethnography is grounded in the positivist scientific paradigm. In keeping with the positivist paradigm in qualitative research, ethnography was theorized and practiced as an objective study of other cultures, groups, and societies, researched through field work immersed within the culture being studied, and data were derived from researcher-as-participant-observer's thick description in the form of field notes, observations, and records. Findings from ethnographies or ethnographic texts were accepted as value-free, therefore, objective and reliable.

With origins in anthropology, ethnography as a methodology gained validity with the works of Bronislaw Malinowski and Margaret Mead. Malinowski's (1922) *Argonauts of the Western Pacific* is based on a study of the indigenous culture of the Trobriand people living on an island northeast of Papua New Guinea. Malinowski's research is foundational to giving ethnography a methodological direction and theoretical grounding in the study of social behavior in cultural contexts and professionalizing the use of terms such as field work, field notes, and participant-observation (Firth 1957). Similarly, Mead's (1928) *Coming of Age in Samoa* is a study of adolescent girls in Samoa on the island of Tau and examines social categories such as adolescence, gender, social norms, and family to serve as a comparison with similar categories in Western culture, presenting ethnography as firsthand study of non-Western cultures in local settings. Such early ethnographies were instrumental in establishing many of the tenets of present day ethnography such as field work, field notes and participant observation. According to Denzin and Lincoln (2005), the modernist moment (1950–1970s) in qualitative research builds upon traditional ethnography and brings ethnographic work into the realm of education, chiefly, the classroom. During this phase, ethnographers in the social sciences studied the structure, process, relationship, and conventions of a specific issue within a given culture that impacted the social order. Examples of ethnographies from the field of education included research into school culture (Burnett 1969), the world of students (Cussick 1973), identity and socialization (King 1967), success and failure of students in formal systems such as the education (Rosenfield 1971), urban school culture (Smith & Geoffrey 1968), and the connection between schools and society (Wolcott 1967).

By the 1970s, ethnography as a methodology was challenged presenting an epistemological crisis in representation stemming from how knowledge of other cultures was constructed within unequal relations of power and subordination articulated through categories, hierarchies, and binaries. Early ethnography constituting a study of the "Other" as evidence of primitive, indigenous, non-Western cultures represented unequal power relations between the researcher and the researched (Smith 1999). With its disciplinary roots in the imperialist era, ethnography as a methodology that represents or speaks on behalf of cultures and subcultures carries with it implicit relations of inequality between ethnographers identified as belonging to Western civilization and "primitive" societies and cultures that were colonized or "discovered" by the West. According to Deleuze (1994), the modern world is one of simulacra that is a failure of representation as it brings about a loss of identity rather than a portrayal or depiction of the subject under study. The challenge to representation of other cultures is voiced by several theorists such as Baudrillard, Derrida, and Foucault. Baudrillard (1983) challenged traditional representation to argue that there is little evidence to suggest that reality of the subject is being represented and that the conventional relationship between the researcher and the researched is neither truth nor valid. Derrida (1987) argues that representation of any content in speech, writing, or art creates a difference from the original across the passage of iterability as the original is nothing outside its rendering, leaving gaps and silences in representation; there is always a surplus and excess of meaning or difference. Speaking of the formation of subjects as objects through apriori discursive conditions, Foucault (1972a) speaks of "depresentification" of the subject in opposition to representing the subject. Said (1978) critiques the West's notion of "Orientalism" for being neither a mirror of reality nor a true representation of knowledge about "oriental" cultures. In the above examples, the known and accepted forms of representation began to show symptoms of crisis challenging the researchers' ability to represent another's reality or the terms under which the researcher constructed knowledge.

In the 1970s, two important questions emerged from this crisis: who has authority to represent whom or who has been given voice to speak for others, and what political purpose do such representations serve? Because these questions challenged the main premise of traditional research methodologies and their ontological, epistemological, and axiological assumptions, it became possible to examine and critique the political agendas of the researchers and rendered the act of representation problematic. For example, the breakdown of representation and critiques of ethnographic knowledge production raised questions about the process of conducting ethnography and undermined the objectivity of the researcher and subsequent truth claims reported from the research.

Subsequently, the 1970s witnessed an emergence of diverse qualitative research methods that embraced researcher subjectivity absent in previous methodologies. Going beyond the research convention of the outsider studying "an-other" culture or researcher as objective-participant-observer, this emergent and diverse range of methods included narrative, autobiographical, and lived experience as qualitative data with analysis of data as interpretive and open-ended. Emergent methodologies such as narrative, autobiographical, and autoethnographic inquiry validated personal experiences, thoughts, feelings, and observations as a medium for exploring, examining, and understanding the social contexts of education, therefore, having epistemological significance (Maréchal 2010). Oppositional in content, method, and purpose emergent methodologies rejected the conventional binary opposition between researcher and the researched, self and other, personal and political, and objectivity and subjectivity that drives positivist epistemologies and methodologies (Ellingson & Ellis 2008). By the 1980s, the crisis of representation questioning positivist and behavioral paradigms including traditional ethnography gave way to a call for research into the lived experience of race, class, gender, and other differences with emphasis on self-reflexivity in qualitative research.

The crisis of representation had two major consequences for ethnographic research in education. The first consequence was the questioning of traditional ethnography's claims to a normative and stable researcher self and the culturally inferior "other," foundational truth and timeless knowledge; ethnography's complicity with imperialism; and the objectivity of the ethnographer in reporting timeless truths about "other" cultures. The second consequence was the generation of research methodologies and methods that validated autobiographies, narratives, and lived experiences of the "other" through the politics of identity grounded in race, class, gender, sexual orientation, and other differences. For many scholars, research voices in the first person is a postmodern response to the crisis of representation and identity giving way to interpretive forms of inquiry (Smith and Watson 1998), self-reflexivity (Lather 2000b), and alternative forms of methodological texts such as autobiographical work from the margins (Ellis 2004).

Autobiography as a research methodology in the field of education in general and curriculum studies in particular emerged from this crisis of representation (Pinar et al. 2004; Greene 2000; Miller 2005). From the 1970s, much of qualitative research emphasizes the process of research with interpretive possibilities in contrast to positivist research that emphasizes numerical data and measurable variables. With greater focus on the process rather than product, qualitative researchers explored and examined the politics of identity and cultural difference, the constructed nature of reality/knowledge, the relationship between the researcher and the subject being researched, the what, when, why, and how of participant and/or researcher's experiences, knowledge, and practices. Thus, autobiography as a method for understanding educational experiences emerged as "a knowledge producing discipline with its own method of inquiry" (Pinar 2000, p. 400).

Calling for autobiography as a method, Pinar (ibid.) states that understanding curriculum issues is directly related to the lived educational experience of students, scholars, and researchers, especially those who are raced, classed, gendered, and ethnically diverse or marginalized from mainstream cultural norms of being white, middle class, and heterosexual. Pinar speaks against the othering of those who do not fit the normative definitions in which the other's sense of self and world is undermined, objectified, and silenced (Pinar 2004). Pinar notes that the dominant culture sustains the status quo in education through its grand narrative that excludes autobiographical voices of those who are outside its cultural and social norms. Typically, anyone who is not within the white, middle-class, male circle is excluded from the mainstream cultural and educational narrative. Pinar advocated a reconstituted self that is not a robotized or mechanical automaton calling this exclusion "the nightmare that is the present" (ibid., p. 13).

Hence, the power of the autobiographical method validated disenfranchised voices restoring a sense of the self and reclaiming marginalized life stories by writing against the official text of exclusion or misrepresentation and challenging the assumption of universality, and categorical and hierarchical thinking. In response to Pinar's call, many curriculum scholars explored the relationship among school knowledge, lived experience, and education. Opening possibilities, the autobiographical method was taken up by scholars in American Studies, Black Studies, Women's Studies, and African Studies among others offering "privileged access to an experience (the American experience, the black experience, the female experience, the African experience)" (Olney 1980, p. 13). The "privileged access" suggested an emergence within theory of the increasingly political nature of autobiography as a method—the politics of identity in autobiographical inquiry and autobiographies of marginalized resistance grounded in lived experience. Autobiographical inquiry departed from ethnographic writing to "a different sort of organization (or disorganization)" (ibid.). At the same time, autobiographical inquiry of the 1970s emerging from the margins rejects traditional autobiography as a genre that privileges the generic white male voice above all others. This departure from traditional and conventional forms of ethnography and autobiography created spaces for much of feminist autobiographical writing and theorizing as an example of the politics of identity or the crisis of representation addressing the inclusion of women's life-work in research and scholarship.

Women have a special relationship with autobiography as is evident from the literature. What is unique about women's scholarship on the politics of identity, such as Grumet (1988), Miller (2005), Ladson-Billings (1997), bell hooks (1998), and Greene (2000), is that they combine theoretical writing with autobiographical work in diverse ways. Grumet writes about her experience with bringing women's personal experiences into the professional arena by introducing the writing of autobiography as a classroom assignment and students' reaction to this assignment. As a classroom instructor, Miller also writes about her experience with autobiographical writing by interweaving her classroom experience with those of her students as a way of giving voice to the personal and professional lives of teachers and students. Ladson-Billings identifies with Black, antiracist, feminist educators who write about their teaching lives. She writes about her struggles trying to help African American children stay in school and transform their experiences through curriculum change. Similarly, hooks writes as a feminist, antiracist, Black educator, and her writing addresses preservice teacher educators, although not confined to them. Interestingly, she combines the autobiographical method with theoretical writing influenced deeply by Freirian philosophy to propose that teachers' personal lives are political. Autobiographical writing and theorizing about women teachers' private and public lives provides an important method for women scholars to articulate research on lived experience. Thus, the autobiographical method is set apart—viewed through personal subjectivities, sexualities, and experiences hitherto unacknowledged as worthy of critical research in education.

Greene (ibid.) believes that teachers as researchers who write about the intersection of the personal and professional lives directly confront decades of teacher education programs that separate teachers' private lives from the curriculum and deny the use of life stories in curriculum practice. According to Greene (ibid.), Grumet (1988), and Miller (2005), identity is specifically and historically placed; therefore, academic knowledge and curriculum practices are tied to who we are and how we think as teachers, students, and researchers. Such scholars challenge dominant scholarship that validates objective and value-free knowledge and call for an affirmation of autobiography and life stories that highlight the notion of identity of the teacher-researcher, the politics of location, and question who has claim to truth of voice. Rather than referring to themselves as teachers or researchers, autobiographical scholars consciously adopt a methodology that combines the autobiographical method with the writing of the text in the first personal legitimizing the self subject of research that uses life stories to gain insights into the larger culture or subculture (Dyson 2007).

The literature on the autobiographical method represents, contests, and constructs a personal and contextual understanding of how lived experiences, perceptions, and interests of teachers, scholars, and researchers shape their research questions, the theoretical frameworks they use, and the methodologies they develop in the construction and understanding of academic knowledge in education. Autobiography as a research methodology honoring lived experience challenges the traditional aims, objectives, and processes of educational inquiry, theory, and practice. It is particularly visible in teacher education, in autobiographies of cultural difference, women, gay, lesbian, queer, ethnic, and racial minorities, in life stories from everyday classroom experience, in art and aesthetics, and environmental education. During this era, the articulations of personal knowledge and life experiences as the focus of serious scholarship presented possibilities for transforming educational research methodologies, which in turn influenced curriculum change.

Writing and reading autobiography as pedagogical engagement in the classroom and practicing autobiography as a research method that privileges lived experience offered many possibilities, but poststructural readings of lived experience revealed that certain issues in autobiography as a study of lived experience remain unresolved. First, any gendered, raced, and classed identity might translate into essentialism as it tended to see identity as a fixed, static form that was inadequate for understanding the complexity and dynamism of changing identities (Gilmore 1994). Second, lived experience did not engage in class issues: "While celebrating inclusion and stressing sensitivity training, such an approach fails to adequately analyze power relationships and leaves structural injustice and inequities unchallenged" (Wang & Yu 2005, p. 29). Third, and critical to any form of self-reflective inquiry, the awareness of differences in others did not necessarily lead to interrogation of the raced, classed, and gendered nature of one's own position. Poststructural scholars began to take up the task of addressing some of these gaps.

A particularly influential work articulating the new language was Britzman's "'The Question of Belief': Writing Poststructural Ethnography" (2000). Britzman, an exemplar in challenging the kinds of knowledge that knowing cannot tolerate or questioning whether there can be a knowledge that exceeded the limitation of humanism, spoke the new language of poststructural possibilities. Autobiographical method as lived experience addressed exclusions through autobiographical narrative in order to explore the racial and gendered constructions of difference and how they affected the status of educational knowledge, history, and culture. Lived experience challenged our need for knowledge, which affected what we recognized as valid knowledge and the ways in which we shape our needs by the politics of difference. Britzman (1998) also asserted, "I mean to signal more than just how one comes to recognize, imagine, and contain signs." Instead of the recognition of identities of difference, she argues for "proliferations" that "exceed—as opposed to return to—the self" (p. 85). Speaking of the experience of listening to a preservice English teacher's stories, followed by extended interviews, Britzman (1989) tried to capture the lived experience of the teacher and analyzed her own difficulties through the process. Britzman realized that however hard she tried, knowledge of others and of the self remained partial and uncomfortable, making them "guilty readings" (2000, p. 38) of other people's lives. This is precisely what poststructural readings claimed to do—unsettle, disturb, and provoke.

In her collection of essays, *Lost Subjects, Contested Objects: Toward a Psychoanalytic Inquiry of Learning*, Britzman (1998) discussed the conceptualization of sex education, a queer theory of pedagogy, an antiracist curriculum, the relations of love and hate, and the "contentious historicity" of Anne Frank, and suggests that the person and the context are mutually constitutive. The essay "Queer Pedagogy and Its Strange Techniques" focused on the alienation experienced by those whose sexuality is not situated within the "normalcy in classroom sites" and whose exclusion contradicted the very terms of social justice that is the purpose of education. Britzman offers a new language of the "knowledge of bodies" to speak against "bodies of knowledge" and the latter's reactions to anything that "unsettles normalcy's immanent exclusions" (p. 80). Britzman considered recognizing, if not understanding, the constructed history of queerness—and "rethinking of the self as an effect of, and condition for encountering the other as an equal," as an essential precondition for the "education of education" (p. 81). Britzman's argument asked for the inclusion of anxiety, ambivalence, aggression, desire, uncertainty, and other emotions that are inconceivable in the educational imagination, claiming it is time educators and researchers addressed this troubling absence in the curriculum. To question what we know, how we come to know, and the value we place on what we believe we know, or think we know, is perhaps the strength of a discursive lens—to trouble, interrogate, and complicate any given notion of truth.

By the 1990s, curriculum scholars generated diverse educational research methodologies and methodological tools that moved from autobiographical inquiry and the politics of identity to poststructural critiques of traditional autobiography and ethnography. Curriculum scholars using poststructural methods showed an unusual and dynamic relationship to autobiography as a research method by recognizing women's ways of knowing (Lather & Smithies 1997) and critiques of feminist methods of autobiographical writing (Britzman 1998). Lather and Britzman challenged the notion of identity as fixed and unchanging to write in terms of the plurality of women's lives as multiple and contextual subjectivities. As a feminist deconstructivist, Lather (2000b) questioned the authority of essentialist feminist identities and the basis of historical knowledge, to suggest "the ruins of feminist ethnography as the very site of possibility" (p. 285) for teacher educators and researchers in the process of unlearning traditional concepts and becoming comfortable with not knowing. Britzman as a queer theorist complicated the feminist analysis of patriarchal and gender issues with notions of difference within difference and performative sexualities. Britzman (2000) spoke about teachers challenging the authority of knowledge and opening it to new readings, as autobiography is "not about capturing the real already out there" (p. 38). Feminist poststructural autobiography in education illustrates, more than any other, that autobiography is interpretation; therefore, autobiography is as much constructed by those who write autobiography as those who write about autobiography.

Poststructural scholars continued to challenge generic definitions of autobiography and position autobiography as a discursive effect that should be read alongside other discourses of the times. Rather than use the customary "autobiography," Gilmore (1994) focused on the limits of traditional autobiographical language and conventions, and sees the nature of autobiography changing from lived experience to a discursive practice. According to Gilmore, poststructuralism and autobiography have a "shared interest in theorizing the subject" and the poststructural "performance of questioning not only intersects with but powerfully structures contemporary interests in autobiography" (p. 3). From a feminist poststructural perspective, Gilmore rejected any traditional forms of autobiography that establish a stable historical identity through representational hierarchies of race, class, gender, and sexuality as terms that heighten power or undermine it. There is no attempt at universal or absolute knowledge; rather, her emphasis was on the partial sense of knowledge or situated knowledge that is produced from the material and situational conditions of people's lives. Thus every autobiography is seen as contingent, relational, and intersecting with the context of specific locations accounting for differences in each story.

From the perspective of postfeminist and poststructural scholars, autobiography as a discursive effect becomes the site for destabilizing traditional meaning, new meaning making, and pushing autobiographical understandings toward multiplicity that addresses exclusions. Gilmore's autobiographics can be seen as an educational discourse that disrupts traditional forms of autobiography and develops in line with other poststructural discourses on multiplicity, fragmentation, disruption, and proliferation. The poststructural discursive site for disrupting the traditional site of autobiography and identity politics becomes the very site where autoethnography emerges as a methodological possibility.

As an emergent qualitative research paradigm within qualitative educational research in general, and curriculum inquiry in particular, autoethnography, thus, has its origins in ethnography, autobiography, and poststructuralism.

Autoethnography as a qualitative research methodology

Autoethnography as a qualitative research methodology offers a perspective different from traditional ethnography of early anthropologists by positioning the researcher's personal lived experiences or subjectivity at the heart of the research (Ellis & Bochner 2000, 2006). What makes autoethnography critical, according to Ellis (2004), is the use of autobiography as well as ethnography, or "part auto or self and part ethno or culture" (p. 31) in ways that create "something different from both of them, greater than its parts" (p. 32). It is the "greater than its parts," the linking of the personal to the political in terms of engaging with larger issues in culture, society, and education that gives certain forms of autoethnography its critical edge. Writing about the intersection of the personal and larger issues, the autoethnographer takes a political stand on social, cultural, and educational matters (Reed-Danahay 1997). The critical autoethnographer's standpoint is that the production of knowledge is neither innocent nor politically value-free. Rather, the production of knowledge is subjective representing specific interests and political standpoints that are situated in particular contexts producing partial knowledge that is culture bound and mediated within power relations of race, class, gender, and other differences.

As a qualitative research methodology, autoethnography is multidisciplinary. Ellis (2004) defines autoethnography as "research, writing, story, and method that connect the autobiographical and personal to the cultural, social, and political" (p. xix). Maréchal (2010) defines autoethnography as "research that involves self-observation and reflexive investigation in the context of ethnographic field work and writing" (p. 43). For Spry (2011), autoethnographic work is a "critically reflective narrative representing the researcher's personal and political intersections/ engagements/ negotiations with others in culture/history/society" (p. 53) or how we make meaning of our experiences in relation to others. As a postmodern response to the crisis of representation, autoethnography offers transformative possibilities from where the researcher is the voice of the other coming into a deeper understanding of various forms of difference and the connections between lived experiences and the larger sociocultural-educational world of norms and exclusions (see Anderson 2006; see also Goodall 2000).

Autoethnography challenges positivist epistemologies about whose knowledge is privileged and heard and whose voices silenced or marginalized. The interest in autoethnography as a method also stems from the ways in which ethnographic texts consisting of personal stories offer researchers and readers multiple cultural understandings of self in relation to "others," creating spaces for cross-cultural interaction (Muncey 2010). As an oppositional decolonizing research practice that counters the ethnographic texts of history and culture filtered through Eurocentric eyes, autoethnography offers those who have been historically subjugated the space to reclaim voice and experience (Smith 1999). Within spaces of memory and interpretation the enactment of the autobiographical self and other provokes questions of who is the self and what is the relation of the self to the other. The autoethnographic space for rewriting of lived experiences and its connection to cultural norms and exclusions is "an ancient scroll upon which is written the stories of one's movement through the world" (Spry 2011, p. 49). Autoethnographers question traditional autobiography's notion of the coherent, stable subject of history as well as early ethnography normative and foundational self in relation to the "Other." What does it mean to be black, white, or brown? What does it mean to be a girl behind bars, suspended or expelled from the school system? What does it mean to resist school norms? Who constructs these norms and with what consequences? Autoethnographers complicate these questions to incite reconceptualization of teaching, learning, and curriculum change.

In taking a political standpoint and actively engaging in movements committed to change for those who have been historically marginalized, the critical autoethnographer rejects positivist research for its claim to objective social science represented in traditional ethnography. The notion of the researcher positioned as an objective observer who reports about cultures and peoples from a neutral lens is derived from early ethnography in which researchers studied a culture or a social phenomenon as outsiders. In contrast, the autoethnographer is the main participant/observer/subject of the research when the emphasis is on the telling and analyzing of personal stories and cultural narratives. From the autoethnographer's standpoint, traditional ethnography as a colonial enterprise is a misrepresentation of "other" cultures that reinforces the oppressive power relations between dominant and subjugated peoples. In rejecting traditional notions of research as objective and the findings of research as objective knowledge, the epistemological and methodological stance of the autoethnographer is to give voice to subjective, personal stories, feelings, thoughts, and lived experiences of classed, raced, gendered, and other forms of oppression.

The subject of autoethnography begins with the researcher's personal experience to engage in broader social, cultural, and educational issues often overlooked in research—issues such as raced, classed, and gendered experiences. Examples of autoethnographic research that begin with the personal and move to larger social, cultural, and educational issues are autoethnographies on bereavement and loss of loved ones (Spry 2011), loss of motherhood and adoption stories (Jones 2005a), eating disorders (Saukko 2003), losing a father (Wyatt 2008), experiences of personal or collective trauma (Behar 1997), marginalization of urban street life (Bochner & Ellis 2002), the discourse on HIV (Lather & Smithies 1997), and criminalization of juvenile offenders (Sharma 2010) to name a few. Questions that autoethnographers ask to connect the personal to broader cultural, social, and educational practices and discourses are for example, what is my experience with race? How does race function in social, cultural, and educational discourse? How does it get constructed, regulated, and sustained? What are its social, cultural, and educational effects? What action does this new understanding of the personal, social, cultural, and educational experience provoke?

Three interrelated concepts inform the theory and practice of "doing" autoethnography: the performative I, the constructed other, and the connection between the self and other as embodied knowledge production or autoethnographic performative praxis (Spry 2011). The process of making meaning of our experience with others is grounded in the autobiographical telling of the performative "I" in relation to the raced, classed, gendered different "other." As a methodology, the work of the performative "I" or the autoethnographer is to engage in social, cultural, educational difference, disrupt existing power relations, and intervene in oppressive practices that label, categorize, and exclude (Butler 1997). The autoethnographic enactment of the performative "I" in relation to "other" is a process of knowledge construction for social and educational change. The autoethnographer in questioning taken for granted forms of knowledge, unsettles received forms of knowledge to expose the power/ privilege/ knowledge systems of control both in and outside education, and out of the tensions negotiates, collaborates, rewrites, recreates an embodied curriculum from multiple voices and perspectives.

Throughout the writing process, the researcher must be conscious of how performance, voice, and embodiment are used to disrupt and deconstruct cultural as well as methodological practices with a strong sense of commitment to the enactment of a "critical cultural politics" (Denzin 2006, p. 422). According to Butler (2005), the process of deconstructing knowledge and the construction of new forms of knowledge that emerge from the critique are not innocent, rather, they are pedagogical and political practices whose meaning is deeply embedded in cultural beliefs and attitudes toward race, class, gender, sexual orientation, and other differences. Therefore, self-reflexivity is critical to autoethnography as the act of telling the researcher's life stories and lived experiences in relation to others is also a representation of the self and "other" filtered through the autoethnographer's norms, values, and beliefs (Ellis 2007, 2009). The autoethnographer has to answer the questions: How did the autoethnographer write the research? How was the data collected? How has the subjectivity of the autoethnographer influenced the research? How does the autoethnographer hold herself/himself responsible for knowing and telling other people's stories? The self-reflexive researcher continues to be mindful of the process and product of autoethnography as any methodology that deconstructs, challenges, and critiques dominant forms of knowledge is already always implicated in those very same dominant cultural narratives. In "doing" autoethnography, or telling stories of the self in relation to others, the autoethnographer is responsible for the telling of others' stories and how the "other" is represented by the performative "I."

Similar to other methodologies in qualitative research, the autoethnographer employs several steps toward being mindful of the ethics of conducting research that consists of the telling of life stories. As personal experience is the starting point for autoethography, and may involve participants' personal stories as well, review by the Institutional Review Board (IRB) is an expected requirement. In keeping with the IRB requirements the researcher must maintain transparency in reporting institutional affiliations, funding sources, change of names and places for protection of participants, and acknowledge the what, when, why, how questions stemming from the researcher's influence on the research. The researcher has to protect the privacy of the participants represented or implicated in the autoethnographic text by use of pseudonyms and altering or removing identifying details such as names, places, race, gender, and institutional affiliations.

The researcher also conducts a member check by showing the interpretation to participants implicated in the research, allowing participants to respond, and acknowledge how participants feel about how they are being represented. At the same time, when writing or interpreting the data, the researcher must be mindful of balancing the authenticity of personal stories, making meaning of others' personal stories, and inciting transformative change (Jones 2005b). Autoethnographic methods of data collection include personal and interpersonal stories told in different genres and forms; biographies, autobiographies, narratives, storytelling, journaling, field notes, personal observations, interviewing; personal, institutional, and policy documents; archival, historical records, and artifacts; maps, sketches, and photographs; poetry, art, and other aesthetic forms of expression; and media images and live performances. Evidence from personal and cultural experience also found in field notes, interviews, and/or artifacts are described, and then analyzed through the interpretive lens of race, class, gender, ability, profession, or through poststructural reading practices such as deconstruction and discourse analysis in order to think differently about the experience.

Autoethnography as a research methodology presents a variety of perspectives and draws from different theoretical approaches that create a multidimensional analysis and interpretation of data to reconstruct meanings of an experience, personal story, or the text in relation to the broader social, cultural, and educational texts. What lends meaning to the analysis is the reconceptualization of the experience and interpretation of the experience in relation to the identity of the researcher, participants in the research, and the reader. In analyzing personal lived experience several validity questions are considered. For example, Ellis (2004) notes that when reading autoethnographic texts, the reader must feel the events and the interpretation described are "lifelike, believable, and possible" (p. 124) and the extent to which readers are incited to understanding themselves and others differently. Ellis asks autoethnographers and their audiences to look for validity in the narrative truth of speaking about lived experiences and personal stories in terms of what happens to researchers, participants, and readers and look for generalizability in terms of opening up the discussion rather than closing down the conversation.

Reporting the findings of an autoethnography might be in the form of a traditional journal article, a scholarly book, a literary piece or nontraditional reporting of research in the form of art creations, dramatized live performances, or audio-visual media productions. Analysis of data makes use of poststructural lenses and reading practices such as deconstruction and discourse analysis. Through the analytical process, the autoethnographer deconstructs and recomposes the self, the other, and the broader social and cultural landscape. The production of autoethnographic knowledge is "a critique of self and society, self in society, and self as resistant and transformative force of society" (Alexander 2005, p. 423).

When the subject of research is personal narratives that counter grand narratives of society, culture, and education, the epistemic responsibility of the researcher in critiquing dominant and oppressive forms of knowledge and constructing personal and embodied knowledge is articulated in the use of critical self-reflexivity to guide the research. Self-reflection deploys memory, interpretation, and recursivity to evoke thick description of personal experiences. In addition, a self-reflexive autoethnographer calls attention to the implications of the research and the autoethnographic text in terms of what political arrangements or institutional policies are legitimized in the research process and who is affected by this process. Saukko (2003) suggests "introspective interrogating" (p. 352) of one's own understanding of the self in relation to social, cultural, and educational discourses, what new realities the research creates, and to what effect.

Self-reflexivity is an ongoing practice of critical reflection, even a moral imperative, of "seeing the self see the self through and as the other" (Alexander 2005, p. 423) and acknowledging that the researcher is not only producing subjective partial knowledge but is implicated in the very forms of knowledge and systems of oppression being critiqued. Thus, the critically conscious, self-reflexive autoethnographer works with, through and against epistemologies and methodologies to offer transformative possibilities via critique, interpretation, and social action (Humphreys 2005).

While the notions of redirecting attention to personal stories of lived experience that are intimately connected to curriculum knowledge, including silenced voices in educational theory and practice, and questioning sexism, racism, and other forms of discrimination have tremendous possibilities, they are not without pitfalls. Goodson (2003), commenting on the personal and professional knowledge of teachers, states, "Like all new genres, stories and narratives are Janus-faced; they may move us forward into new insights or backward into constrained consciousness—and sometimes simultaneously" (p. 24). He suggests caution in the use of personal stories, saying that their "appeal is substantial after long years of silencing, but the dangers are more shadowy" (pp. 31–2), as the stories might create new ways of silencing and sometimes silence the very voices to which they supposedly claim to give voice. Schools are linked to the social, economic, and political systems that dominate them and that stories should, therefore, be "particularized" and "historicized" so that they are linked to broader social and political stories if personal narratives and autobiographical sources are to translate into social activism and classroom practice.

A strong critic of autoethnography that slips into the personal realm without engaging in social critique or cultural meaning-making, Delamont (2009) expresses concern over the ethics of telling personal stories of the self and other in relation to informed consent and confidentiality of those being researched. Further, according to Delamont, autoethnographers are strong in describing personal experiences but fall short of a deeper analysis of their data in terms of how personal experiences highlight social and cultural practices that might benefit from critique. Keeping in mind the above critiques, Chang (2008) cautions autoethnographers of the following: (1) over emphasis on self, (2) strong narration but weak in analysis and cultural interpretation, (3) exclusive dependence on personal memory as data source, (4) negligence of ethical standards with regard to others in self-narratives, and (5) inappropriate application of the term, "autoethnography."

Speaking of his own experience with autoethnographic work and the challenges he faced in persuading reviewers about the validity of his work, Holt (2003) admits that evaluating autoethnography is problematic. He suggests evaluative criteria for autoethnography and advises that autoethnographers keep in mind that the crisis of representation refers to writing practices, and therefore, autoethnographers must be mindful of how they respond to the culture being studied or represented. Speaking of the criteria for evaluating autoethnographic texts, Richardson (2000) suggests readers examine how the narrative contributes to our understanding of social events, how the narrative resonates with the reader, and if the construction of social meaning opens the reader to new questions or incites social action. In terms of the research's generalizability this responsibility includes the autoethnographer and the reader (Chang 2008). The autoethnographer reconstructs personal experience to shed light on social and cultural processes, however, it is the reader who validates the autoethnographic text by constructing meaning of the events as well as constructing new knowledge by reinterpreting events in their own lives (Richardson 2007).

Diverse autoethnographies

As a qualitative research methodology, there is a diverse range of autoethnographies that overlap in their philosophical and methodological commitment; however, each autoethnography is distinct in the intersection of the researcher's historical, social, and political location, theoretical perspectives, critical tools for analysis, and modes of writing. Notable autoethnographies are the analytical autoethnography such as Ellis' (2004) *The Ethnographic I: A*

Methodological Novel About Autoethnography, cultural-narrative that can be read as autoethnography such as Scheper-Hughes' *Death Without Weeping: The Violence of Everyday Life in Brazil* (1993), and autoethnography as performative in Spry's (2011) *Body, Paper Siege: Writing and Performing Autoethnography*. Research that attempts to understand contextual experience through social and cultural discourses that shape them makes autoethnography critical to exploring multiple, discursive realities as opposed to the "realist project of making sense of the social reality" (Saukko 2003, p. 34).

Ellis' *The Ethnographic I A Methodological Novel About Autoethnography* weaves autoethnography as a research methodology with doing autoethnography. As one of the leading proponents of autoethnography, Ellis rejects traditional realist forms of ethnography and the ontological and epistemological assumptions that frame it. In her rejection of traditional ethnographic methods that misrepresent the "other," Ellis turns toward postmodern and poststructural stand for questioning how the "other" has been represented in history, society, culture, and education. Ellis advocates evocative autoethnography where storytelling that is found in literary works is used as a research technique that keeps the integrity of personal and emotional experiences in the research. She suggests forms of research that engage with concrete action, emotion, embodiment, self-consciousness, and introspection (Ellis 2004, p. xix) to make meaning of personal experiences and shed light on historical, social, cultural, and educational experience.

According to Ellis, autoethnography is research, writing, and methodology that connect the autobiographical and personal to the cultural and social. In her methodological novel, Ellis narrates personal stories about a fictional graduate course that she teaches to engage in methodological issues such as what is autoethnography, ethnographic roots of autoethnography, how to conduct autoethnography, how to conduct interviews, researcher's identity in relation to the participants, the blurring of fact and fiction, ethical issues concerning the relationship between the researcher and the researched, confidentiality and the role of the autoethnographic "I." Drawing from her experience as well as the experiences of her students, the novel is set in a fictional class in which Ellis teaches the process of doing and writing autoethnography as a methodology simultaneously doing and writing autoethnography. During the course, Ellis' students discuss several topics such as domestic violence, bicultural identity, breast cancer, and sexual relationships through the telling of personal stories and connecting these lived experiences to broader social, cultural, and political issues. Delving into past experiences, Ellis and her students tell their stories, analyze the past, and reread their past differently in the present context of their lives. Throughout the methodological novel, Ellis and her students follow two overlapping discussions: one that follows the interpretive, narrative, autoethnographic research, and the other, the therapeutic telling of personal stories related to emotional experiences, such as illness, death, and divorce and their connection to the larger cultural narratives. Ellis' methodological novel is an example of emergent forms of inquiry that offer alternative possibilities for making meaning of the self and others situated in cultural contexts.

Bringing together critiques of early ethnography, autobiographical narratives, and poststructural analysis in an autoethnographic text is Scheper-Hughes' *Death without Weeping: The Violence of Everyday life in Brazil* (1993). As a health worker/researcher Scheper-Hughes talks about her own experiences then moves to broader social issues to present a critique of traditional understanding of mother love and child death in the context of extreme scarcity and chronic hunger in the Brazilian shanty town of Alto Crucifix Hill. Going beyond her own experience, Scheper-Hughes speaks about the women in Brazil and their raced, classes, and gendered experiences with cultural expectations and norms in relation to women's bodies, hunger, illness, medicine, violence, motherhood, and parenting, to present an unsettling view of mother love that transforms how we talk about these issues in different contexts. Providing testimony of women's experiences, Scheper-Hughes attempts to understand her own lived experience, her changing perceptions around issues such as mother love, and to change societal and cultural perceptions around some of these issues.

Community autoethnographers use their personal experience of researchers-in-collaboration to illustrate how a community manifests particular social/cultural issues. The focus on women and the discourse around mother love unsettles the literal and traditional meaning of maternal love as a sacred emotion. Scheper-Highes reveals the everyday violence of poverty, hunger, disease, and infant mortality as normalized through social, medical, and economic discourses. The telling of trauma of the people of Alto Crucifix Hill displaces all understandings of maternal love and brings to surface the lethal dynamics of global production, medical knowledge, cultural contexts, social practices, and institutional implication in writing history and death for those who live outside the margins. Scheper-Hughes' text can be read as a discourse on mother love and the inscription of women's roles written into culture. Subverting traditional research methods such as ethnography grounded in positivist humanism, Scheper-Highes rewrites a counter discourse to the discourse on mother love dislocating all forms of research that claim absolute and foundational knowledge.

Spry's (2011) *Body, Paper, Siege: Writing and Performing Autoethnography* is a performative autoethnography that offers how to do autoethnography by drawing connections between performative embodiment and cultural knowledge as an engagement with self-reflection and social justice. Writing in the first person, Spry describes the purposes and processes of performative autoethnography as a critical, reflexive, and "often forgiving" (p. 15) methodology that centers the body as the locus of knowledge; one that enables "a subaltern narrative revealing the understory of hegemonic systems" (p. 16). Spry draws the intimate connection between the sacred trinity of body, paper, and stage—the embodied self in place and time, interpreting and writing the body as a cultural text, and the critical and performative body on stage that opens personal experience to political transformation.

According to Spry, autoethnography opens research to performative possibilities through embodied forms of knowing. For Spry the engagement of the self and other begins with the self in relation to the self as a cultural text. When doing autoethnography, the researcher begins with "an experience—or a series of experiences—that changed your life in some way, or that was somehow transformative in terms of how you think, act, or see the world" (p. 123). Using the performative I, Spry suggests creating thick description through the use of metaphors that show the "inbetweeness" of self/other/culture/language in relation to social cultural and political issues. According to Spry, autoethnography is written from the margins as a challenge to systems of domination that have silenced the voices of certain groups of people because of their race, class, and gender. This "culture of absence" is addressed through the telling of autoethnographies of performing bodies, analysis of "cultural codes and expectations" (p. 49), leading to agency and transformative possibilities.

The role of the critical autoethnographer is to use the body as evidence in telling stories of power and privilege, analyzing forms of power and privilege, and critiquing systems of power and privilege. Spry sees autoethnographic telling of one's story as a challenge to hegemonic representations in culture and history of dominant narratives built upon exclusion and marginalization. According to Spry, what makes autoethnographic telling of embodied life stories transformative is the "ontological tension between its epistemological potential and its aesthetic imperative" (p. 109); between the construction of new knowledge that highlights or sheds light on cultural norms and writing an aesthetic text that is healing and reflective. Spry makes the argument that performative autoethnography should disrupt "dominant narratives" (p. 69), unsettle social norms and expectations, and focus on how the body can tell a counter story that enhances self-awareness through self-reflection. At the same time, Spry cautions that autoethnographers must question their own implication within the cultural norms that are being critiqued. Spry validates the process of writing and performing as a way of making sense of personal pain and exclusion to larger sociocultural events. Narrating the personal pain of losing her mother to cancer, Spry articulates the cultural text of her "mother's authorship" over her life, and the power of telling her story that helped her emerge out of her grief reclaiming her voice.

Practitioners of autoethnography ask fundamental questions about the construction of one's identity and that of the "other," question assumptions and values that define inclusions and exclusions in the curriculum, and advocate the use of self-reflection as self-transformative. One reason why autoethnography as a qualitative research methodology is powerful is because it allows for specific, important interpretation of experiences not as fixed categories identified with race, class, gender, and other differences that reinforce exclusion through consolidation of categorical identities, but because it goes beyond any form of shared experiences or identities toward "problematics" that do not totalize, stabilize, or consolidate. Autoethnography allows for a critical exploration of research in education as a site that recognizes autobiographical telling as knowledge that has educational relevance and meaning. Different forms of autoethnographical inquiry across disciplines share a common driving force—a desire to understand the self and to recognize the self as a site for knowledge production, therefore as an educational endeavor. As a site where the marginalized struggle to claim recognition of their voice, identity, and subjectivity, autoethnographic work serves as a challenge to our understanding of what curriculum considers an academic or scholarly enterprise.

Bringing autoethnography as a qualitative research methodology into curriculum inquiry, ethnography, autobiography, identity, self, and voice are problematized as terms that cannot be used without acknowledging incompleteness, contingency, contextuality, and multiplicity. It is not enough to confront positivist, technocratic, and rational aims of traditional curriculum development; alternative modes of questioning that are self-reflexive make for a deeper understanding of curriculum change. Learning how to write lesson plans and memorizing facts and figures that constitute traditional curriculum development are distortions of curriculum but also allow the possibilities for complicated conversations inciting curriculum change.

To ask questions in relation to curriculum developed around technocracy, bureaucracy, standardization, measurement, and methodologies as key to understanding knowledge that gets critiqued or/and validated in curriculum inquiry is significant. It is one where the understandings we have held and the consequences of our subsequent research and practice are unsettled through autoethnography. The fundamental beliefs that define curriculum development at various historical junctures make us conscious of the limits of prescribed curriculum frameworks. To think beyond our known scope of what makes knowledge possible and subvert the tendency to silence or erase what does not fall within our own understanding of things is what emergent forms of critical curriculum inquiry offers.

As an autoethnographer, I am excited with the notion of being a scholar-woman-mother-teacher-researcher writing an account of my lived experiences in relation to the lived educational experiences of girls behind bars to question, critique, and transform broader social, cultural, and educational issues. Such questioning can shift our knowledge from stability and certainty and force us to recognize not just the way things are but why they are so. At the same time, they create a need for relinquishing established truths we cherish, to question the historical and specific conditions that make such knowledge possible, and incite inquiry into the intimate connection between key frameworks, practices, and assumptions in educational research and its relation to critical curriculum theory. Indeed, if critical curriculum theory must envision an inclusive tomorrow, it must understand the realities of curriculum historically, as lived experience of self in relation to other, as educational practice and as social change. Continued interrogation of curriculum knowledge, process, and assumptions is critical. Autoethnography as a movement toward forms of "knowing through not knowing, knowing both too little and too much" (Lather 2000b, p. 285) is a departure from taken-for-granted humanist notions of the subject as self-knowing and positivist methods focused on evidence based knowledge as truth. This departure positions the next three chapters in the writing of autoethnography as a transformative space for telling life stories that attend to the failures of representation by addressing the question: Who is a young girl behind bars? Moving forward, the next chapter is a gesture toward "stuttering knowledge" (Lather 2001, p. 207) through autoethnographic accounts of girls behind bars reclaiming education in transformative spaces.

5

Embodied Life-stories and Counter-stories

Introduction

The chapter situates this qualitative study within three "postfoundational" discourses: poststructuralism, postfeminism, and autoethnography creating the space for writing critical autoethnography. Autoethnographic spaces make possible the weaving of three discourses critical to the curriculum of girls behind bars reclaiming education in transformative spaces—poststructural readings of the subject, disrupting the "political imperative of feminism" (Lather 2001, p. 199), and co-telling of lived experiences. Poststructuralism offers critical reading practices to interrogate the legitimacy of the fixed, essential, universal subject in relation to lived experience and multiply positioned subjectivities (Gilmore 1994). Postfeminism enables interpreting on several registers of experience such as sexual difference, gendered embodiment, and desire for change and suspicion of the subject (Butler 1990). Autoethnography offers a position from where I can speak by "both getting out of the way and getting in the way, as we tell stories that belong to others" (Lather 1997, p. xiv), always aware that the telling of others' stories is a guilty reading of other people's stories, implicating me in the story even as I create my own. In what follows, I disrupt discourses on the fixed, essential, universal, female educational subject of detention, rehabilitation, and education; validate lived educational experience and interpret multiple subject positions of girls behind bars; and open possibilities for reclaiming education through transformative spaces.

For me, autoethnography refers to an educational practice and a discursive site that offers a specific set of methodological and epistemological premises for engaging with difference. The complexity of my experience of teaching starkly contrasted with the institutional representations of girls behind bars, and the straightforward aims of rehabilitation and education. Institutional representations in the literature on detention, rehabilitation, and education failed to account for students' unsettling lived experiences as they played out in my classroom. Likewise, the educational standards and measures proved inadequate for academic empowerment. Desperate for answers, I turned to special training in mentoring at-risk youth and followed this with enrolling in professional development courses at graduate school. Two things changed my search for solutions—Pinar's autobiographical theory of curriculum and poststructural interpretive reading practices.

In the first phase of my research, I draw heavily from Pinar's autobiographical theory of curriculum to learn more about the lived experience of students through self-representation via autobiographical writing. While autobiography had a profound effect on my understanding of exclusions and inclusions in the organization of curriculum knowledge, the very concepts evoked by autobiography such as self, identity, and difference raised questions for the philosophical assumptions embedded in them. I developed an autobiographical writing project in my class; however, during the process of writing, students challenged my presumed right to tell their stories and altered the terms of my research by refusing to write and taking back ownership of their life-stories. Rather than express themselves through language that gave me power over them, students renegotiated to paint their discontinuous lived histories on canvas.

The disruption to the autobiographical writing was a turning point in my research leading to the second phase of my study—from written life-stories to stories on oil and color. Students reversed my planned "data collection" into a site for undoing those very themes of identity, self, and knowledge that I presupposed in planning the autobiographical writing project. It is worth noticing that students introduced elements of unreadability and undecidability into the project, as a counter-position to mine, compelling me to turn toward poststructural readings that create space for irreducible differences rather than produce generalized and transparent identities. I turned toward poststructural interpretive frameworks to explain my focus on subject positions rather than identity and discursive constructions rather than dialectics. For the purpose of this chapter, I focus on students' written autobiographies and move to life-stories on canvas in the next chapter.

The possibilities and limitations of Pinar's autobiographical theory of curriculum and its significance to studying the lived histories of girls behind bars are examined in the first section. I describe the autobiographical writing project as part of an English assignment for eleventh and twelfth-grade students. I situate my work within autoethnography and its intersection with autobiographic, postfeminist, and poststructural thought. Therefore, I turned to a more complicated exploration of the life-stories of students through poststructural reading practices evident in the works of Baker (2001), Butler (1990), and Lather (1992, 2000a). Touching upon the critical breakdown during the autobiographical writing project as it played out in my class, I use Rigoberta Menchú's problematic testimonial to elaborate on the crisis of representation of the autobiographical self effected by discursive challenges to truth, knowledge, and identity.

In the next section, I turn to the autobiography of Amanda, a student. My aim is to deconstruct the modernist notion of the individual and read Amanda's life-stories as multiply situated within discursive practices. I resituate Amanda's life-stories within historical and philosophical discourse to ask questions about the constructed nature of experience, how Amanda as a subject of discourse is constituted, and how detention practices and school policies constitute Amanda's experiences. The constructed life-stories of Amanda reveal the impact of exclusion bringing to light the injustice of epistemological, Cartesian, and modernist categories of representation and the premise on which detention and detention identities are constructed and perpetuated. My purpose is to give an understanding of the complexity of the histories of girls behind bars and the conditions of their existence through critiques of normative practices and the historical processes that produce experiences and make exclusions possible.

I reread the autobiography of Katy, another student, from a postfeminist perspective in the subsequent section to interpret her life-stories as multiple accounts of "becoming-woman" (Kennedy 2000, p. 28) that consist of continuities and disjunctures. In the context of girls behind bars, this process of becoming is "a continual processual movement in time, with no finality, no fixed positioning" (p. 16) that poses numerous questions on what it means to be viewed as "becoming-woman" rather than a "woman." I posit that modernist notions of individuality and the positivist assumptions of education based on prediction, measurement, and control have not allowed a place for subjectivities in understanding difference. I also call for a rethinking of students not within fixed identities or categories that erase differences but rather as subjects-in-the-making whose affects are "becomings" through the possibilities of changing subject positions.

The autoethnographic project

Autobiography to critical autoethnography

In this section, I set the premise for my autoethnographic study. I begin with Pinar's autobiographical theory of curriculum for studying the lived educational experience of girls behind bars and their attempts at reclaiming education. I briefly discuss the initial phase of my data collection. Subsequently, using Menchú's historic testimony, I outline why and how my research project on the telling of other people's life-stories offered a transformative space dramatically changing to an autoethnography of girls behind bars.

As a multidisciplinary form of writing, autobiography is an established presence in literature, history, anthropology, sociology, and psychology (Pinar et al. 2004). Invoking the import of autobiography as a method for understanding curriculum, Pinar (2004) claims autobiography is "a knowledge producing discipline with its own method of inquiry" (p. 400) and a form of educational and philosophical inquiry based on personal experience and expression (Pinar et al. 2004; Grumet 1980; Greene 2000; Miller 2005). Pinar's (2000) autobiographical theory of curriculum challenges the objectives, methods, and process of schooling that creates "hollow men, obedient automatons programmed to make the correct computations, strangers to themselves and to others" (p. 375). Pinar argues against alienation of certain groups of students affected by a school curriculum founded on cognition, intelligence, test scores, and evaluation methods ignoring spontaneity, and emotions. Instead, Pinar prefers to focus on the process of educational experience as opposed to a total bureaucratization of the term "education."

Pinar (2004) notes that the dominant culture sustains the status quo through its grand narrative that excludes autobiographical voices of those who are outside its cultural and social norms. Accordingly, dualisms such as male/female, heterosexual/homosexual, and civilized/barbaric act as alienating practices in educational philosophy and research that categorizes and construct difference. Typically, anyone who is not within the white, middle-class, male circle is excluded from the mainstream cultural and educational narrative to be undermined, excluded, or silenced (Pinar 2004). Calling the science-driven educational practices, "the nightmare that is the present" (ibid., p. 13), Pinar advocates a reconstituted self that is not a robotized or mechanical automaton serving positivist aims of education. Hence, the power of autobiography from disenfranchised voices partly restores a sense of the self and world to reclaim their side of lived experience by writing against the official text of exclusion and challenging the assumption of universality and sameness.

Responding to the call for transformative action, Grumet (1980, 1988) uses feminist theories to give autobiographical accounts of educational experience, which is very different from traditional autobiography or traditional classroom curriculum. Grumet (2006) critiques school structures and policies that separate students' personal stories from curriculum knowledge as what she calls the "semiotics of schooling: AYPs, EOGs, EOCs, 93rd percentile, Level III, Ramp Up, NCLB" (p. 47). In trying to experiment with bringing funds of student knowledge into the curriculum through class assignments, Grumet states that some students were uncomfortable being asked to give a private response to schooling; others became defensive about revealing their personal lives in the classroom; a few were outright hostile to this unusual class experiment of writing autobiographies within political spaces.

Following Pinar's autobiographical theory of curriculum, and Grumet's engagement with personal and political knowledge, I set out addressing the silence of girls behind bars by co-creating transformative spaces to write life-stories. Through autobiographies, I attempted to translate tension in my classroom into a curriculum moment for understanding the lived experience of students. In writing autobiographies, students used the present conditions of their lives to reflect on the past, interpret life-stories, connect lived experience to broader social and educational issues, and opened discussion for reclaiming education in transformative spaces.

In the context of my classroom, traditional forms as well as oppositional autobiographies were inadequate to the telling of complex lived experience of girls behind bars that played out in my classroom. Girls behind bars' lived experiences marked by discontinuities and breakdowns as well as my involvement in the telling of their stories called for a different kind of autobiographical inquiry— one that would work out of autobiography and yet challenge traditional forms of writing the self. Autobiographical writing, represented in western canon privileges patriarchal voices relegating women and women's voices to the background making women's life-stories as inquiry: a form of talking back and resisting the "othering" of women's ways of knowing. The writing process was further complicated by the unique relationship I had built with students, especially when they had no contact with the outside world. To be called an aunt, a mother, a grandmother is unusual for a teacher, but in the special circumstances of detention, where the need for bonding was palpable, defining the student–teacher relationship within familial terms made it difficult to keep a formal distance between us and threatened to become immobilizing.

In search of spaces from where to explore life-stories as possibilities for reclaiming students' lives the autobiographical project started as a writing assignment that grew into a process of self-discovery for the students and for me, with unexpected twists and dramatic turns. In order to protect personal information of the research participants and the sensitive nature of the data, pseudonyms were used. In the summer of 2007, I taught an English composition course to eleventh- and twelfth-grade students three days a week in 90-minute blocks. The class consisted of 16 students between the ages of 15 and 19 who were working toward a GED or high school diploma and were to be in detention for nine months or longer. These were to be my participants in the research who would write autobiographies three days a week for six months. The autobiographies were not to be graded, and students had the right to opt out of the research project without repercussions. Officially, the writing project began in May 2007 with IRB approval.

According to the state's juvenile justice laws, juvenile offenders cannot give informed consent for any kind of research; hence, the director of the facility discussed the research project with students before giving official consent aligned with IRB approval guidelines. At the time, I had concerns that I was asking students to write autobiographies and personal stories while informed consent had to be signed by the director rather than the students. The director's consent for the research study was given with the understanding that all data and subsequent analysis would have to be approved by the facility, pseudonyms would be used, and no photography or audio-taping would be allowed in keeping with safety and security regulations of the detention facility. Although I discussed the research with students several times, I am not certain that students understood the long-term impact of their participation on my work. Throughout the research process, even as I write this, in spite of the need to make students' counter-stories heard, I am troubled about using students' life-stories for academic purposes. In spite of IRB approval that protected the participants to some extent, I had some concerns.

I was conscious of the ethical issues involved in my role as a teacher and authority figure on the one hand and researcher on the other. In an ideal situation, students should have the right to tell their stories and exercise their agency on their terms. Representing girls behind bars who do not have the right to give informed consent is fraught with ethical questions of confidentiality, ownership, and the vulnerability of participants. In simple terms, the researcher is the one who reaps immediate benefits in terms of research and scholarship. Besides, if I aim to rewrite students' life-stories to draw attention to larger structural and institutional processes that promote detention and create inequities, then I am also complicit in the production of knowledge when I include and exclude stories based on my subjectivity and context.

As a teacher and researcher I am afraid of my complicity in the production of academic knowledge that in turn is complicit in influencing educational practices one of which is the processing of students from school to the prison pipeline. I am aware that I am using students' life-stories to get to larger social and institutional networks that perpetuate racism, sexism, homophobia, and other biases. I am also aware that students' stories hold the key to understanding lived experience or the role of institutions in shaping detention, rehabilitation, and education, but also the key to change—the struggle for social justice and equality begins with how difference is viewed, and knowledge about difference is produced and circulated. In the light of these tensions I discussed and outlined the autobiographical research project with students several times and at different stages of the autobiographical project.

The data for this study was gathered in two phases; the first phase is elaborated in this chapter and the second phase is discussed in the next chapter. Data consisted of students' official case sheets maintained by the facility, students' self-portraits, and my field notes. I kept detailed notes on my interaction with students, the process of autobiographical writing, and paid close attention to my own lived experience. I kept a journal from the first year of my teaching at the facility and used the journal entries to supplement field notes written as "the story of the self who has stake, asks the questions and does the interpreting" (Goodall 2003, p. 60). I kept detailed notes on my interaction with students, the process of autobiographical writing, and paid close attention to my own lived experience as a "colonized other" learning to teach in a detention classroom. Students' autobiographies were analyzed as counterstories to official, institutional narratives of girls behind bars through multiple lenses.

As I began to collaborate with students on autobiographical writing, students voiced numerous questions. At first, most students responded with doubtful statements such as: What is there to write? Everything is in my intake sheet—read it. What do you want to know? Why do I have to write about myself? Is this for a grade? No one wants to know about my life. Why can't we just read

Maya Angelou's life? Does it have to be in proper English? Do I really write about myself or just all the good things? Who is going to read this? Through the recovery of personal stories, previously silenced, I wanted to give a new reading of girls behind bars.

The students and I expected honesty from each other, and established a supportive and trusting atmosphere in the classroom so students could write without any threat or fear. This is of special significance in a detention classroom, as students are familiar with the routine of confessional therapy and group counseling wherein silence is construed as refusal of prescribed therapeutic treatment. Furthermore, autobiographical writing is testimonial and confessional and can be used against students by the detention facility.

As a class we settled on some basics such as a range of topics, those who wished would share their autobiography with the class, that I would not discuss their stories with others employed in the school, that the writing assignment would not be graded, and that I would not expect accurate punctuation and spelling! An afterthought was added—I would have to voice my personal life and let them read it. The assignment consisted of stories, excerpts, narratives, poems, memories, journal entries, and events drawn from students' past histories and educational lived experiences. Students worked on their autobiographies from May 2007 to November 2007 without interruption. The initial brainstorming consisted of topics listed below:

- A timeline of my life
- Brief sketches of my life
- A happy moment/sad moment
- Person who has had a positive/negative influence
- How would I describe myself?
- How do I think others view me?
- A time when I experienced rejection/intense love
- Any part of my past that I could change
- A place from my childhood that is unforgettable
- If I could achieve anything, what would it be?
- Why am I in detention?
- How would I describe my educational experience?

After much reflection and deliberation, students agreed to write as well as speak about their experiences. To tell or not to tell? The telling is a complex unraveling of exclusion and silencing as well as a fascinating portrayal of voices of resistance and possibilities for transformation. At times students were keen to tell their stories, at other times the struggle to tell life-stories that cannot be spoken was apparent.

After six months of consensus on writing, reading, and discussing autobiographies, in the first week of December, students refused to write any further. This was a turning point in my study. Reading this as a disruption to my research plan, I took some time to recover from this loss of direction. I felt powerless as students had taken back the right to tell their stories on my terms. I reflected, how do I give back to students what I had claimed as mine? How do I renegotiate the terms of the autobiographical project and regain their trust? Were students afraid I would misrepresent the particular historical contexts of their experience? Were they reclaiming the production of knowledge about themselves? Did the disruption call for new modes of thinking?

Out of this crisis, the students and I had to rework the project as they redirected their autobiographies toward life-stories portrayed in oil, reclaiming their education to write life-stories on their own terms. What complicated the writing project was that the autobiography itself that had transformed into a site where power, authority, and trust were being challenged in ways that placed the students and me in contradictory positions. It was at this point that I turned to postfeminist and poststructural reading practices in education for interpreting life-stories.

With a change in the class dynamics where the students decided to paint self-portraits in oil and in the context of the breakdown in my plans, the research moved from autobiography to critical autoethnography. I realized that when students tell their life-stories, as a researcher I have an active role in autobiographical remembrances and in reconstructing experiences from my own subjective lens. For example, when students transformed the autobiographical project moving from writing autobiography to painting self-portraits in oil, I interpreted their move as resistance to my streamlined plans that suited my research intentions rather than their personal knowledge. The reversal of the writing project indicated to me that teacher knowledge is a partial knowing and that there are always deeper aspects of experiential and embodied knowing that I would, perhaps, never understand or know. Although the scholarship on teaching in detention recognizes the importance of a teacher's ability to learn about difference from students' lives, it fails to acknowledge that received knowledge as established truth is a highly contested concept with transformative possibilities.

I do acknowledge my complicity in shaping the discourse by opening autobiography to contested interpretations, knowing that interpretations are positions that are continually breaking down. Deconstructive reading offers multiple interpretations of autobiography as a text providing a space for transforming the conditions of impossibility into the condition of possibilities for a different set of experiences. I also acknowledge that my complicity does not end with interpretations of students' autobiographical texts but that "the self's engagement in fieldwork could not be suppressed" (Okely 1992, p. 9).

Students as autoethnographic subjects can be viewed as telling multiple testimonials rather than a single, universal, fixed truth. I interpreted students' resistance as muddying the distinctions between self-representation, representation, knowledge, and truth. Students' testimonials, like Rigoberta Menchú's story, challenged the ways in which positivist and humanist research is conducted, specifically the position of the researcher and subjects in the research troubling the transparency of the research process. When doing research, it is impossible to draw the line between subject-researcher, the construction of knowledge, claims to truths, the discourses that shape subjects and subject positions, and researcher's implication in legitimizing certain stories. Therefore, I will briefly outline Menchú's story to show how autoethnographic work pushes the boundaries of knowledge and truth when doing research that draws together our stories—mine and my students' stories.

Rigoberta Menchú is a Guatemalan woman who championed the Central American people's struggle against the US government, multinational companies, and the indigenous political and military elite who joined forces with the United States. Elisabeth Burgos-Derby, a Venezuelan anthropologist, records Menchú's story, then translated, as *I, Rigoberta Menchú: An Indian Woman in Guatemala*. The book was widely acclaimed, and Menchú received the Nobel Peace Prize in 1992. Thereafter, David Stoll, a US anthropologist, found discrepancies in Menchú's famous *testimonio*. He published a book, *Rigoberta Menchú and the Story of all Poor Guatemalans*, that held Menchú accountable for manipulating the truth, made his allegation through speeches, and himself became a controversial subject.

Menchú responded by admitting that parts of her story were not literally true but argued that it is a larger story that must be read in a historical context, a story meant to draw world attention to murderous exploitation in Guatemala and other Central American countries, under the sanction of the United States and its European allies. In response, Western intellectuals, the media, and political figures immediately entered a long-drawn conflict over Menchú's story, Stoll's story, and the nature and politics of truth and its representation for political purposes (Arias 2001; Scheurich & Foley 2000; Zimmerman 2000/2001).

At the very heart of the Rigoberta Menchú controversy is the question about whether those who make stories public, their own or others, ought to tell the truth. Lather (2000a) writes of:

> the price subjects pay to speak the truth about themselves out of forms of reflexivity, discourses of truth, forms of rationality, and effects of knowledge, we learn how people undertake to speak truthfully within the forms of power exercised and how they are put into play. (p. 156)

With Menchú, truth becomes less of a truth and more of what Lather calls "truth-effect" (p. 154). Lather (2000b) claims that "the differences between truth and fiction is, finally, undecidable" (p. 155).

In the context of the "problematic of accountability to stories that belong to others," Lather (2000b) speaks of the "epistemological paradox" (p. 284) faced by feminist poststructural, autoethnographic work that simultaneously dislocates and constructs knowledge. Postfeminist and poststructural concepts, particularly critical autoethnography, offer possibilities for troubling received forms of knowledge (Britzman 1995, 2000, 2009), producing knowledge differently, and questioning the researcher's complicity in interrupting (Lather 2004). Autoethnography creates a "textual space wherein the culturally and historically changing epistemology of the self find[s] particular expression" (Gilmore 1994, p. 85).

Writing out of autoethnography, Lather (1992) attempts to move educational research from traditional positivist representation to "less on what is true and more on how particular discourses produce 'truth effects'" (p. 96). Research that attempts to understand contextual experience through social and cultural discourses that shape them makes autoethnography vital to exploring multiple, discursive realities as opposed to representation. Lather (2001) advocates "postfoundational possibilities," a counter discourse to "lovely knowledge," dislocating all forms of research that claim absolute and foundational knowledge (p. 202). In sum my autoethnographic work aims to show that girls behind bars, rehabilitation, and education can be "reinterpreted, re-stored, reinscibed" (Derrida 1995, p. 256) through the possibilities of changing subject positions.

Life-stories and counter-stories

Amanda's life-stories

In this section, I present Amanda's life-story. Amanda's counter-stories draw attention to the ways in which gender discrimination sets up certain groups of students for the school-to-prison pipeline. There is a double injustice when young women like Amanda are sexually abused, then placed in detention as part of their gendered treatment. In Foucauldian terms, I interpret multiple tellings of Amanda's life-stories as "statements" that position her as a subject of competing discourses. Foucault reminds us that:

> The subject of the statement should not be regarded as identical with the author of the formulation. It is not in fact the cause, origin, or starting point of the phenomenon of the written or spoken articulation . . . it is not the constant, motionless, unchanging arena . . . (1978, pp. 95–6)

If subject formations are determined and inevitable due to historical forces, subject positions that resist and disrupt are also part of the same historical moment. Therefore, to take detention identity as an object of inquiry is to analyze subject positions, in part, as the effect of discourses that place students within the discourses of detention. Amanda's self-representation is discursively produced, not restricted to any fixed interpretation.

Amanda's original case sheet recording her biography had been misplaced at the facility; hence, below is her biography given to me by her case manager, the official designated to "manage" her "case." Amanda's institutional story is brief:

March 2, 2007

Amanda: White seventeen-year-old female, with history of drug and alcohol abuse. She has been sexually abused and must undergo individual therapy for sexual abuse and group therapy for substance abuse. Her school record is sketchy and she has been repeatedly expelled from numerous schools. There is no record of her grades although the last school she attended did not want her back. Hence, the facility is advised to help her take the GED exam rather than return to school. Caution for the staff—Amanda is a "substance abuser," "self-harmer," and "at-risk."

My telling of Amanda's story:

When we first met, Amanda and I connected immediately. My first memory of Amanda was a young woman who had an absent look on her face, deep in thought. When I asked her about it, she informed me she had a "lot to think about." She said she was angry for being in a facility where students were "dumb" and "without hope" because she knew she could do better. She was also angry that when arrested no one was willing to listen to her side of the story because she was "punished for serving time for earlier crimes." Amanda was different from most of the girls in her class in small ways that were magnified under conditions of detention. She was polite and careful not to use inappropriate language in the class, was a good listener, and took pride in herself, holding her head high at all times. In the classroom, she was enthusiastic and determined to score high.

I learned many things from Amanda. One of them was the language used in detention that was so much a part of students' vocabulary yet unfamiliar to me. She made a list for me called "Sharma-dictionary" and often tested me by asking what some of the words and terms meant. Apart from legal terms from the world of juvenile justice, the dictionary consisted of slang for drugs, words and phrases used for detention staff, and an entire repertoire of codes that students in detention substituted when planning collective resistance. For example, when a student was going through a drug withdrawal it was referred to as "jonesing," being isolated meant "holing," and "fishing" meant socializing a new student into the ways of detention.

Amanda's dictionary gave me the privilege of entering the secret world of girls behind bars and earned for me the respect of many students. In their eyes, knowing the hidden codes critical to their lives distanced me from my institutional affiliations with the facility. My lack of awareness of the hidden curriculum of institutional policies of detention and the juvenile justice system, my limited awareness of the cultural nuances within American culture, and my obvious Indian ways of existence assigned an outsider status to me that was not lost to students, creating a kind of shared, though unspoken, intimacy between us.

Students labeled as "challenged" had no difficulty learning what related directly to their lives, were creative when motivated, and had a lot to teach me about their life as well as shedding light on mine. I also learned some disturbing aspects of myself as a teacher, chiefly that I tended to pay more attention to students who were either high scorers and loved the English class or those who were diagnosed with behavioral issues. I was guilty of focusing on two ends of the class spectrum and, perhaps, not connecting with many students who went unnoticed because of their silence.

Below is Amanda's first autobiographical testimony:

October 12, 2007

Hello, my name is Amanda and I am 17 years old. I was born to the parents Linda and so-called father John or Josh. I am not sure which one is my dad . . . I was abused physically and sexually. I was sexually abused by my brother for which he hit me a couple of times and I was physically abused by my dad. I always went to school after that but, I was really bad all the time.

I was about 14 years old when my brother tried to force himself in me. This was at nighttime and everybody was sleeping except for me. My brother came into my room, locked my door, and pushed me on my bed. He began to take off all of my clothes and I was screaming, crying, and trying to get him off, he just continued . . . This is when they diagnosed me with a sleeping disorder and put me on meds. I also began to see a psychiatrist once a week. That never worked and the abuse seems to get worse. My brother continued to come to my room at night. He would still do stuff to me anyways. I did not want to tell my mom as she had earlier refused to speak to me when I told her about dad being abusive. I know sometimes my mom does not like me and we don't have the fun that we had when I was little. So I began to self-harm with my nails and was sent to isolation rooms at different facilities where I was on suicide watch. Okay, I was cutting myself, I was not killing myself. See, there is a difference.

I ran from home many times until I was arrested and sent into a placement. I was so bad that I was moved from placement many times. That is how I got here. Most days I hate this place [detention]. I hate the way staff treat us saying we manipulate staff. I do not want the girls to think I was flirting with staff so I told everyone I am gay. Now I have to pretend that I am. But it protects me so I will continue to say I am gay. I have to become organized and get my head out of my butt. In order for me to leave this facility, my county wants me to complete this whole program and get my school credits. I know I have a lot of work to do but if I can shut my mouth, stay quiet, be compliant then I can complete this program and graduate. I need to go back to school as I get straight A's in school. I love drama class because I do not have to be Amanda, I can be anyone I want. That is why I changed school so many times because in a new school I can start all over again. That is what I thought. But in the end you still remain yourself. I tried hard to hide my past, be good, follow the rules, make good friends but I kept slipping back to my bad ways. If it is not one thing, something else gets you whether it is school or home.

I don't need drugs or sex to get a rush. I can cut myself, and although I don't feel pain, when I cut myself I can watch the blood drip and it kind of makes me feel good. That was the other reason I saw a psychiatrist. I think the psychiatrist was a nice lady but she has no idea what it feels like to live my life. She wants me to become okay but I am okay. She is the one who wants to fix things for herself. She doesn't realize that talking about the same thing doesn't help. So I don't speak to her anymore.

In another autobiographical telling, Amanda handed me a poem, which she claimed was her "happy side." The poem is a play on remembering and forgetting. Below is Amanda's poem:

You and Me
You are my memory and I am forgetfulness
You make me remember the good things while I want to forget the bad
Which is me? You or me?
You remind me of the days at the beach, just rolling in the sun, sand in my hair
I have never had so much sun, sand, and fun before
And then there is Me
The Me that wants to forget I have a bad life, bad family, bad grades
Bad is a bad word for Me
When was the last time Amanda and good were used in the same sentence?
When I was one, or two, or three years old?
Oh, You are bad too because you remind me of the good that is not for Me
I am used to betrayal so what if memory betrays me too
Memory, you are forgiven
It is harder to forgive Me
And all the things I will never forget

Was Amanda reminding me that even though she wanted to forget the trauma of her past, I was constantly reminding her to stay in her memories? Complicating Amanda's memory and history, illustrates the difficulty of an autobiographical writing project. Amanda is troubled by the institutional story of her life that documents and constructs her as a fixed subject of detention and the story she is retrieving from memory as well as interpreting through her changing subject positions. Her testimony opens autobiographical transformative spaces from where she is able to tell her story on her own terms.

Knowledge is always being mediated on many levels such as between the "autobiographical I," the autoethnographer, and the reader. Amanda is not a fixed object nor a fixed subject under surveillance but part of changing multiple discourses that attempt to fix Amanda as well as offer transformative possibilities for changing the discourse. For example, the institution sees her as a detainee who is a "substance abuser," "self-harmer," and "at-risk"; Amanda sees herself as a victim who is "physically abused by [her] dad," and "really bad all the time." She also sees herself as a student who "got straight A's" and asserts that in spite of what others, specifically, the psychiatrist might think, "I am okay."

A disturbing element of Amanda's autobiography is her history of sexual abuse. Amanda's gendered experiences and subsequent survivor strategies are directly connected to juvenile injustices that label some students as juvenile delinquents without fleshing out the connection between female victimization, survivor strategies, and what gets diagnosed as delinquency. Statistics on sexual abuse continue to increase by epidemic proportions, making gendered discrimination a part of the pipeline for girls locked up in detention facilities across the United States. Once in detention, survivors like Amanda are further pathologized through a narrow curriculum of rehabilitation strategies, psychological evaluations, and the disciplining of gender.

Early feminists would read Amanda as a typical case of women's oppression under patriarchal domination; however, complicated stories are interwoven through Amanda's subjective histories along uncertainty and ambiguity. As a victim of abuse, Amanda's resistance takes the form of memory, silence, desire, and conflict that does not mirror sexual disturbances with transparency. Childhood trauma consists of many unexplained aspects that impact women's emotional and mental development (Herman 1992).

Sexual abuse in the family contains elements of father–daughter desires as well as increasing anxiety over sexuality, leading to a highly charged and complex relationship. For example, Amanda describes the abuse inflicted by her brother but only hints at the violence perpetrated by her father saying, "when I told her [mom] about dad," suggesting abuse though never explicitly saying it. She again extends the suggestion, remembering, "my mom refused to speak to me," yet never really explaining the strained relationship with her mother. It is not clear why Amanda's mother refuses to speak with her, and this can be interpreted as undercurrents of sexuality and resentment, blurring the boundaries between victim and perpetrator.

Another problem in Amanda's autobiography is the psychiatrist's confessional therapy that Amanda rejects as meaningless. In a sense, the psychiatrist's repeated retrieval of Amanda's memory of past trauma is an attempt to fit Amanda's experiences within the normalizing discourse of women's response to male domination and victimization. Whereas Amanda destabilizes discourse on sexual abuse, the psychiatrist attempts to preserve the unity and stability of Amanda's victim story as it sustains Amanda's gendered experiences as fixed truths. By problematizing Amanda's experiences, I bring attention to the multiple competing discourses that complicate the effects of sexual abuse. I also wish to create space for multiple understandings of the experiences of girls behind bars by mobilizing controversial issues such as incest and desire long taboo in academic discussions. I do not mean to minimize Amanda's lived experience of gendered abuse by her brother and father. I do submit that her self-representation has wider implications and complicated readings that emerge.

Through my interaction with Amanda, talking about her life, reading her autobiography, in subsequent conversations with her, and my interpretation of her life-stories, I was confused as to how to respond to her. I did not know how to understand Amanda. On the one hand, as a child, Amanda's life has been one of subjection within various discourses. On the other, Amanda refuses all counseling, making me wonder if Amanda is rejecting help or if the help that is being offered ignores her lived experience. In creating such a powerful image of her self-harmed body as an instrument for speaking, Amanda disturbed and unsettled my schooled notions of curriculum or how I should teach in the classroom. I had never experienced anything quite like Amanda's self-harmed body and found it hard to keep the images out of my mind.

At the same time, I felt the image evoked by cutting and self-harming, such as "I cut myself I can watch the blood drip and it kinds of makes me feel good," is Amanda exercising power not only in the shock value of the act but also in the control it gives over her own body and emotions. When I think of my own growing up, I can see a teenager who rebelled against authority at home and in school. Perhaps the circumstances of my childhood, the stability of family, and the love that I got at home protected me from the conditions that threatened Amanda. In spite of the loss of my father, I had older brothers and sisters who in immeasurable ways protected me and were sensitive to my feelings. Now when I think of Amanda, I am aware of how little I knew about the trauma of physical, mental, and sexual abuse and its silence in curriculum issues.

In detention, where the right to speak is restricted to counseling and confession, Amanda looks for alternative ways to express herself outside the conventions of language. Self-harming behaviors as a gendered practice more common among women detainees of all ages, has been recognized as a serious psychiatric disorder, but remains undertheorized as personal testimonies and counter-stories of those who have survived multiple forms of marginalization and abuse. My own understanding of detention as well as how to respond to Amanda's self-harming assumed the powerlessness of those who are forced into silence, yet Amanda disrupts my ways of knowing by generating alternative expressions of resistance when she speaks of embodied experiences that challenge traditional discourses. By refusing to speak during counseling, directing her anger and frustration inwards and cutting herself, Amanda reveals a desire to escape the oppressive discourses of detention and rehabilitation.

I told Amanda I wished she would accept her counselor and psychologist's help. At the same time, I understood that Amanda was not searching for rehabilitation through the possibilities in rational thought; rather, she turned toward her body, in the intersubjective realm of her own lived embodiment and feelings. I was torn between the traditional authority of detention and the desire that Amanda's experiences would be understood under a different set of terms. For me, Amanda's institutional representation, her self-representation, and my interpretation of the many versions of her life tell the story of a young woman who resisted the power of others to control her life, a life that she maps free from the institutional surveillance that attempts to hold her captive. Amanda takes back control by refusing to speak, controlling what she can say, is allowed to say, or is forbidden to say. However, her story, her silence, and her life were beyond my understanding or beyond anything I was trained to respond to. I interpreted Amanda's reactions as born out of multiple discourses—history, memory, detention (surveillance), and rehabilitation (counseling).

The dominant discourse positions her as a young girl behind bars, a victim of patriarchal domination, and a dangerous and violent offender. The result is that when Amanda writes about her subjectification, there is a reliving in the reading of it; yet, her multiple portrayals dislocate the discourses that render her a passive victim or a powerless subject without agency. My training at the facility speaks of Amanda's responsibility in making poor decisions that need rehabilitation and correction. Nevertheless, she claims, "I am okay." While both discourses code and fix her in contradictory ways, Amanda is not a subject who can be overdeterminedly fixed; rather, she is subject-in-the-making who can use silence in dangerously subversive ways to mystify and reclaim control of the institutional and social space she occupies.

The dominant discourses of teaching do not provide me with the medium or the space for expressing ambiguous or contradictory positions. Through lived experience, Amanda invites me to live within a curriculum space that is transformative as she reclaims education. My own lived educational experience of deciding at 16 to leave the small town I grew up in and opting for a liberal arts education a thousand miles away in New Delhi or choosing my spouse contrary to the traditional "arranged marriages" that young women my age relied on, positioned me to disrupt discursive practices. The unraveling of Amanda's changing subject positions relocates my memory. If dominant discourses constitute the subject, validating lived experience and changing subject positions unsettle dominant discourses of teaching and provide possibilities within curriculum for transformative change.

An English teacher for decades, I have gloried in the privilege of words as rational expression of thought. Now 17-year-old Amanda has displaced the clichéd English teacher's faith in language and challenged the relation between silence and speech. In articulating her embodied ways of knowing, Amanda has challenged every known way in the institutional curriculum of schooling inscribed within the conventions of language, power, and knowledge. Was her self-harming incidental or was it historical apriori? Or was Amanda's self-harming a search for embodiment through knowing too much and knowing too little? I would never fully know.

Multiply situated subject-positions

Katy's life-stories

In this section, I offer my autoethnographic portrait of Katy, a young girl behind bars, not to grasp the essence of her identity but to deconstruct how her life has been constructed. I begin with an institutional representation that predicates her, my reading of her life-story, followed by Katy's self-representation. Subsequently, I reread all three articulations of Katy's life-stories to disarticulate them, in a manner of speaking, in order to provoke a reading of Katy as a multiply situated subject. In reading Katy's subject positions, I am prompted to look at my own.

Below is Katy's institutional case sheet:

March 12, 2007

Katy: 18 years, White, female. Religion unknown. Hair blonde. Eyes brown. Identifying marks tattoo on ankle, scar on L cheek, scars on both upper and lower arms. Reason for referral: Domestic assault. Offense: battery, Delinquency Issues: Drug and alcohol usage, runaway. Under court custody: Release date to be fixed with caseworker. Treatment: Counseling. Attend assault and battery group counseling. Individual counseling: Anger management. School attendance: Regular. Additional information: Has two year male child in foster care.

Referred into detention by: County and high school

My telling of Katy's life-story:

I was introduced to Katy in the middle of a reading of Shakespeare's *Romeo and Juliet*, and Katy jumped right into the role of Juliet's nurse as if born to play the part. At the time, I wondered if Katy felt comfortable at her new placement because she was socialized into detention and was in a familiar environment because of a long history behind bars. Secretly, I wished she felt comfortable because she loved Shakespeare. She was the first student who stopped by on her first day at the facility to ask me about wearing a *saree*, a traditional Indian dress. She told me she was fascinated with *Bollywood* dance and showed me a few steps. *Bollywood* is India's Hollywood.

I enjoyed Katy in the class as she threw herself wholeheartedly in all the things she was good at doing. Katy was not popular with the other students at the facility. She dressed immaculately, which is quite a feat in detention, where students have no control over the uniforms they have to wear that are often ill-fitted and wrinkled. She found ingenuous ways to iron her clothes by sprinkling water and spreading her clothes between mattresses, watched her weight, and did push-ups in my class, joking, "I have to stay fit as you never know when I have to run for my life!"

Katy had plans to graduate from high school and regretted that she had lost her honor roll status for being "locked up." Katy often challenged me in class and chastised me when I did not have answers to her questions! I was the teacher, should I not be knowing everything, she once asked me in frustration. She told me she could not understand why I knew "so much" about American literature and "so little" about American history. One of my greatest challenges teaching in an American classroom was the discrepancy between my ability to situate English and European literature in context and a complete lack of it when teaching American literature—never had I imagined a student in a detention classroom to question this gap in my teaching—and I respected Katy for this.

Below is Katy's autobiographical account. Katy loved writing letters to herself, so for Katy the autobiographical writing project was a dream come true!

October 4, 2007

A moment in my life when I felt loved . . .

Nothing stands out that would be important. A time when I felt unwanted was right after I turned my foster dad in for an argument that turned physical. It is sad that I don't remember the reason for the argument but we argued, and it was my first step into hell. All I remember is we argued, he hit me and I threw something at him. He picked me and threw me down the stairs. I had a bloody nose, a split lip, cuts and bruises, bumps all over. I went to my neighbor's house for the night and no one looked for me. That hurt even more. My neighbor took me to school, told my principal and the police came. The patrol officer in school took my statement, photographs and documented everything. But after it was over, I regretted speaking about it. This cycle was repeated many times and I know that the police or the school would not do anything. Because they blame me for it. Why? Because I am a girl who is supposed to be sensible not argue with my parents. I was sent home and then it would start again. My family has never been the same again. Even though this is my foster family when I was little we were happy as a family. Now they do not trust me and I do not trust them. I want to be with them and I don't want to be with them. I love my family but then I don't. This is never going to end. I can't remember some of the things . . .

What else should I write about? School? I am not who the girls think I am. I was. I am. Who am I? Especially in these clothes, and these shoes. Am I becoming like them? The girls here don't like me because I don't like telling them why I am here. I feel it is in my hands to do well in school and do well in life. All the girls here are not bad. Some are good girls just got in trouble because of friends or family. They know I have issues as I have scars on my arms and legs. I mutilate my arms and legs because it makes me mad when people tell me I am beautiful. I want them to know I am smart. Not beautiful. It is not about being beautiful anymore, as I have to change my old ways. I have to change for myself not for my looks or for my family or for my friends. That's how I was raped in ninth grade and have a baby who is with his adopted family. I am happy he is a boy because girls have to take care of themselves all the time. I want to have children but not till I can finish school. My county case worker says I should take the GED exam but I will not. I will go back and graduate from my high school as GED is for those who are dumb. I like going to school and I get good grades even though my teachers treat me like I am trouble.

How do I read Katy's autobiography? In other words, how do I read the three tellings of her life to answer the question "What is a young girl behind bars?" Several dimensions of Katy's autobiography are significant. Katy's institutional case sheet portrays her as "delinquent," her self-portrait disrupts the institutional discourse that is marked by her silence and absence, and my experience with Katy oscillates between the institutional and Katy's representation. What do Katy's subject positions tell me about the categories that define knowledge of girls behind bars? Whether it is a loss of voice, or imposed silence, a misrepresentation or her own fantasies and desires, Katy makes it difficult for me to locate a stable identity, or fix a central "I," within her many subject positions.

Katy's story does not unfold through a linear development. Her memory drifts back and forth to reveal a story of violence and abuse until she refuses to remember. She confronts the powerlessness imposed by family violence with her own inability to articulate what her memory attempts to forget. The more she struggles to forget, the less she is able to comply with institutional scripts—the longing to tell is far greater than the forces that silence. Katy disrupts the institutional story by authoring her own script when she feels she is being read by others. Katy's autobiographical excerpt challenges the essential, humanist self to situate her experiences historically and culturally within discourses that she creates as much as they create her. By underscoring "I am a girl" and questioning, "Am I becoming like them?" Katy represents herself as the prototype "other" who is transformed from an example of a delinquent educational subject to multiple subjectivities and changing subject positions.

In recreating her lived experience within the context of school and family, she drops the "I" to become a "we" in relation to "them" saying, ". . . when I was little we were happy as a family. Now they do not trust me and I do not trust them." In creating an opposition, she is drawing boundaries that revolve around domination and subjection. While she draws discrete lines between "we" and "them," the underlying commonality in her positions revolves around the axis of gender represented through, "I am a girl," "All the girls here . . .," and "I was raped . . . and have a baby." Within the world of distinct boundaries between home and school, "we" and "them," and "victim" and violence, the primary feature of her subjectivities remains gender.

Katy reconceives the notion of gendered violence separate from any common understanding of trauma, as there is no single way of telling traumatic experiences (Felman 2000). Her autobiography shows how trauma and violence can paradoxically make her victim and survivor at the same time, exposing the troubling reality of the gendered nature of conditions that have made her experiences possible (Felman & Laub 1992). Katy's trauma emerges from the confusion she feels in reporting her father's abuse and then regretting it because of having lost her family's trust over it.

Katy recognizes the repetitive cycle of abuse and the subsequent guilt and rejection but is unable to move beyond it. She has begun to believe that her life is a "hell" of her own making and one that she has entered without any turning back. She grapples with her changing subjectivities—a challenge to the binary assumptions of being a victim or perpetrator, innocent or guilty, "good" or "bad." Saying, "I regretted speaking about it," she sees herself between keeping silent and resisting it, contradictory and confusing and continues to struggle for some form of meaning in her discontinuous life. She not only challenges her own need to speak and feel but also complicates the notion of voice by speaking in new ways. When Katy speaks up, she regrets it; when she is silent, she is alienated from the other students, who "don't like me [Katy] because I don't like telling them why I am here." Watching Katy, I realize the contradiction in my own attitude. At times I advise students to make friends and learn to live with each other; at other times, I expect them to stick close to the disciplinary rules that state no student should speak to another.

At times Katy tried to follow norms and at other times she resisted the fixed educational subject of detention. For Katy, writing becomes an act of reflection and reclaiming education as she traces her lived experience, the memories of events reconstructed as she recreates a transformative autobiographical space for reenvisioning her educational experiences. It also gives me the autoethnographic opportunity to interpret her life in the context of a new reading of her lived experience as the historical silencing of her embodied speaking in contrast to playing out the cultural script for a girl behind bars. Katy's delving into the past calls for a misreading and mistreatment of her place in history (Felman 1982) as her lived experience unsettles the "delinquent" subject to validate lived experience and voices silent in the dominant discourse of education.

Between Katy's desire to do well in the school system and the desire to be herself, she creates an image of herself in relation to the Cartesian (good/bad) and the ontological self (Who am I becoming?) and many other images of self-representation in between. Lost in the fixed representations of her identity, perhaps what she sees herself becoming, she struggles to represent herself as anti-Cartesian and anti-ontological. Rather, she creates an identity that is the "other" from the norm yet one that retains shades of the historical self and the original "other."

Refusing any coherent identity, Katy claims a subject position separate from any scripted other, where meaning resides in what she chooses to call herself through subject positioning, reimagining the legacy of a woman who refuses a normative translation. In rejecting being called "beautiful," Katy denaturalizes traditional forms of sex, gender, woman through a renewed commitment to subjective knowing that gives meaning to her changed subject position from "beautiful" to "smart." As she moves back and forth between different subject positions, Katy blurs boundaries between subject and object, between representation of prescribed categories and a refusal to recognize the self within the rigid markers of sexual and gendered identity.

At other times, Katy indicated how conscious she is of her gendered presence by speaking of the need she feels to look her feminine best. In one of her autobiographical entries, she writes:

> I have to make sure I look my best even when I am locked up. My hair and my eyes are the most beautiful part of me, so I take care of both. You never know when a great guy is all over you and what if he is the right one. So I tell all the girls here to look good, don't let yourself get ugly.

In the encounter between her gendered self-representation through autobiography and interpretation of her self-representation, Katy confronts the limits of writing autobiography—what Derrida (1981b) calls the law of genre—that the genre of writing autobiography and the question of gender are two sides of the same coin. In Katy's context, the inadequacy of the autobiographical genre throws the representation of gender and identity in educational discourse into question, calling in new modes of curriculum for Katy to reclaim her education.

In writing about her lived experience, Katy offers a space for transformative understandings of her contradictory positions as an educational subject of detention that is within, and without the gendered identity of woman. As a subject, Katy is positioned multiply rather than singly. She is not simply young, or woman, or delinquent, or student, or mother, or teen. She is a subject that is irreducible and embodied, ever changing and complex, a subject-in-the-making or "becoming-woman" (Kennedy 2000). Her lived experience produces subjectivities of struggling to finish school, claiming motherhood, getting lost in her search for herself, confronting categorical understandings yet not knowing how to handle uncertainty, disrupting the very laws of genre and gender that restrict her self-representation.

Students' life-stories bring together residual memory, subjective manifestations, and institutional, historical, and discursive identities. The intersection of lived experience, subjectivities, and changing subject positions, makes it difficult to represent a harmonious or a fixed portrait of what precisely is a young girl behind bars. The montage of lived experiences defies any final representation. Students' stories are not representations of ethnographic or autobiographic portraits. They are counter-stories shaped by lived experience.

The counter-stories of Amanda and Katy are a counter discourse to the official script of education in detention, a "form of discourse which ultimately matters, a discourse against power, the counter discourse of prisoners we call prisoners and those we call delinquents—and not a theory of delinquency" (Foucault 1977, p. 194). The scripted curriculum of education in detention assumes that teachers are responsible for students' empowerment; however, the lived experience of teaching girls behind bars reveals the power, powerlessness, and possibilities of curriculum knowledge for transformative change.

Discussion

Marking a theoretical shift from the unified, humanist self to self as subject of discourse, poststructuralism challenges generic definitions of autobiography and see autobiography as a discursive effect read alongside other discourses of the times. Poststructural scholars connect historical and generic exclusions to absence or erasure such as "the absent body" and inclusions such as the politics of identity to "subject-in-the-making." Rather than use the customary "autobiography," poststructuralism focuses on the limits of traditional language and conventions and sees the nature of autobiography as changing lived experiences within discursive practices better expressed as autoethnographic interpretation. Autoethnography can be read as a discourse that develops in line with other poststructural discourses on complexity, multiplicity, and disruption (Lather 2000a). In the autoethnographic method there is no attempt at generalization; rather, the emphasis is on partial sense of knowledge or situated knowledge that is produced from the multiple intersections and contexts of people's lives. Autoethnography makes space for destabilizing traditional meaning, new meaning making, and pushing singular understandings toward multiplicity, thus creating conditions for "interruptions and eruptions with resistance and contradiction as strategies of self representation" (Gilmore 1994, p. 42).

Through autoethnography I began to understand the beginnings of my own teacher transformation. I began to recognize the constructed nature of terminology such as "offender" that overtly states or covertly implies teaching students has an ethical imperative. There is not enough evidence in the literature justifying that the practices advocated actually transform offenders' self-detrimental or "delinquent" behaviors. When some experts on teaching speak of ethics and reformation under the rehabilitative ideal they do not clarify their own positions or give a clear account of their conception of what constitutes "good behaviors" for girls behind bars. Besides, teachers who follow an empirically defined path to achieving the rehabilitative ideal depend on phrases such as "altering behavior" by "re-forming character and habits" of female youth offenders as an important objective of detention. These objectives are based on arguments that expect sameness from all students regardless of their specific histories or differing life experiences.

When girls behind bars are unable to conform to the model school, family, community, and gendered self, or when as educators we hold them responsible for their assumed failures, there is a grave sense of injustice in the violence done to students who are nonnormative or the causes and effects used to define their failures. As Derrida (1995, 1981b) teaches us, it is not that the subject is not important. Rather, the subject is indispensable to any account of knowledge, history, philosophy, education, therefore, curriculum. Closely associated with formal schooling and standardization of learning and teaching, is a complex set of exclusions in the curriculum, a troubling reminder of knowledge that is repressed or silenced—contingencies that make the experience of detention possible. Standardizing out of nonnormative students from public education in this process of exclusion is the most troubling note of all. As long as teaching in detention classrooms fails to recognize the intimate yet complicated relationship of subject positions, history, and context to the struggles of the lived experience of girls behind bars, teaching in detention will continue under the notion of effecting rehabilitation through the discourses of standardized teaching and testing practices.

Are teachers simply mediators between institutional structures of the prison and educational systems? Troubling and overlapping concepts such as gender, trauma, memory, and subject positions in institutional contexts call for an analysis that is disruptive indicating the complex issues at hand that require intricate unraveling as well as weaving lived experiences into the curriculum. How might educators teach girls behind bars within such complex disruptions of the rules of educating in detention? When detention is an unstable site of constant breakdowns reclaiming education emerges from transformative curriculum possibilities. The next chapter positions transformative curriculum possibilities for bringing to the forefront silenced voices and lived experiences of girls behind bars.

6

Guilty Readings of Other People's Stories

Introduction

Guilty readings of other people's stories is the autoethnographic telling of life-stories of young girls behind bars painted on canvas. This chapter offers embodied life-stories of girls behind bars as counter-stories that question and unsettle the notion of a normative, universal identity and knowledge produced and validated within ontological categories, binaries, and hierarchies. The representation of certain groups of students in the juvenile detention system combined with school discourse of identifying students by sorting, labeling, and tracking students through officially sanctioned norms privileges certain groups of students while fast-tracking others into detention. Students' counter-stories evidence institutional discourses that racialize and gender certain groups of girls to shape, categorize, and at times, predicate their detention.

In previous chapters, I claimed that the discourse of education in detention constructed as historical apriori conditions emerged out of social, legal, scientific, and educational need to conform young women to predetermined conditions for experience. I also attended to the discursive practices that position students as subjects as well as historicized the subjectivities produced. Students' autobiographies, as I earlier posited, reveal that education in detention is not a representation of a fixed identity but a series of historical, social, and cultural discourses that constitute educational subjects who are always in the process of becoming. Readings of life-stories validated students' lived experiences breaking the silence that shrouded their lived histories, contesting existing fixed notions of girls behind bars, and opening new ways for thinking about difference. The point was not to justify students' victimization or to condemn their life choices. Rather, I examined the struggle between disciplinary, powerful norms of the juvenile justice system and the diverse young women held under its authority. In so doing the aim was to question the gendered discourse that constructs girls behind bars as representations of various disorders, highlight the causality of social and institutional structures that lead to detention for certain groups of students, and interpret counter-stories of resistance as girls behind bars become agents of knowledge production to participate in the struggle for personal and political transformation.

Using gender as a category of analysis and the body as the locus or space for struggle and change, I interpret the life-stories of girls behind bars through postfeminist and poststructural lenses to disrupt the combined institutional discourses of the juvenile justice and the school system. Life-stories are interpreted to show young girls as subjects constituted by discursive practices on the one hand, and as embodied subjects who are agents of knowledge on the other. Challenging binaries, hierarchies, and categories central to normative constructions of identity, the body is interpreted as a contested and transformative space for creating and negotiating multiple forms of knowledge engendering possibilities for curriculum change.

Grounded in the ontological category of "woman" and given epistemological significance through history and culture, gender as a central discourse in defining woman's identity is deployed to discipline the female body, sexuality, and desire (Smith 1994). In spite of reproducing cultural scripts, the performance of gender is a contested site that also produces embodied forms of knowledge absent in the curriculum and is contradictory to the cultural script. Students' counter-stories highlight that girls behind bars rewrite the codes of "gender" portraying their experience of "woman" as epistemologies of resistance that enact forms of knowledge forbidden in traditional curriculum discussions. Students' life-stories articulating different forms of desire—lesbian desire, desire for death, and desire for silencing family secrets—are deconstructed through Butler's (1993) notion of disruptive performativity as an enactment of critical resistance against the exclusion of difference.

Autobiographical writing framed within the epistemological and ontological language of the categorical identity of "woman" validated student voices and life-stories long silenced in curriculum conversations. While autobiographical theory of curriculum provided space for recognizing lived experience, and initiated the writing of autobiographies, six months into writing, students rejected writing autobiography as another mode of representation not on their terms. Challenging the terms of the writing project, students chose to paint their life-stories on canvas in oil and color. The challenge was an act of resistance by way of asserting their right to produce knowledge on their terms. The choice of painting self-portraits as a different mode of reading and writing autobiography emphasized students' "otherness" from the conventional, autobiographical "I" and the identities I was constructing of them.

By taking control of their life-stories, students distanced me from their sense of "otherness," to challenge my institutional affiliation and the power I held over their writing as an English teacher. In reclaiming the terms of telling their life-stories students were also challenging my role as a researcher as the "knower" who owned their life-stories and had assumed the right to tell them. The move from writing autobiography to self-portraits painted on canvas is not to suggest that linguistic and nonlinguistic discourses are contradictory. Rather, I will use this unsettling turn in my writing project to suggest that the relationship between the subject and discourse is such a complex and dynamic one that it defies the fixed structures of language and the humanist need to define, contain, and anchor meaning and therefore fix the subject. Students' resistance to the writing project suggested that discursive relations embedded in philosophy, history, and culture extend beyond linguistic meaning and naturalized categories. By rejecting linguistic frameworks in favor of life-stories on canvas, students compelled me to think outside the confines of traditional autobiography as well as beyond popular media representation of "women behind bars" or self-representations of "life-stories from prison." The disruption to the autobiographical writing was a turning point in my research leading to the second phase of my study—from written life-stories to self-portraits in oil and color. Students reversed my planned "data collection" into a site for undoing those very themes of identity, self, and knowledge that I presupposed in planning the autobiographical research project.

When autobiography strains the very basis on which identity depends or when the discursive constructs for understanding girls behind bars such as sex, gender, and the female body are under question, then autobiography calls for a different set of tools and a different medium of expression. Clearly, the tools were not ones that would locate women's self-representation in canonical genres (Lorde 1984) of writing autobiographies in which students are already scripted on historical documents that have been scratched over and rescripted many times (Foucault 1984b). Rather, a montage of life-stories was especially suited to asking questions about the philosophical "I" and the price of suppression, repression, and silences imposed by a stable, coherent, gendered self. This study emerged through a combination of autobiography and postfeminist, poststructural thought to critique and reconceptualize how we think and speak about girls behind bars, not as fixed identities, but as active agents whose subjectivities are always-in-the-making.

In this chapter, I expand my study of girls behind bars to rereading students embodied counter-stories of resistance as performing gender through various forms of desire played out in differing contexts and contingent relations. While desire as a form of knowledge production is important to this discussion, it is a means to move thought beyond the cultural conventions of "woman," the "female body," and "sex" and their relation to the social and institutional norms of gender and the expectations that accompany the norms. Using gender as the starting point, in the first section, I begin with the life-stories of Chantia, a student, to explore lesbian desire as working against generic categorizations of gender toward a complex interweaving of epistemologies of resistance emerging from her changing identities, subjectivities, and subject-positions. The next section discusses Brittany's life-stories, where contradictory forces and feelings represent forbidden desire through a death wish. My aim is not to romanticize suicide but to read her life-stories as epistemologies of resistance enacting the presence of difference and "otherness" outside naturalized binaries of man/woman, subject/ object, or life/death. This is followed by Rochelle's life-stories in the next section, a site for the "unthought in education" (Britzman 2003) knowledge that is taboo, often kept secret. The epistemologies of resistance presented are drawn from students' self-representations on canvas, the initial autobiographical writing project, field notes on biographical and institutional information on students, and intertextual interpretation of lived experience in relation to educational norms and curriculum enactment.

In this section, theatre is used as a metaphor for telling performative and resistant life-stories of the "other," to disturb the certainty of a fixed identity, and to challenge the ontology of a universal young girl behind bars. What emerges is a crisis of epistemology created by students' counter-epistemologies—epistemologies of resistance compelling us to recognize the failures of the production of knowledge in educational discourse, question the basis of what knowledge is considered of most worth, and our own roles in the production of curriculum knowledge. In what follows, I examine the ways in which girls behind bars create a space for embodied life-stories out of historical representations and disciplinary techniques that regulate and repress them. I will emphasize that the women I study are interpreted as performative subjects-in-the-making (Butler 1990; Kristeva 1984) who are marked by differences and, although constituted by historical apriori conditions, exceed their own experience through a shifting indetermination of the "pragmatics of 'becoming'" (Kennedy 2000, p. 92).

Sedimentation, iterability, and performativity

Chantia's lesbian desire

In telling and interpreting Chantia's life-stories, I draw heavily from Butler's work on gender to distinguish three interrelated concepts critical to exploring the discursive effects of gender on the subject of detention: sedimentation, iterability, and performativity. The concepts provide ways of thinking about life-stories of girls behind bars as a contested site of knowledge historically, socially, culturally, and institutionally grounded. Keeping in mind "the politics of knowing and being known" (Lather 1992, p. 91), I first present my field notes describing Chantia, a student's self-portrait on canvas, followed by my interpretation of Chantia's lesbian desire.

In reading Chantia's lived experience, expression of desire is interpreted not as a force that threatens patriarchy or as an effect of trauma but as a nonnormative presence that continually disturbs the norms of gender and identity, revealing the contested nature of both. Chantia's lesbian desire does not resignify her body or her identity; rather, it presents the experience of possibility to resignify the body as a disruption to the unity of expected and normative identity recognized by the juvenile justice and the school system that attempt to define and regulate student desires. Chantia's lived experience reveals that gender or identity does not exist altogether as historical apriori but come into existence performatively as active resistance or enactment of agency.

My descriptive field notes and interpretation of Chantia's self-portrait on canvas:

January 16, 2008

Chantia has described her life through objects dotted across the canvas. She calls the self-portrait, "My coat of many colors." The background is bare white canvas, stark—I have to search for the colors. A dresser, a chair, a bed, red high heels floating in the air. A window on the right side has two ashtrays full of cigarette ends and smoke trailing as if curling right out of the canvas frame. The drab shades of brown for the furniture and the shaded white for everything else come alive with the occasional red, the only other color used. Where is she in the picture? She is of course present everywhere on the canvas but her body is significantly absent, but there is a hint of an erotic presence on the bed, the dresser, even the red high heels. The two ashtrays evoke presence and absence. There are blotches of red on some of the cigarettes in both ashtrays. The suggestiveness of intimacy pervades the portrait. I did not know that Chantia is an artist who can evoke and suggest with a few strokes of the brush but I am amazed at the layers of complexity her work embodies.

I tell and interpret a young woman in detention, Chantia's life-stories, drawing heavily from Butler's (1997) work on gender to provide ways of thinking about life-stories of girls behind bars as a contested site of knowledge historically, socially, culturally, and institutionally grounded. Why gender? Girls behind bars such as Chantia labeled black lesbian predators, and who defy conventions of womanhood are considered "sexual delinquents," therefore, they are specifically counseled in character education to control sexual behaviors and are placed in therapy to contain their sexuality. At the detention facility, where heteronormativity was an expectation and any other sexual orientation was addressed as a sexual disorder, Chantia was open about her sexual choices in the classroom and talked about being a lesbian. I was aware that because Chantia openly expressed her sexual identity, other students were advised to stay away from her. Chantia did not see herself as a predator and in retaliation preferred to be in the isolation room than sit with the other students. When staff at the detention facility constructed her as an African American lesbian predator, Chantia countered by saying she was proud to be a black lesbian but that she was not a predator.

Officially, the detention facility identifies Chantia as an African American student and the only difference in identity that was acceptable within the institution was her race. However, if her identity was to be marked by difference, Chantia preferred to be recognized by her sexual orientation, that is, be recognized as a lesbian than as an African American. Thus, I suggest that Chantia's identity or subjectivity does not exist altogether as historically determined by institutional discourse of race and gender but also comes into embodied existence as a performative choice. I reread my first impression of Chantia's self-representation through the political implications of Butler's notion of performativity. When a normative act is enacted and repeated as an exaggeration or an understatement in order to subvert what the act that is being repeated represents, it becomes a performative act of subversion. For example, Butler's use of drag as an example of performativity of gender is a mask, a representation, and something that exceeds both the mask and the representation. Chantia's self-portrait as performativity contests representation, questions the stability of its own existence, and reveals the problem of disentangling or opposing representation and performativity.

As a survivor of sexual abuse, Chantia constructs her own counter-stories that speak of racism and sexism, of shame, guilt, denial, silence, sexuality, intimacy, desire, recovery, and possibility. As Chantia tells her stories, changes the medium and the silence of her narrative, she contests the institutional script of her body and her sexuality, knowing that she has the ability to contaminate the script by painting her life-story. Chantia's self-portrait can be read as a subversive act; the images inscribed on the canvas resisting institutional inscription through a disruptive absence.

I interpret the high heels and the blotches of red on the cigarettes as evoking lesbian desire in the twin representations or mirror images of the heels and the ashtrays. Chantia's self-representation reflected in the red heels and the red on the cigarettes suggest two women rather than a man-and-woman and questions gender as a category of analysis by which "the sex one can *see* becomes the gender one must *be*" (Gilmore 1994, p. 10). A rereading of her portrait shows how gender and sexuality is experienced and represented as a form of lesbian desire when "sex does not become gender become heterosexual desire" (p. 12). Butler asks, "To what extent do *regulatory practices* of gender formation and division constitute identity, the internal coherence of the subject, indeed, the self-identical status of the person?" (1990, p. 16). Similarly, Chantia is challenging the ontological category of "woman," and the constructed system of defining female essence or roles of bride, wife, butch, mother, sister, or dyke. Butler argues that:

> the category of sex imposes a duality and a uniformity on bodies in order to maintain reproductive sexuality as a compulsory order ... I would like to suggest that this kind of categorization can be called a violent one, a forceful one, and that this discursive ordering and production of bodies in accord with the category of sex is itself a material violence. (1993, p. 17)

As a performative subject, Chantia performs the interruption of naturalized categories of gender and sex by keeping the two female bodies out of the picture, challenging the viewer to define and violate what is invisible, therefore unknown.

When legitimacy of gendered roles of a man-and-woman relationship depends upon their being repeated, Chantia interrupts the scripted role of gender by refusing to play the scripted part of a heterosexual woman portraying two women leaving traces of lipstick on the cigarettes. The red heels and lipstick can be interpreted as conventional representations of "woman"; however, the repeated image in the second pair of heels and the red on the cigarettes is suggestive of a woman-and-woman relationship subverting the convention of man-and-woman relationship through lesbian desire. A subversive performance such as lesbian desire, like drag, is useful in revealing that every performance of a gendered action is an imitation of an imitation (Butler 1990). In Butlerian terms, there was never an original, natural gender, or man-and-woman relationship that is imitated. For Chantia, being able to engage in imitation as subversive performances opens the possibility for new meanings to the role for "woman" that subverts the claims of ontological, essentialized categories of "woman," "sex," and "gender." Deconstruction of categories such as woman or gender has epistemological implications for it highlights the arbitrary nature of knowledge production as a discursive construct representing political interests in what knowledge is valued, silenced, or excluded.

The notion of performativity is part of the ongoing poststructural critique of the subject of history, its representation, the language of representation, agency, and subjectivity. Embedded in the metaphor of performativity is the notion that its dramatic immediacy make it a nonrepetitive process (Butler 1997). Accordingly, Chantia's performance can never be repeated in time, place, or context; therefore, subjectivity in her performance cannot be pinned down to any apriori truth or presence that is being represented. Butler links performances to textual reading practices, therefore to interpretive frameworks, by connecting "iterability" and "performativity" to forbidden forms of knowledge that include lesbian desire.

According to Butler (1997) the expression of any language or "utterance" is part of the apriori structures of philosophical representation in language. For example, the term "woman" not only evokes a particular image but also means a particular set of norms that sets "woman" apart yet creates a universal category of "woman" representative of all "women." However, between context and utterance is a space of undecidability and uncertainty unknown to the subject/speaker that does not abide by the norms or the apriori condition. It is this deviance from the norm, this nonrealization of the apriori conditions, that constitutes Chantia's disruptive performativity or the act of the performative lesbian whose only certainty is its nonrepeatability suggested in the theatrical absence of the two lesbian bodies never fully captured.

Chantia's failure to adhere to the norms creates a rupture between the apriori conditions of detention and the determined effects of utterance. This results in an instability of norms in the category of "woman," the predetermined female subject of history and its representation, and opens a space for resistance and transformation by changing the rules of representation through iteration. Chantia's portrayal of lesbian desire, which she calls a coat of many colors, interrogates the limits of a single, unified, unchanging representation, stubbornly refusing to be classified into categories.

While Chantia underscores the impossibility of normative behaviors, she also constructs a performative gender. She does this by resignifying her position against heteronormativity, which under the gaze of detention becomes a subversion not only by the absent bodies in her picture but by the power of discourses that produce absent bodies when subjects like Chantia embody forms of knowledge such as lesbian desire that are silent in traditional curriculum conversations. Similar to the notion of performativity contesting the concept of essential stable identity, so does Chantia rewrite subject-positions by challenging the norms of "heterosexual imperative" (Butler 1993, p. 3). The self-portrait is not just a subject position that Chantia embues but is performative as it unravels the contingent nature of subjectivity, identity, the body, and knowledge. By contesting heterosexuality as an imposition, Chantia exposes the constructed nature of heterosexuality or "the utterly constructed status of the so-called heterosexual original" (Butler 1990, p. 41). Butler argues that the debate between subject-positions "misses the point of deconstruction" (p. 9) because deconstruction does not mean, "everything is discursively constructed" (p. 8). Rather than a utopian world, Butler (1993) agrees with Derrida that discourse is messy; it excludes, erases, and stigmatizes all that does not fit within its field, but that exclusion, erasure, and stigma are disruptions that unsettle discourse. As Butler translates and expands Derrida's deconstruction to give it yet another meaning—for Chantia, construction of epistemologies of resistance is an ongoing process, not a single performative utterance—the repeated and repeatable activity makes her performative utterances possible.

Derrida's (1992) concept of reiteration and Butler's (1992) use of it provide a way to understand construction of knowledge as a dominating force but one that can be resisted. Similarly, Chantia cannot speak or act without conforming to a script, but she can never conform to duplicate the script. Therefore, the undecidability of reiteration is a kind of repetition and something else altogether. The "re" suggests sameness or representation, however, the "iter" indicates performativity or the sense of otherness enacted as resistance to forms of fixed representation. When Chantia opts to be sexually different, she reproduces the category of "sex" or "woman" by virtue of her biological sex and destabilizes both categories in the course of this reiteration through nonnormative sexual utterances of gender performed through lesbian desire.

As an effect of a reiterative practice, gender, sex, and woman are categories that acquire their naturalized effect partly because the range of language available for articulations of performative sexuality is nonexistent except as an all-encompassing "otherness"—yet it is also by virtue of this reiteration that spaces for possibilities are opened. Rather than a constituted scripted sense of who Chantia is, the constitutive instabilities in such constructions as sex, woman, dyke, butch, deviant, and delinquent defy and exceed the normative by becoming that which cannot be wholly defined or fixed. This instability is the deconstituting possibility that is part of repetition (Deleuze 1994), the power that resists and undoes the very effects by which categories are stabilized.

Interpretive possibilities put the normative categories of sex, woman, and dyke, butch, deviant, and delinquent into a performative chaos. Reiteration means to repeat and change, hence the iterations of sex, woman, gender, is an "enactment that performatively constitutes the appearance of its own interior fixity" (Butler 1990, p. 70). What represents a stable identity is a discursive effect. What is not represented in Chantia's picture must be present in what is represented, which, according to Butler, is what exceeds representation—"the impossible within the possible" (1993, p. 236). Without a language to articulate new possibilities, resistance disrupts categorical definitions, however, performativity is the space for articulating the new language of instability, multiplicity, and change.

As a subject, Chantia comes to recognize her sense of agency only retrospectively in relation to historical conditions penetrating the stability of the conditions with her absent desire that displays a disruptive performativity. Embodiment offers Chantia the possibility for resistance through which her subjectivity is dispersed between the erotic pull of desire and the feeling that lesbianism is something that is supposed to be hidden behind pretenses—the red high heels, the smudged lipstick on ashtrays, the mystery-performing embodied knowledge that makes the conventional, the disruption, and the representation come alive.

Suspicious montage of subject-positions

Brittany's death wish

I present my rendering of the self-portrait of Brittany, a student, and read it alongside excerpts from her written autobiography to create a suspicious montage of subject-positions that defy a single, stable identity. Although Brittany perceives her life separate from the various subject-positions she portrays, she nevertheless desires a death wish by refusing all the different subject-positions she portrays or imagines for herself. Interpretation of her autobiography reveals a fragmented montage of life-stories that disrupt the humanist notion of a prior self, and complicate her wish for death as represented in the portrait. Complicating the desire for death, Brittany's death wish is simultaneously a desire to destroy the historical apriori conditions that constitute her life experience as well as create possibilities for existence outside the apriori conditions.

My field notes on Brittany's self-portrait on canvas:

January 16, 2008

Calling her self-portrait "DETENTION IS NOT BRITTANY" Brittany has drawn six matchstick figures in black paint around a single large matchstick hangman with a caption printed below, "BRITTANY IS NOW DEAD." The hangman has a mound of pills at its feet and the hangman's noose is strung out of intravenous needles. Brittany's composition seems out of some medieval morality play with only the religious cross missing. What a dark, sobering self-portrait from a sixteen-year-old young woman; almost one I wish she had not painted. The image of death is depressing. Should I speak to her about this, then, perhaps not? The hangman is enclosed in concentric circles. Five matchstick figures are numbered marking a period in her life and a corresponding caption. One reads, "7 Brittany learns to talk back," another reads, "15 Brittany will not speak," a third reads, "8 Brittany loves no one." One of the captions says, "11 Brittany is raped," another says, "Brittany has no mother," and the last one says, "16 Brittany cannot remember." Do I really want to see such a disturbing rendition of Brittany? Teaching Brittany will never be the same again. My insisting on test scores and grades in the class now feels like a repetition of violence in her life. I am not sure what I feel seeing her life-stories.

Revisiting childhood, Brittany is pushed to the limits of experience, ultimately claiming she cannot remember, even as she is haunted by vivid images on canvas. I asked Brittany what the numbers on her captions stand for and she declined answering my question. Hence, I interpret the numbers as marked periods in her life that indicated her age. To me, her self-images speak of suicide, drugs, and alcohol that reveal the complexity of her existence and the conditions that have written her life into detention. Her painting suggests she is either creating stories to lose herself or to cope with the regulation of institutional restrictions within detention. Her self-portrait can be interpreted as a shutdown of all feelings caused by loss of self or loss of connection with her painful past, making her question what it means to exist in relation to a self that does not wish to live.

Autobiographical writing in the third person gives Brittany the fluidity to create personas when she cannot extricate herself from her tangled life. As a child she recalls small acts of rebellion, "7 Brittany learns to talk back," and of being alienated in "8 Brittany loved no one." From her autobiographical writing I learned that at age eleven she carved into her skin, "Brittany is dead," which is a recurring statement in her life. The concept of a previous identity that she does not refer to as an "I" is further complicated by the interplay of denial of the self and desire for self-destruction in portraying her life through the images and captions of refusal and death. If I was wondering why the caption "Brittany has no mother" was not prefixed with a number like all her other captions in the portrait, her autobiography partially filled the gap, informing that she was repeatedly beaten and humiliated by her mother. For example, she recalls in her written autobiography, "I was called the bed-wetter, and my mother made me stand in the corner for the rest of the night." Part of Brittany's pain is that she now has no contact with her mother and is fighting desperately to return to her mother. According to the facility's records, the courts have issued an order restraining her mother from making any contact with Brittany. In her autobiography, Brittany has written that "the pain of not having a mother is greater than having one."

The matchstick figures can be interpreted as the new selves she keeps creating to shut out her past or to close herself off from others, especially the physical and mental abuse by her mother. Her writing reveals that violence kept her "alive," saying, "I know my mother's violence kept me alive and safe from others as no one could get close to me." Her court records show that she escaped from her mother's abuse by running away several times, and her subsequent homelessness and prostitution finally ended in detention. In her autobiography, she explains the experience of prostitution: "Brittany needs to feel without knowing who she is feeling," revealing her desire to connect with others yet mistrusting close relationships. She continues saying, "I wanted to get away from home and I needed a friend. So I became a prostitute." It is paradoxical that her need to feel loved, wanted, and safe while fulfilled by "strange old men in strange old beds but they treat you nice," distances her from home, family, friends, and community.

Brittany's self-portrait on canvas as well as her written autobiography contains telling accounts of the ways in which her gender confounds her subjectivities, at the same time, produces subjective effects. Her story incites me to reflect about what my own gendered identity—historically, culturally, and subjectively—and how meaning can change upon reflection on the process of signifying a self or signifying multiple positions. It reminds me of my own changing positionalities—from a gendered subaltern existence in India to a raced immigrant in the United States—the many faces of the generic Eve or subject-always-in-the-making.

Being and existing as a young normative woman does not come naturally to Brittany. Her life-story enables a reading of the way an individual becomes a subject, how a young woman becomes a subject of detention. My reading of her subject-position is not neutral, nor am I making any truth claims about Brittany's life. Nonetheless, her nonnormative subjectivity as a young girl behind bars who is portrayed with a noose around her neck is troublesome: Brittany's hangman story is not an example of every young girl behind bars who experiences unpredictable and contradictory effects. What I am offering is an interpretation through a partial knowing of Brittany's lived experience and her own fragmented account of her subject-position and what she desires for herself.

Brittany's attempts to claim her identity though forgetting can be read as attempts to distance herself from or escape the effects of apriori conditions through her desire for death, the very condition discourses constitute and represent. The contradictory inclusion and exclusion of "I" from the discourses with theatrical statements such as "Brittany has no mother" and from its contradictory and complicated meaning is a way of creating subject-positions at the cost of betraying her identity—performativity of negation. If death wish is a form of performativity that challenges all forms of representation, it is also a challenge to performativity itself in its representation of that which is perhaps a mask—in this case, death as a mask for life. She insists on refusing an "I," which she replaces with "Brittany," then denies Brittany life saying, "Brittany is dead" and makes the overarching claim, "Detention is not Brittany." In her ability to continually unsettle the conditions of her identity, to actively resist it is an elusive "other," one that I will never fully be able to read, is always beyond interpretation.

In her autobiography, Brittany writes that at seven when she first learned the meaning of detention, it explained the outside world; detention was the only home she previously knew. She says her father was "never getting out" of prison and her mother "had me in prison so I would not be a crack baby. I was born a crack baby anyway and that too in prison, my whole family is in prison, you tell me, where do I go when this [detention] is home and when it is not home?" Yet it is a world that evokes mixed feelings in Brittany.

The withdrawal from her past and what is familiar, she realizes, must be disowned through the act of refusal, through forgetting. She discovers how she can reverse the identity that is expected of her by denying her own existence, asserting, "Brittany is dead." She uses theatrical performativity to control the context of detention, which has become problematic because although it is the only world she knows, she recognizes that it is a forbidden place that should not traditionally be called home. By complicating her own feelings toward detention, she can retain her position in detention by refusing not to be, yet affirming her presence of it. She has thus produced, in liberating herself from detention, another set of constraints, another subject-position she will have to perform—one that anticipates death before transformation.

Hence, self-portraits do indeed produce new possibilities for existence, for it is possible to deconstruct something that is constructed to begin with. Part of the challenge of identity for Brittany is to deconstruct and to de-essentialize the concept of detention. Performativity, according to Butler (1993, 1997), is the productive iteration that materializes effects via performance and is not to limit the subject's performance to a single identity. Autobiography and self-portraits on canvas are useful; however, Brittany complicates the relation of image to thought by articulating death over life. At the same time, the evocation of death implies an awakening.

Arguably, the constructed self who is "woman" exists in her desire for nonexistence; it is as constitutive of the subject as the multiple irreducible selves she constructs. It is not surprising that the blank outside the death circle on her canvas, which she claims portrays her lack of feeling, is actually her feelings most profoundly expressed in her deliberate attempts to disconnect from the rest of the world. As she writes, "That spot outside the ring is for me. I don't want anyone else there because I have no feelings for anyone anymore." When Brittany wants to reassure herself that the world she has shut out, paradoxically, is all around her, she cuts herself, marking her body to speak what the portrait cannot do for her. As she notes, she lacks feelings for other students and her distancing can be read as a nonnormative response.

Earlier, during the autobiographical writing project when other students accidentally made body contact, Brittany felt her space was violated; the experience overtook her so completely that she abandoned the portrait and etched on her body instead. When she felt she was losing her crafted hangman identity, she connected with her own body by cutting into her skin, but this called notice to her because of self-harming. What Brittany showed during the autobiographical project is that written meaning had collapsed for her as she lost the ability to connect the written word with meaning. Instead she moves back and forth between writing her autobiography on paper, painting it on canvas, speaking of it when I did not see her perspective, and carving on her own body. There is a breakdown in form, content, and experience as Brittany turns a fragmented self into subject and object, the doer and the deed. Moreover, by telling her story in the third person, she challenges my external gaze imposed on her that forced her to create a distance between the autobiographer and the reader. The authority to tell her life-story, she seems to say, can be reclaimed at any time.

Brittany's identity presupposed within the binary pressures of "remembering" or "forgetting" exceeds both "remembering" and "forgetting" to show that categorical difference between one identity and another within the same person does not hold its own truth claims. As Lather (1996) says, the certainty or intelligibility of any claim to truth in relation to the other is undecidable. All the more reason why her silence is performative—the power of remembering a story of difference or forgetting a story to construct difference. By painting her life, Brittany challenged traditional ways of writing autobiography through form and content by inscribing on her body. Subverting linguistic norms, her portrait creates a new space outside convention for making meaning of discontinuous and fragmented life-stories. The identity on canvas is hard to locate as a disjunctive and suspicious montage of portraits complicates it. Who is Brittany—hangman, autobiographer, teen, young woman, or all of these subject-positions depending on the intersectionality and the contexts of her life? Marginalized by the discourse of detention, Brittany exists on the boundaries that make her suspicious of any identity imposed on her and leads her to embody knowledge forbidden from curriculum.

Brittany's splintered autobiographies make visible the particular in lived experience against the universal subject to emphasize not only the difference among girls behind bars and the contexts in which those differences are constructed but the differences within the same subject where one subject-position contradicts the other. Brittany's oppression does not need any further silencing by theories, practices, and institutions of power. As both Chantia and Brittany reveal, the discourse on gender historically predisposes women to certain forms of violence written into the juvenile justice system and implicates all educators, for in this silence is perpetuation of violence against girls behind bars. Put differently, Brittany's counter-story has everything to do with what is forbidden in school knowledge: embodied subject matter and subjectivity. Students' life-stories reveal the institutional and discursive all contribute to the "otherness" that defies any labeling or categorizing. In Brittany's graphic montage, gender becomes a representation of the female body as a mark of identification. It is also the site where gender and violence are linked. Gender as the female body is the historical apriori condition of her identity. Violence is intertwined in the self-representation of her gendered identity. The reconceptualization of the female body as a site for resistance, even one marked by a death wish, is a displacement of gender rewritten on the scarred body—the marks rewrite the cultural script imposed on her to socialize and normalize.

Epistemologies of resistance

Rochelle's family secrets

Rochelle's life portrait invokes a subject that speaks against the discourse that men are the speaking subjects of history by using a form of silence giving meaning to the historical discourses that are ever-present in her life portrait. She produces a new set of epistemologies of resistance, bringing to the forefront differences that contradict her subject-positions and are in opposition to the norm, institutional, and stereotypical definitions of her experience. Rochelle's deliberate silence challenges my attempts at defining under the normative or generic representation of African American woman. She does not offer a straightforward story in her self-portrait. I have interpreted Rochelle's life-story because of what I know about her life and through my experiences with her, as a willing participant in painting her autobiographical portrait on canvas but resistant to the autobiographical writing project. When she agreed to craft her life-portrait, I understood that in presenting herself as an artist, she was making a subversive statement on many levels.

My field notes on Rochelle's self-portrait:

March 3, 2008

Rochelle's self-portrait tells multiple stories. A first impression of Rochelle's por-trait is a large heart-shaped face on the canvas. This is a grotesque heart, out of place and out of proportion. On close inspection, the face has heart shaped features replacing a nose, mouth and eyes. Instead of a body, two grey wings hang from the neck. The portrait is named, "Ghetto secrets in my heart." Before I could tell Rochelle what I thought about her portrait, she explained that the heart stood for many things for her—not dreams, not love, but her many secrets. While the face is painted in a smudged pink, the rest of the canvas is bare with streaks of grey. Between the streaks are three tiny pairs of eyes that almost go unnoticed under cover of grey. There is an indefinable sense of pain in the grotesqueness that I find very unsettling. What was I expecting? Had I underestimated autobiographical work? Or had I underestimated lived experience? Do I really want to know more than I already know about students? It is hard to read Rochelle because she has so many complex sides to her.

There is no background on Rochelle's canvas—the lack of details mime the starkness of detention. The images also evoke repression and silence. The portrait is a very sober rendering of her life represented in a self-image that denies her body, her beauty, and her sexuality as she asserts her subject-position, not herself as object but as a subject who chooses what and how she will tell her story. The heart-shaped head in the portrait is severed from the body; instead wings substitute for the body. The heart looms large and dominates the canvas. Her African American presence rendered in the shadows behind the image is in the telling of her existence and the conditions of her survival. Through the contrast between the giant heart-shaped face and the minute half-concealed eye images, the powerlessness she feels against the stereotyping and representation of feelings is dramatized. The reduction of African Americans to a status of objects is evoked and represented in the pairs of eyes. The Foucauldian gaze that has "ghettoized" her existence is ever-present through the half-hidden eyes.

The central heart image is a deliberate device that exaggerates and subverts the traditional objectified media pose of a face considered beautiful and a figure with a perfect score. In her disfigured portrait that has wings for a body and a heart for a face, the deliberate fragmentation claims that emotions are no longer repressed or hidden simply because they are not a unified whole. Historically, black identity has been critical in defining and shaping the selfhood of black women in their search for freedom from white oppression and black male domination (Lorde 1984). In spite of decades of racial politics, however, there is no one single African American identity within the United States or authentic black self the world over (McKay 1998). This is not to deny that gender is a major force in black women or in Rochelle's life.

In the classroom, Rochelle rejects the victim story to present herself as self-assured and resists the destructive impact of her losing control of her different lives. The severed head suggests a sense of something over the edge of pain, a reliving of terror underlies the horrific, unspeakable memories. Rochelle's records at the facility document that in her teen years she has undergone repeated sexual violation at the hands of her father, her uncle, her boyfriends, and an aunt. She has been held in detention several times, partly because of her mother who was sentenced to prison repeatedly, twice because of incorrigibility at school, and this time because she sought revenge by stabbing a boyfriend in the stomach for physical assault. At times she accepts socialization into the juvenile justice system, and at other times she is desperate to leave detention and move on with her life. The revelation of some form of trauma lingers throughout—child rape, violence, beatings, tortures—half-buried under the smudged pink face and the repeated heart images that run through the piece.

Rochelle challenges every life-story that represents her to reinvent her autobiography through self-portraits that not only breaks away from but also complicates her lived experience. There is a sense of dislocation and disarticulation through the pain and trauma in her self-images. The giant shaped heart embodies her painful experiences; the grotesqueness of the image dislocates clear identities and collapses boundaries between her silence and her compulsion to speak in metaphors that depict her horrific experiences. Rochelle's self-portrait is the story of a young girl behind bars who is compelled to tell her story through repetition of her fixed institutional narrative represented in the pairs of eyes in her portrait and her own ability to reinscribe as well as interrupt the narrative. Her resistance to writing, in a sense, reinscribes her oppression; however, the embodied silence complicates the telling of her own life-story and her self-portrait interrupts the narrative of her oppression and trauma.

Self-representation brings back the female body to the fore as a counter discourse to the conventional detention narrative of young women who go through therapeutic counseling for being sexually active. It is impossible for Rochelle to think of herself without bringing her body into the picture. Using her absent body in the portrait as a strategic intervention, she pushes the limits of known thought, challenges what has been spoken about girls behind bars and how it is articulated in official documents and in popular media stories. Rochelle uses the absence of her body performatively to reconstruct forbidden memories and epistemologies of resistance that implicate the body in its own absence and exceed all previous telling. She is unable to think about herself or her body outside violence. Her rape, her escape, her trauma, and her revenge, her absent body are the site of many disjunctive stories marked by a sexuality that has threatened to destroy her.

Somewhere along Rochelle's resolve to remain silent slips beyond voice and voicelessness to suggest a narrative memory of gendered trauma within the fragmentation of her own particular experiences (Felman 1982). Lorde (1984) speaks of transforming secrets and silences into language and asks women who choose to speak through silence, "What are the words you do not have? What do you need to say? What are the tyrannies you swallow day by day and attempt to make your own, until you will sicken and die of them, still in silence?" (1984, p. 41). Lorde speaks of the distortions of Western constructions of "woman" that "systematizes oppression" (p. 114) through simplistic binaries such as good/bad, and inferior/superior. Rochelle refusing to speak out her secrets yet speaking through the epistemological spaces between the distorted images in her self-portraits opens possibilities for examining and resisting the distortions created by the historical apriori conditions that shape as well as misshape her experience.

It is not clear where the historical apriori that conditions her experience ends and where performativity that de-sediments collective memory of history through subject-positions begins. Rochelle performs a need for taking her subjective life-stories to a more public space from where the experience of violence is not visible only through detention and punishment, as a public spectacle (Foucault 1977), but as complicated forbidden epistemology to be peeled on many levels. At the facility, the students and some of the staff members constantly reminded Rochelle of her physical beauty, which she refused to speak about or acknowledge. Rochelle's body is a constant reminder of her sexuality and her desire for intimacy.

In Rochelle's silence is a disruption of the convention of all that is sacred and safe in the classroom. She internalizes the physical and mental threat posed by those around her and by the demands imposed on being considered beautiful, by denying her face any beauty. She disfigures her face, depicting it with grotesque, unreal features in the form of distorted hearts, challenging attempts to turn her into an object of desire that represents a subjection to repeated violence. The effects of violence on Rochelle are disruptive to every kind of convention and thought. In Rochelle's life-stories, the codes of filial relations are violated with her father's abuse, the sanctity of friendship is threatened by her boyfriend's abuse, and the aunt who sexually abused her shatters even the familiar feminist narrative of patriarchal domination. What is all the more unsettling is how she attempts to find meaning in her life. Rochelle's is not a portrait of a beautiful body or her sexuality; rather, it is theatrical performativity beyond the limits of normative intelligibility. In the portrait replacing her body with wings can be interpreted as distancing her body from her sexuality only to reaffirm the connection between them.

Knowledge of forbidden secrets is reinforced by her experiences as she traces, erases, and rewrites the historical and cultural script of her body. As she tells her stories, changes the medium and the silence of her narrative, she moves her institutional story from the fixed position of detention, creating gaps in the story for multiple interpretations. She recognizes the limits of the cultural script of her body and her sexuality, knowing that she has the ability to contaminate the script by exposing the disjunctures and the gaps in the coherent, unified construction of a young girl behind bars. Her denial in silence speaks of her bodily inscription, only to reject the destructive effects of repetition through reconstitution of her life-story. Self-portrayal becomes a subversive act; the images inscribed on the canvas continually reconceptualize her subject-positions saturated with historical significance yet transforming the inscription into a disruptive unmasking and unmaking through silence and secrecy. As a survivor of rape, Rochelle constructs counter-stories that speak of pain, danger, shame, guilt, denial, silence, sexuality, intimacy, patriarchy, desire, threat, recovery, and possibility.

Discussion

In reading students' life-stories, I am confronted with what it means to know and be known by the "other" as much as what it means to be the "other." Students' life-stories are the space from where I cannot escape the consequences of failure to acknowledge the price of ontological and epistemological certainty. Embodiment situates subject-positions not on the epistemological foundation of certainty but as performative continual of knowing and uncertainty regulated through contexts and contingencies. Students' counter-stories set in motion epistemologies of resistance that challenge subject/object, mind/body, objective/subjective, dichotomies as knowledge that counts. In producing knowledge that is forbidden through embodied manifestations of desire, passions, and anxieties, students' counter-stories can be read as counter discourses to the prevailing discourse on girls behind bars.

Autoethnography incites interpretations of embodied knowledge that counters the invisibility, marginalization, and distortions of popular representations of girls behind bars. Enabling a rich multilayered form of writing, autoethnography decentralizes the "I"; rather, it makes room for articulations of the researcher and the participants through history, memory, and changing multiple subject-positions (Lather 2000b). This is not to claim that I was an objective researcher; rather, I was as much an involved participant as researcher. For example, as a woman researcher, I was very conscious of the way students' educational experience played out through their bodies and the centrality of gender in shaping choices they made. In detention, rules are useful in explaining the structure and process of offending and justifies the rationalization of subsequent teaching against "unacceptable social behaviors." For example, female youth in detention such as Chantia who defy conventions of womanhood are considered "sexual delinquents" and specifically counseled in character education to control sexual behaviors and contain their sexuality. Speaking of gender as a performative concept rather than as a category that contains, Butler (1993) asks, "Is there a way to link the question of the materiality of the body to the performativity of gender? And how does the category of 'sex' figure within such a relationship?" (p. 1). I found myself torn between trying to teach by disrupting any expression of sensuousness or embodiment, and the urge to acknowledge the ingenuity with which students use the body to express subject-positions.

It is hard for me to read students' self-portraits as life-stories when I am implicated in them. I admit I am interpreting their life-stories, corrupting the past to create a readable present, but reflectively. Knowing students personally, I did not find it possible to make meaning of the portraits with total clarity, nor do I claim that the meaning is the same for me today as it was when I first viewed them. The challenge to my writing of their stories counters the fixed identity implied in autobiography. As noted earlier, I had concerns that I was asking students to write autobiographies and personal stories when informed consent had to be signed by the director rather than the students. The director's consent for the research study was given with the understanding that all data and subsequent analysis would have to be approved by the facility, pseudonyms would be used, and no photography or audio-taping would be allowed in keeping with safety and security regulations of the detention facility. Although I discussed the research with students several times, I am not certain that students understood the long-term impact of their participation on my work. Throughout the research process, even as I write this, in spite of the need to make students' counter-stories heard, I am troubled about using students' life-stories for academic purposes. In spite of IRB approval that protected the participants to some extent, I had some concerns. I was conscious of the ethical issues involved in my role as a teacher and authority figure on the one hand and researcher on the other.

In an ideal situation, students should have the right to tell their stories and exercise their agency on their terms. Representing girls behind bars who do not have the right to give informed consent is fraught with ethical questions of confidentiality, ownership, and the vulnerability of participants. In simple terms, the researcher is the one who reaps immediate benefits in terms of research and scholarship. Besides, if I aim to rewrite students' life-stories to draw attention to larger structural and institutional processes that promote detention and create inequities, then I am also complicit in the production of knowledge when I include and exclude stories based on my subjectivity and context. As a teacher and researcher I am afraid of my complicity in the production of academic knowledge that in turn is implicated in influencing educational practices such as the processing of students from schools into the juvenile justice system.

The move from writing autobiography to self-portraits on canvas is a disruption that exceeds the limits of writing and the limits of my knowing. Self-portraits through an artistic medium that is not dependent on the embeddedness and organization of language were especially valuable for reading autobiographies of those who are marginalized. From this perspective, the interplay of the detention self/I/subject-position was not wholly defined by the historical apriori conditions but performed by students in social, legal, scientific, and educational contexts. This does not mean that the authority of the speaking "I" is unquestioned by virtue of its marginalized identity or instability of subject-positions. If one life-story of students' denies the existence of the other, it is also rendered questionable by the other. Life-stories that contradict and play against each other have generative possibilities. Revisiting their life-stories, students question the apriori conditions that have laid out their experience of gender, woman, and the female body to create possibilities of telling their histories within historical and philosophical frames as theatrical performances of gendered subject-positions. The move from apriori conditions to subject-positions that perform within undecidability corresponds to an epistemological shift from history written by dominant discourses to contingent and contextual positions that contest practices that normalize, predict, or standardize.

Each story, however fragmented, intervenes in the authority of any one story becoming the authority that speaks for all stories, thus displacing any single identity's claim to be the norm. In disrupting the category of woman or gender, students are not denying identity per se; rather, they are questioning the terms on which identity has been coded and inscribed for young girl behind bars as apriori narrative. Opening ways to question and subvert the construction of identity and acknowledging the contingent and contextual nature of all claims are ethical conversations, providing the means to construct the terms by which identity is both represented and subverted.

Thus, students' embodied resistance challenging existing representations, breaking the silence about students' experiences that simultaneously confirm and question gender stereotypes. For example, Chantia reveals a sense of self-righteousness in her self-representation of being a victim of heterosexual normativity and speaking from the authority of the autobiographical lesbian "I." As a counter example, Rochelle refuses simplistic morality, offering instead a pained silence without wearing the badge of victimhood. Brittany complicates the insights of Chantia and Rochelle, critically reflecting on her subjectivity that calls into question the effects of her changing subject-positions. Against this, however, Chantia recognizes the liberating effects of subversion even when her sexuality is stereotypically depicted. Thus, portraits generate multiple discourses out of the complex and contradictory existing conditions of their lives.

Turning to poststructural reading practices provides critical concepts such as deconstruction, sedimentation, iterability, and performativity, within which all forms of the normative and the nonnormative are contested practices for analysis of lived experience. Deconstruction attacks the assumption that structures of meaning are stable, universal, and ahistorical. Deconstructive analyses uncover what is deemphasized, overlooked, or suppressed in a particular way of thinking or in a particular set of beliefs. Deconstruction does not claim that concepts have no boundaries; rather, it reveals that boundaries can be parsed in multiple different ways as they are inserted into new contexts, opening new interpretations (Derrida 1988).

Iterability means that the insertion of texts into new contexts continually produces new meanings that are both partly different from and partly similar to previous understandings (Derrida 1982). The multiplicity of deconstructive meaning produced from different contexts requires us not only to recognize others as others but also to be open to them and their perspectives. Thus, deconstruction (Derrida 2001) contains an ethical imperative both to question our own beliefs and to understand the contexts of others. In a sense, performativity offers a space out of the deadlock between the historical apriori conditions that predetermine and the notion of deconstruction that opens aporias of meaning (Spivak 1987).

History and philosophy foreground the construction of detention knowledge. The play of meaning or interpretation does not imply a loss of political will. The political agenda is to generate possibilities of different perspectives through the situatedness of all knowledge, which is why questioning is an ongoing process. The art project is an intertextual effort to read one text in another, one subject-position in and against the other that restricts all forms of classifications and categorizations. The image of sedimentation is useful here—layers of knowledge, texts, discourses that merge, mesh, confront, refute one another before any one discourse or text can settle. If there is repetition of existing discourse, there is a revision of interpretation if the self is established as a philosophical and historical category; interpretation confounds the distinctness of self, identity, subjectivity.

The power to naturalize a woman can put all the categorization associated with woman into a "productive crisis." Sedimentation is a key concept that captures how discourse becomes knowledge. In the performative utterances "young women in school" or "girls behind bars" are examples of performative utterances and practices. As such utterances gather, layers of meaning and practices are assumed, and with accumulation they sediment into knowledge. The category of "woman" is naturalized over layers of sedimentation. Hence, instability and indeterminacy are built into the process of naturalizing. The students found it impossible to escape the structures of their lives, but it was possible for them to turn their lives into "messy" ones, meaning, to digress from the script.

A poststructural emphasis on interpretation and play of language and meaning is not to abandon my political agenda. It is to actively consider and reconsider modernist enlightenment thought to generate possibilities through different perspectives on girls behind bars. I admit the play of interpretive politics is not neutral. In selecting particular forms of knowledge to resituate at the exclusion of others, I am acknowledging the situatedness of all knowledge, including mine. Educational equity requires reconfiguring the intellectual and political space education and its bearers occupy not as an end in itself but as a form of self-reflective inquiry into how much we shape what and how we teach and, therefore, who we teach.

Political acts such as performativity take place within specific contexts in which different forms of oppression such as sexism, racism, and homophobia are being contested. If I take the context of detention out of students' lives, there can be no interpretation for an utterance such as the silenced voices of "young girl behind bars." Two thousand years of philosophy teaches us that the child is a construct that is open to interpretation within various contexts (see Baker 2001). Although context puts limits on interpretation, contexts and contingencies themselves are unlimited. To remove context by generalizing, standardizing, and normalizing is to subsume all differences, reducing students to a fixed identity. When interpretation of actions is conscious of context, it enables us to accept the incompleteness of all knowing and the violence that is perpetuated in the certainty of fully knowing. For this reason, the life-stories of students bring a wealth of knowledge and experience into the classroom that expands the way we view difference. It is a form of privilege to have students open their world to our teaching a world that education or rehabilitation literature has not engaged.

Life histories and counter-stories need to be told—what happens to girls behind bars needs to be brought into the public space that is education. Students' stories need to be heard—stories of girls behind bars who are oppressed and marginalized—and have survived. Girls behind bars are capable of powerful refusals—not to participate in my research, not to engage in rehabilitation or therapeutic practice—that permit them to reclaim agency, however temporally, in a system that consistently deprives them of autonomy and the right to privacy. In disrupting the categories used to define and discriminate, students are not denying identity per se; rather, they are questioning the terms on which identity has been coded and inscribed for girls in detention.

Students' life-stories bring focus to how we decide what knowledge is acceptable, what is forbidden, and in whose interest. Juxtaposed with the pursuit of knowledge is the exclusion of particular forms of knowledge. Opening ways to question and subvert the construction of identity and acknowledging the contingent and contextual nature of all claims are necessary conversations to provide the means to construct the terms by which identity is both represented and subverted. Reworking embodied stories as experiential knowledge in education begins with reading of absences in the curriculum. Rereading students' counter-stories subverts misrepresentations that forbid, contain, and exclude their lived experience from curriculum knowledge.

7

Agents of Change, Not Subjects or Objects of Discourse

Introduction

Agents of Change, Not Subjects or Objects of Discourse, draws together teachers, curriculum developers, policy makers, and educational reformers as agents of change in the struggle for social justice. This book works out of the impasse between historical apriori conditions that shaped students' existence and lived educational experience of students that run counter to the conditions that shape lived experience to investigate the following questions: What is a young girl behind bars? What are the historical apriori conditions that constitute young girls as objects to make the experience of detention possible? How might the notion of a multiply constituted subject of discourse contest the historical apriori conditions that predicate detention? What frameworks and methodologies offer possibilities for the telling of life-stories from multiple voices and counter voices? How do girls behind bars reclaim lived educational experience as curriculum knowledge? How do girls behind bars create spaces for gender as a site for transformative curriculum possibilities? What are the implications for curriculum when girls behind bars are viewed as agents of knowledge production? How do girls behind bars reclaim education in transformative spaces? Exploring the above questions by way of unsettling scripted and institutional representations of girls behind bars bring new insights into the complicated, multi-layered life-stories of students. Opening the discussion, this chapter calls for reinterpreting reading and writing life-stories to understand the social and political realities of knowledge production, its implication for inclusive education, and renewed participation of all communities of educational practice in reimagining how we view and act upon cultural difference.

Revisiting various reading practices, the chapter engages educators in ongoing examination and reflection on dominant discourses of knowledge production in teaching, learning, and policy to reposition young girls behind bars not as subjects or objects of discourse but agents of change. Advocating writing, reading, and interpreting life-stories toward curriculum change, this chapter offers tools and strategies to all teachers, curriculum scholars, policy-makers, and educational reformers to participate in creating transformative curriculum spaces. Countering positivist ethnographic and traditional autobiographic research life-stories of girls behind bars are presented and analyzed through interpretive tools from critical scholarship that participates in the work of honoring lived experience in curriculum inquiry, theory, and practice. Autobiography provides the space for reclaiming lived experience as curriculum knowledge; poststructural reading practices offer tools for critique as forms of agency; postfeminist deconstruction offers a lens for gendered stories mobilizing the language for articulating difference in the curriculum; and autoethnography creates methodological spaces for interpreting life-stories to produce curriculum knowledge.

Dominant discourses and lived experience

There is a deep divide between the institutional and ideological structures of education and detention and the lived experience of students evidencing the failure of education in detention as an intervention for rehabilitation. Institutional structures such as the juvenile justice and school systems, and their practices are informed by theories derived from evidence-based research, developmental psychology, and cognitive learning (Baker 2001). Many of these theories stem from the European Enlightenment's notion of rationality as a major organizing principle for the success of institutions but offer conditions that position marginalized students on the fringes of mainstream education that is critical to understanding the construction of goals, interactions, and practices of schools as well as detention (Arrigo 1999). Accordingly, traditional curriculum knowledge does not engage with the life-stories of students and dismisses knowledge students bring into the class as disruptive if their experiences complicate simplistic binaries and categorical thinking. In keeping with the emphasis on rationality, school practices are built along hierarchies, binaries, and categories that define students based on norms and deviations. The normative is included in school curriculum while its opposite, that is, difference is excluded. The process of inclusion and exclusion creates a deep divide between teachers and students or a gap between "us" and "them" marginalizing students who are different as the "other." The notion of a culturally different deviant "other" in opposition to a modernist normative "self" is an uncritical representation of girls behind bars.

Social and academic knowledge has consequences for students who are different. As a social construct, institutions such as schools do not exist in isolation but are linked to other institutions. For example, the discourse on standardized testing, academic success or failure, and student accountability is directly linked to academic tracking of students. An analysis of statistics on academic tracking reveals how race, class, and gender are also being simultaneously tracked. Evidence of scholarship on the education of youth behind bars shows that one in three youth arrest is female and between 7 to 21 years—more than a 200 percent increase between 1987 and 2002 (Snyder & Sickmund 2006). Further, scholarship reveals that minority students' dropout rate is higher with minorities over represented in special education, special services such as English language learning services, and detention facilities across school districts, and underrepresented in college enrollment. While "successful" students are tracked toward college, those identified as failures are tracked for detention restricting options and resources of those who need it most leaving them underprepared and underserved. Schools as institutions that prepare students for other institutions track some students for college and others for detention directly implicating education, schooling, and teachers in the discourse on girls behind bars.

What is ignored in dominant discourses of knowledge production is how agency is articulated within specific sites of domination, such as detention. To see girls behind bars as an uncontested, unified object of education, or detention or rehabilitation is to presume and reproduce a polarity between teachers and students, "us" and "them," the teacher as the knowing self and students as the other, and reinscribe students' exclusion. When institutions representing social justice such as the school and the juvenile justice system normalize detention or when detention is offered as treatment for being different, there is a double injustice done to certain groups of students—first such students are discriminated for being different, then they are normalized into detention. In many ways, the institutional normalization of detention and the pedagogic function of education in detention are acts of violence that derive meaning from the importance given to rational thinking that positions certain forms of difference for detention (Meiners 2007). However, the everyday acts of such violence normalized into the daily routine of detention leaves educators ill-equipped to process or address the lives really at stake. In addition, the war against drugs, homelessness, teen pregnancy, and prostitution are all experiences of violence that make detention predictable for some young girls (Crenshaw 2001). When educators lack training on how to address students' lived experience, their resistance, their call for help, or their self-destruction, there is a reinscribing of institutional oppression. Any strategy, intervention, or understanding of curriculum change has to be context dependent that takes into account the intersections of race, class, gender, and other differences; otherwise, there is further exclusion by the treatment options prescribed for girls behind bars.

Resisting and disrupting discourses

I began with the question of whether a young girl behind bars could be defined as a category representative of all girls behind bars. At stake is not whether it is still possible to refer to a universal identity "young girl behind bars" as a recognized representation of certain groups of students in education as the label "young girl behind bars" is a construct, one that serves many purposes but denies the complexity and multiplicity of the lived experiences of "young girl behind bars" constituted through the exclusion of cultural difference in the curriculum. Students' life-stories dramatically contests the notion of "What is a young girl behind bars?" as stabilized in detention and educational literature as delinquent, dysfunctional, and as subjects in need of correction. The composing of life-stories do not deny the self, however, interrogating the construction of the stable, normative, universal subject of modernity as unchanging is necessary. Students' diverse and multidimensional life-stories illustrate a notion of the self not as a given, predetermined entity but a historical construct contingent upon what discourses we prioritize in education, therefore, a self that is subject to change. Girls behind bars are capable of powerful refusals—not to participate in my research, not to engage in rehabilitation or therapeutic practice—that appear to permit them to reclaim agency, however temporally, in a system that consistently deprives them of autonomy and the right to privacy. In disrupting the categories used to define and discriminate, girls behind bars are not denying identity per se; rather, they are questioning the terms on which identity has been coded and inscribed for them as apriori narrative.

Opening ways to question and subvert the construction of identity and acknowledging the contingent and contextual nature of all claims are necessary conversations to provide the means to construct the terms by which identity is both represented and subverted. Reworking embodied and experiential knowledge into education begins with a reading of absences and a rereading of students' resistance to racism, sexism, and homophobia, and their subversion of misrepresentations that forbid, contain, and exclude them from school knowledge. Whether it is the ontological construct of the universal "being" or an epistemic subject constituted by forms of discursive practices, manifestation of the modernist self can be subverted through critical investigation of the dominant discourses that are privileged in education. Critically examining, questioning, and unsettling dominant discourses of knowledge production makes spaces for reenvisioning curriculum practices that recognize lived experience of all students.

Using oppositional methodologies

Delineating the link between education and detention and reenvisioning curriculum is made possible when teachers see themselves as researchers, study lived experience, and analyze their own assumptions about teaching and learning. Self-reflexive tools for research have the power for raising teacher consciousness and effecting change. Research as a practice offers educators, curriculum developers, educational reformers, and policy-makers the language, resources, and methods for conducting inquiry into the social and institutional relations that produce the conditions for detention. When educators examine their own assumptions, beliefs, and practices in relation to students who are culturally or academically different they are also disrupting as well as generating knowledge.

The absence of lived experience from dominant narratives of education in detention demand ontological and epistemological shifts through oppositional methodologies representative of the voices and experiences of girls behind bars. The original framework of the study grounded in autobiography provides evidence that life-stories of students challenge fixed stereotypical portraits of girls behind bars. An autobiographical theory of curriculum offers a framework for understanding the educational experience of girls behind bars validating lived experience addresses exclusions through autobiographical narrative in order to explore the racial and gendered construction of difference and how they affect the status of educational knowledge, history, and culture. Lived experience challenges our need for knowledge, which affects what we recognize as valid knowledge and the ways in which we shape our needs by the politics of difference.

Understanding the complex relationship between education and detention requires diverse methodological tools and theoretical strategies for analysis.

While autobiographical theory of curriculum enables examining the politics of identity and the exclusions in curriculum, the turn to critical autoethnography and use of poststructural tools offer a complex understanding of students' shifting and contextual subject-positions. Poststructural unpacking of detention as a concept argues that if historical apriori conditions constitute detention, students' experiences troubles detention as a concept, a practice, a technique, and an institution, thus changing the dominant discourse and suggesting possibilities for change. For example, studying the impact of race, class, and gender differences in the lives of girls behind bars not only reveals the ontological assumptions and epistemological "truths" that constitute girls behind bars, but also sheds light on how education and detention shape and maintain racialized, classed, and gendered experiences of students who are culturally different.

As a methodological tool for critique and interpretation, French poststructuralism provides reading practices such as genealogy and deconstruction to trouble how the modernist self has been conceptualized in history and philosophy. Questioning belief systems and interpreting them can be "dangerous, for it uncovers, interprets, clarifies, deconstructs, and challenges all fields of study, including curriculum development models and methods" (Slattery 2006, p. 142). Poststructural critiques that emphasize possibility and change as an ongoing interpretive process in curriculum are transformational because they critique to destabilize the structures of the educational system and philosophies that have defined modernist schooling to shape the educational experience of students. Poststructural tools provide many variations of the decentered self to show the paradox of a subject that exists but under conditions that are unstable and partial, continually producing agents of change.

Reading practices that provide educators, curriculum scholars, policy-makers, and educational reformers tools and strategies for critiques incite curriculum change. Critiques are meant to illustrate the violence and harm that comes with fixed forms of knowledge and the sense of injustice that comes from the exclusion of knowledge embodying difference forbidden from the curriculum. Through systematic critique, teachers, students, curriculum scholars, policy-makers, and educational reformers question their own assumptions about education, their professional and institutional roles in the marginalization of students who are different, and the exclusion of student knowledge from curriculum processes and practices. Deconstructing unpacks how the language for marginalization of difference is sustained through categories, binaries, and hierarchies that define and fix student identities, participate in the normalization of difference and policy emerges to position marginalized students from the school into the juvenile justice system.

In the use of critical methodologies, the aim of this book was not to define "young girl behind bars" but to unsettle it and reposition lived experience as curriculum knowledge. Students' life-stories speak of dislocations, breakdowns, and performances that proclaim their universal representation is an unjust construct. Analyzing and interpreting students' life-stories presents a fragmented, hybrid, subjective self-defying fixed notions of identity to present a montage of contradictory images of the self with a political message for social change. While there may be potential for holding on to an essential identity for strategic purposes (Spivak 2000), such as contesting repression and oppression of marginalized minority groups it is possible to interpret identity neither as a constituted prediscursive subject nor as a fixed and unified knowing self. Rather, the subject is constructed through changing subject positions in and through acts that are performed in particular contexts, relations, and discourse. The subject, then, is a discursively changing construction that is neither wholly predetermined by historical forces nor completely controlled by discourse, because to read the subject thus is to close all transformative possibilities for reclaiming education.

The shift suggested in representing identity such as "girls behind bars" unsettles epistemologically and ontologically predetermined self communicated through educational theories and practices. As a form of communication, language as Saussure (1959) argued is a constructed and arbitrary system reflecting the arbitrariness of the rules and values it expresses. Poststructural reading practices offer tools to educators for deconstructing the arbitrary construction of language under rules and values structured within institutional binaries, categories, hierarchies, and other similar value-laden codes that enable some students and discipline other students. For example, the philosophical construct of binaries used as markers of difference among students identifying them as successful or failures, normal or delinquent is reinforced through institutional practices that support some students for college while others are relegated for detention and correction. When students refuse to abide by the institutional norms of schooling or the social and institutional norms of "woman," or any other constructed and arbitrary norm, they render the normative unintelligible and denaturalize the norm. In denaturalizing the norm the act of agency denaturalizes the nonnormative, underscoring the constructedness and arbitrariness of the norm or the nonnormative of "young girl behind bars."

This chapter calls teachers to participate in critical autoethnography as a methodological space for thinking through simplistic understandings of the gendered educational subject. Who are these girls behind bars? Their life-stories and autobiographies offer spaces to transform their experiences to reclaim their educational needs. Students' lived experience and embodiment become that space for collision affecting each student differently. The work of postfeminist scholars, Baker (2001, 2002), Butler (1990, 1992), and Lather (1997), provide ways of reading that deconstruct knowledge as well as create spaces for resituating the subject of education. Postfeminist deconstructivist reading practices provide educators the language for exploring their own subjectivities toward students' lived experiences. Lived experience opens up the possibility for teachers to think about categories differently, not only of girls behind bars but the politics of other categories that are part of the everyday discourse in education and detention such as "normal," "delinquent," "woman," "female body," "sex," and gender.

Reading students' life-stories as lived educational experience enacted by embodied, gendered subjectivities plays out on many registers of knowledge production. Gendered life-stories of girls behind bars as a counter discourse produces forms of knowledge silenced in education. Using gender as a category of analysis deconstructs the life-stories of girls behind bars as social, cultural, historical, and educational constructs. Interrogating the category of gender revealed the process of dislocation and transformation of other categories as well—woman, student, subject—the discomposition of categories indicated the impossibility of an original generic young girl behind bars and the provisional condition of students' subject-positions. Gender as a contested site serves as the springboard for interrogating other generic concepts that define women, posits that girls behind bars perform gender to reproduce and contest the cultural script written in categorical constructions of "woman," "sex," and the "female body." What is illustrated through students' life-stories is the funds of knowledge students bring into the classroom opening possibilities for a more inclusive curriculum.

In spite of historical apriori conditions that make possible normalized practices of detention, the subject of detention is significant, compelling educators to address its existence. Postfeminist deconstructivist reading of the subject of history and philosophy through a Foucauldian lens sheds light on how the subject of detention is a modernist philosophical and historical construct that can be decentered through systematic investigation. When educators question, unsettle, disturb, and provoke the way classroom knowledge is constructed, they participate in broader discussions about identity and difference, authority of dualistic and hierarchical thought, and educational structures that classify, universalize, and exclude to perpetuate violence. When teachers and curriculum scholars' attend the violence engendered in day-to-day practices of teaching under categorical terms and the "epistemic failure" (Lather 2001, p. 203) of shutting out disjunctive life-stories that do not fit into conventional understandings of knowledge they are also attending to issues of educational equity and social justice.

Autoethnography is a method that validates multiple voices of the marginalized who struggle to reclaim their lives, the autoethnographic telling of multiple life-stories serving as a challenge to our understanding of what curriculum considers an academic or scholarly inquiry. Speaking of using poststructural tools to conduct autoethnographic work, Britzman (1998) urges "proliferations" that "exceed—as opposed to return to—the self" (p. 85). Different autoethnographic forms across disciplines share a common driving force—a desire to understand the self and to recognize the self as a site for knowledge production rather than an unchanging subject or object of history and philosophy (Smith 1999). Oppositional methodologies that validate voices of exclusion as agents of knowledge offer ways to interrogate how concepts have been constructed and deployed in educational settings in order to be able to think out of the deadlock of fixed concepts and move toward transformative and inclusive curriculum practice.

As a discursive site for interrogating, provoking, and creating multiple understandings of dominant discourses within traditional curriculum, autoethnography contests single narratives through critiques of assumptions, beliefs, and foundations of knowledge. Asking critical questions such as how and why certain forms of knowledge have become foundational must be a continuing project of teachers. Studying students' life-stories is a challenge for educators, curriculum developers, and policy-makers; however, students' stories must be told, not silenced. The prejudices embedded in the curriculum are also deeply embedded in those of us who enact curriculum. Therefore, destabilizing traditional meaning, making new meaning, and pushing autoethnographic understandings toward multiplicity makes room for differences, contradictions, and ambivalences in each story. As a political practice, autoethnography offers teachers discursive spaces for curriculum transformations using mixed genres and research methods that do not represent traditional ethnography or the established rules of generic autobiography.

Autoethnography, methodology, and self-reflexivity are important tools and methods for educators to question prejudices and injustices perpetuated simply because they have existed long enough to become normalized. Oppositional methodological tools of analysis offer ways to question the meaning of knowledge and its relation to cultural difference without buckling under the dogma of absolute truth or succumbing to the hopelessness of historical apriori conditions. The ontological apriori being, epistemological conditions of truth, including poststructural possibilities are all contingencies from specific historical moments that must be questioned for their claims to all that is taken to be truth or otherwise—for in making any claim there is a silencing that remains unaddressed. The constructed nature of the subject or any other marginalized voice is paradoxical—embodiment as silence and voice. When students' lived experiences become a knowledge-producing site, it creates space for all forms of knowledge production, histories, embodiment, gender, and desire.

Teachers as agents of change

Lived experience is also the knowledge production site for resistance and disruption unsettling our recognized and learned ways as much as it settles notions of contradiction and change. In the classroom, how we respond to lived experience, how we respond differently to certain types of experience, the inclusions, and exclusions we recognize affect the way teachers and students interact with each other in the classroom. As we continue to ask, "What is the teacher's role in the classroom?" reading life-stories of students offer transformative possibilities. Students' life-stories incite educators to fight complacency, take risks, go against the grain if need be, use the power to listen to students and use the imagination to make connection between history, philosophy, and the present context of teaching.

For example, teachers must make space for students' life-stories to challenge and question the content and process of teaching. Reading into lived experience however uncomfortable reveals the privileged position of teachers and the place of students' knowledge highlighting forbidden curriculum. Students and teachers might be at risk when lived histories are scrutinized and exposed. Nevertheless, in failing to honor students' complex experiences is to lack the will to do so and run the risk of further silencing of certain groups of students. Interpretation of students' life-stories is open to question. However, as educators we can shed light on lived educational experience through the transformations students bring to the curriculum making teachers and students agents of change.

Traditionally, an effective teacher in most classrooms is seen as one who gives students opportunities for self-expression, fosters a dialogic relationship, and allows students to remedy, reorder, and realign their lives according to the academic and social objectives of education. This traditional blueprint of an effective teacher or an ideal classroom, however, does not work for all classrooms as some teachers are caught between a curriculum that emphasizes standardization and control and one that honors students' context and experience as curriculum knowledge. The rules, regulations, and policies in universal education or standardized curriculum are a reflection of the conditions in which they are constituted rather than those it aims to universalize or standardize. The life-stories of students are a counter discourse to the institutional, universalized, and standardized identity of girls behind bars.

Seen from Foucault's perspective, writing and telling personal stories are critical to a wider transformation of teaching and its curricula norms. Speaking of his work, Foucault (1972b) says that:

> when the prisoners began to speak, they possessed an individual theory of prisons, the penal system, and justice. It is this form of discourse which ultimately matters, a discourse against power, the counter-discourse of prisoners we call prisoners and those we call delinquents—and not a theory of delinquency. (p. 194)

Exploring possible understandings through the writing of autobiographies and honoring lived experience is an intervention for inciting students to take ownership of their reading and writing.

When educators use critical reading practices for interpretation of lived experience, they are able to reread their own educational stories differently as discursive spaces troubling the sedimented and embeddedness of all curriculum knowledge. A rereading of one's own life articulates spaces from where essentialist and reductionist notions of teacher, self, woman, subject of discourse, or any other identity that continues to define curriculum can be problematized. Examining and disrupting representations of identities frozen in time and place serve as the springboard from where to begin to think about possibilities of transformation through thinking multiply, contextually, relationally, and self-reflexively. By highlighting students' lived educational experiences, educators can contest any form of universal experiences that totalize, stabilize, or consolidate identities or play them out as historical apriori conditions without possibility for agency and change. By rigorous critique educators ask themselves if they are guiding students to internalize their exclusion from traditional curriculum and to question the extent to which educators advance institutional ideologies and norms rather than assisting students in using their resistance for transformative change.

When educators use critical tools for analysis to deconstruct a fixed categorical construct such as identity they are not subsuming students under the totality of discursive practices but showing the systematic distortions of students' lives when unequal conditions for their experiences are laid out as apriori. The need to define, predict, and control the future of curriculum has restricted the visionary possibilities to what is outside the horizon of known thought and experience—fear of the unthought. The unthought is to know that every understanding of students, teachers, curriculum is partial; that there is always an indefinable realm that is outside discourse, outside the body, outside history, outside memory, outside language—the "as yet unnamable, which is proclaiming itself" (Derrida 1978, p. 293)—a curriculum that is always in the process of transforming.

When teachers identify the dominant discourses in curriculum, there is possibility in critical analysis for political agency. Reenvisioning an inclusive curriculum requires historical knowledge of philosophies that underline everyday practices of education and its relation to education in detention, the categories of analysis such as deviancy and normativity that define educational systems, and how categories have been legitimized over time. The investigation of historical, social, legal, scientific, and educational conditions that make detention possible for particular groups of youth expose the historical conditions of unequal relations underlying curriculum theories and practices. Foucault's genealogy and Derrida's deconstruction are useful academic tools for questioning thoughts and assumptions in the classroom that emerge from philosophy, its humanism, logocentrism, rationality, and fixed reality. For example, questioning the historical apriori conditions reveals how subjects constituted by discourse are subsumed under experiences of subjugation. The argument that detention is a construct in relation to other discourses illustrates the continuity and discontinuities that constitute detention and also delineates curriculum as subject to interpretive and transformative change.

Teachers need to be aware that when expressing exclusion based on test scores, they are privileging academic success over all other differences. Such privileging is oppressive to other forms of knowing that has been historically dominated such as gendered differences and other departures from the normative. The stand teachers take on difference shapes the dynamics of inclusion and exclusion in the classroom, which in turn shapes the ways student identities are constructed within categories and hierarchies that are detrimental for some students. When students resist the status quo in the curriculum how teachers respond to student resistance is critical—teachers have the agency to channelize student resistance toward transformation rather than suspension, expulsion, and detention.

Resistance can be the point of transformation where the intersectionality of identity formation, lived experience, and curriculum lead to agency. Normalization and socialization into detention through suspension and expulsion of students who are culturally different or resistant to normative controls constitutes racial-marginalized subject positioning. The rational forms of knowledge teachers bring into the classroom are structured by institutional power relations that define their teaching identities, identities that under-recognizes situated knowledge of students. Therefore, how teachers as representatives of the institutions that employ them use their power to shape student identities is critical to education as a practice of social justice—do we use our agency to participate in identity and knowledge formation so that all students experience personal and political transformation.

When students challenge the academic goals of the school curriculum, teachers are held accountable for enforcement of standardized teaching practices in a detention classroom. Teachers need several options in addressing institutional demands or the academic and social responsibilities of teaching and learning will not move forward. When students challenge classroom teaching, their challenges serve as critiques of traditional curriculum prompting teachers to be open and flexible in adopting curriculum changes. In confronting teachers, students confront and resist the foundations of teaching and learning within conventional structures and methods that the present conditions of education represent.

In the class, when curriculum becomes the medium for giving voice to universal and fixed subjects, many students opt for silence viewed by many teachers as oppositional behavior. When students do speak up, they are acutely aware of the power imbalance in the student–teacher relationship, and do not consider it safe to speak of their experiences or express their respective personalities. They are aware of facing the risk of reinforcing the very stereotypes evoked by speaking and thinking in ways sharply divergent from the universal normative. Faced with similar situations, many students find themselves in a position that restricts their right to speak or limits their options when the notion of a unified and collective identity of "young girl behind bars" remained uncontested.

Thus, teaching is not a fixed set of rules nor a planned chart of student growth but a situated position in which the tools for teaching keep changing in relation to person, context, time, and place. Students' life-stories and interpretation of life-stories offers possibilities to connect teachers to the students in many ways. Students' life-stories open teachers to the possibilities of viewing students' lives differently and affect the teacher–student relationship, which in turn transforms the day-to-day curriculum. Therefore, there is definitely a pressing need to develop teaching frameworks attentive to the potential in autobiographical work of students. Students' experiences expose knowledge that must be inclusive, and that foundational ideas perpetuate violence in the destruction of cultural and other differences. Educators that exercise transformative agency through collaborative interaction of ideas, actions, and interpretation are able to make meaning of life-stories that can effect social and academic change.

Human interaction, behaviors, and situations are not objects by themselves and cannot always be read as texts that are changeable and unstable—destabilizing history or dislodging philosophy is to see students as human objects without answering questions of human justice. It is to reduce the "other" to a curriculum text or to a textual alterity. It is an acceptance of marginalization, deviance, and further "othering" of the "other." Hence, it is not enough for teachers and students to be oppositional in the struggle for social change. Interpretation is an epistemological concern. The question of epistemology and the transformative possibilities in interpretation are also ethical concerns. The question of difference, the constitution of the self, the performativity of subject-positions, and the construction of the "other" are all ethical issues.

The concept of education and the discourses that constitute education are conceptualized within binaries, most notably, body and mind, emotion and reason, and success and failure. While the mind and reason are given importance, body and emotion are viewed as targets for "subjugation . . . constituted as a problematic and being a visible target for monitoring and intervention" (Baker 2001, p. 574). Detention as an intervention for monitoring lived experience of difference is a consequence of forms of targeted subjugation against difference under the guise of education for rehabilitation. The problem is not always with the binaries themselves but the literal application of binaries at the cost of exclusion. For example, when students are expected to "succeed" at school because we have taught them a prescribed curriculum, "failure" is viewed as a shortcoming or a deficiency in students that needs to be addressed through interventions. This is not to suggest that special services for some students are not needed. Rather, what is recommended is examining the process of labeling students—what is diagnosed as a behavioral or learning disorder is often a systemic failure to address the cause and effect of social and historical conditions that shape the lived experience of difference calling into question education as an institution of social justice.

Lived experience as curriculum knowledge

What might it mean to speak of lived experience of difference as knowledge that counts?

I began the study with Pinar's autobiographical theory focused primarily on curriculum and moved outward to studying girls behind bars under the broad scope of education, specifically in detention. I have come full circle to return to where my journey began—the curriculum. Whether we study education in a broad context, or curriculum as it plays out in the classroom, the modernist methods in curriculum are designed along the Tyler rationale, Bobbitt's efficiency model, Bloom's taxonomy, Maslow's hierarchy of human needs, and Piaget's behaviorism privileging cognitive and empirical theories foundational to current teaching practices in detention classrooms.

Questioning modernist methods can shift our knowledge from stability and certainty and force us to recognize not just the way things are but why they are so. At the same time, they create a need for relinquishing established truths to question the historical and specific conditions that make knowledge possible and incite inquiry into the intimate connection between the history of education and its key frameworks, practices, and assumptions. Indeed, if education must envision an inclusive tomorrow, it must understand the experiences of students historically and performatively. Although traditional teaching acknowledges the authority of the teacher, it does not question reform objectives that disown the life-stories of girls behind bars, thus reinforcing the controlling process of education.

Education for rehabilitation coheres around interconnected issues such as agency and positive identities that are considered normative. Traditional detention literature claims that when students speak in the class their participation indicates a commitment to rehabilitation. The literature assumes that this process of transformation of behaviors is a direct result of successful teaching that has enabled students to take "control" of their lives and make the right decisions. Even though teachers are in charge, the students are responsible for their actions. Traditionally to have educational success is totally under a students' behavioral control as responsible subjects. The simplistic dualism of tests where students fail or pass reinforces the success of students who are performing at the upper level of the testing, whereas it labels others as feeble-minded, idiots, inferior, remedial, challenged, slow, and delinquent. By reinforcing the failure/success dichotomy, educational objectives reflected in the school curriculum place grades at the center of learning rather than engaging the lived educational experience of students.

This chapter calls for a shift in understanding the ontological, epistemological, and methodological edifice we as a community of curriculum scholars have constructed. Life-stories of girls behind bars circulate and are proliferated in schools through suspension, expulsion, detention, special education. Life-stories shed light on how institutions organize and articulate student identities under labels such as delinquent or deviant that silence actual lived experience and in the process exclude certain identities from the primary curriculum of educators. When identities are imposed on students, neither are their real educational needs addressed nor are teachers given the professional help they need to address students' needs.

The consequences of this silencing of difference and labeling of difference under academic subject positioning represents institutional control of difference leading to short-term "treatment" of student identities that in turn lead to long-term consequences such as restricted access to schooling, college, and employment. The "treatment" options provided to students who are nonnormative are deeply grounded in normative structures of subordination such as patriarchy and gender. Additionally, at intersectional moments of their lives, there is collision between intersections such as gender choices, social conditions such as poverty, and historical conditions that mark students under racial lines. When difference is identified in educational theories and practices, isolated, tracked, and marked for treatment under the deficit model of education, tracking students away from education and promoting the production of disabilities to manage cultural difference results. Deficit theories, special education, standardizing curriculum, rehabilitation, and education in detention labels and blames the individual and absolve schools and other institutional and social structures of their role in the processes of educational equity.

What do we resist if as educators we are implicated in all we say, do, and interpret? How does interpretation help educators? Learning to write lesson plans and memorizing facts and figures that constitute curriculum are distortions of the curriculum that beg for change. In interpreting students' autobiographies and life-stories, identity, objectivity, and dualist thinking are challenged as totalizing terms that traditional curriculum relies upon without acknowledging incompleteness, contingency, contextuality, and multiplicity. It is not enough to confront technocratic and rational aims of education whether in or outside detention; transformative modes of questioning that are self-reflexive make for a deeper understanding of students.

Interpretive possibilities, nevertheless, are not without problems. For one thing, interpretation challenges belief systems, institutional systems, and the practices that emerge from them. Interpretation is based on the premise that a text, a subject, a person, a life, a practice, a belief, even a law is complex and has to be deconstructed on multiple registers (Slattery 2006). As Foucault's radical claim of the death of the author or Derrida's suspicion of origins remind us, every text contains traces of previous texts and, therefore, traces of social, cultural, and institutional beliefs.

This is not to suggest any meaning can be ascribed to any text. Interpretation also recognizes that whether it is history, philosophy, people, or event, meaning is not constant or contained but always contingent, emergent, and contextual. The interpretive process takes into account the changing nature of context, time, and place, making space for multiple meanings. For example, as a teacher analyzing a historical or a literary text or a current event rather than accepting absolute authority of a given text, interpretive work engages in multiple understandings and meanings without subjecting all students to the tyranny of a single interpretation. Rather, interpretation comes with a tremendous responsibility for self-reflexivity and recursive thinking before meaning emerges from the text or experience.

Students' life-stories do not represent the philosophical and rational "I am" who is a knowing self. Rather, they explore "how I came to be who I am" or "how can the relations in which I live, dream, and act be reinvented through me" (Gilmore 2001, p. 148). The certainty of a fixed nonnormative identity is transformed through language and action into the performative that denotes changing subject-positions, not delinquency. Instead of judging the student within expectations dependent on patriarchal lineage of gendered values to decide if the student's intelligibility conforms to norms, intervening in normative discourses by shifting the focus toward *how* normative expectations are formed and the arbitrary nature of such claims to truth that define what is normal, what is delinquent, and what to do with the latter opens possibilities/impossibilities.

The impossibility of defining and the complicities of language are evident—"delinquent" names a particular experience or a cultural ordering; it also violates by defining what is nonnormative. Therefore, the term delinquent is not a natural generic identity but can be transformed into difference that disrupts fixed apriori knowledge or practices already in existence. Students' life-stories are lived educational experience that offer opportunities for educators to reflect on how curriculum knowledge as truth is produced and circulated, by whom, in what forms and methods, and to what effects.

Reworking embodied and processual knowledge into curriculum begins with a reading of absences and rereading students' resistance to conventions and misrepresentations that forbid, contain, and exclude them from curriculum knowledge. I have used the naming of the term "detention" as an example to further my intention. Why does the term "delinquent" automatically evoke detention? There is in the use of the term an articulation of meaning, a violence of meaning, and a disarticulation of convention. Although the scholarship on teaching in detention recognizes the importance of a teacher's ability to learn from students' lives, it fails to acknowledge that there are elements and contexts of student experiences that a teacher would never understand or know. In recognizing the subject positioning of all identities, teachers are prompted to examine how their own identities and beliefs are constituted, what is constituted outside their own beliefs and practices, and the conditions of possibility in breaking down the overdetermined differences between "us" and "them." The constitutive "inside" as well as the constitutive "outside," when subjected to question, is a step toward multiplicity of competing heterogeneous discourses in contrast to a single rationalist discourse determining the normal and the delinquent.

I have been aware and reflective of ethical questions, however, telling and interpreting life-stories continues to trouble. The multiple subject positions I speak from are contradictory, confusing, and empowering. For example, I recognize that my privileged position of instructor occupies the same space as my gendered and raced position of being the "other"; and my outsider status as a woman and teacher from India does not fit into the dominant cultural narrative of education in the United States. I have had the privilege of speaking from multiple positions—the positions that restrict my telling also provide the spaces for examining the Foucauldian knowledge/power/inequality/opportunity nexus to reconfigure my relationship to curriculum change. I have arrived at a destination that is contradictory, multiple, complex, and of course, temporary—a process of my own becoming. Identity is important, as is the subject. In deconstructing identity, I have used subject-positions to show the constructed nature of identity, the terms on which identity has been constructed, and by whom. Performativity suggests that there is no fixed identity; rather, the act produces the changing subject-position of the performer, also suggesting that identity can be deconstructed and that rethinking in terms of subject-positions offers possibilities for change.

By voicing the challenges I faced teaching in a detention classroom, I have highlighted the urgency of listening to students' personal stories critical to understanding what enables and disables the teaching relationship. Closely associated with formal schooling and standardization of learning and teaching is a complex set of exclusions reminding us of that which is silenced or ignored—embodied experience. As long as teaching in detention classrooms fails to recognize the intimate yet complicated relationship of self, identity, and subjectivity to the conditions that shape the lives of students, teaching will continue under the notion of effecting rehabilitation through standardized teaching and testing practices.

Call for action

Life stories of girls behind bars signify that students play out life and death battles for survival each day. Students' life-stories are constituted performatively within and against preexisting categories, eluding any permanent definition. Their life-stories mediated through interpretation are forms of agency. In spite of all attempts to interpret meaning embedded in students' histories, their life-stories continue to be partial knowledge. What is significant is not the images of victimization but the oppressive effects of the discourse on righteousness and rational decision-making based on simplistic dualism of regulatory right and wrong, rational and irrational. Students' life-stories, however imposing of meaning, are not articulations coming from delinquent students; they are exercises in negotiating subject-positions without being restricted to a single identity. In other words, students' articulations are effects of philosophical discourses but in their stories there is room for embodied knowledge—lived educational experience that dislodges all attempts at stabilizing the meaning of girls behind bars. When "girls behind bars" is normalized as a category for labeling students who are nonnormative, society, science, psychology, and education are complicit in discrimination against difference. The differences among, between, and within students creates a categorical crisis that demands critical intervention from educators, curriculum scholars, policy–makers, and educational reformers.

In closing is a call to educators, curriculum developers, activists, reformers, and policy-makers for disrupting the connection between schools and detention as part of a complex web of social, cultural, and institutional practices that racialize, gender, and disproportionately impact certain groups of young women by shaping and limiting their academic options and life choices. By calling upon educators, curriculum developers, activists, reformers, and administrators to end the pathologizing of certain groups of students through socially unjust practices and policies counter stories that interrogate the inclusions and exclusions woven into teaching philosophies, policies, and practices affect how knowledge is organized in the classroom, and challenge the types of knowledge that get accepted within the disciplinary norms of everyday schooling.

Evoking life-stories brings attention to the forbidden or disowned conversations in education and the immediacy of attending to difference among students differently. Opening the possibility of curriculum transformation to resituate girls behind bars in contexts that speak to their lives and interrogate the construction of students as delinquent, criminal, and failures resituates educational agenda. Recomposing life-stories provides the occasion for positioning the decentered subject of detention as embodied lived educational experience, marked by convention, history, discontinuity, and displacement. Questioning cannot stop because truth never is—it is always that which is absent; it is the Derridean concept of justice that is yet to come. How do we teach from what we now know about students' absent, silenced, repressed life-stories? How do we talk about knowing too much and knowing too little? If students as educational subjects have no fixed identities but changing subject-positions, how do we teach them not knowing who they are? These are fundamental philosophical questions; however, they are questions that incite fresh inquiry, theorization, interpretation, and transformation. This does not mean that we cannot strive for justice in education, only that as an ideal it is that toward which we must always strive without closure; for not to strive for justice because it cannot be fully realized is as unethical as believing that justice has already been achieved. Social justice should be the starting point of education, not the goal of education.

Girls behind Bars Reclaiming Education in Transformative Spaces

Introduction

Interpretive reading shapes my autoethnographic telling; however, in this chapter the personal experience of situated writing involves the autoethnographic praxis of teachers and students reclaiming education in transformative spaces. This chapter is the turbulent, heartbreaking, and paradoxical world of detention as I experienced it. In the pages of this book my life may not be visible, but this moment I will seize to do just that—dwell on my own positioning, my politics, my lived experience, my emotions—write my own discourse, so to speak. The moments in this chapter exist because of my students. Nevertheless, they are my stories and the voices within my multiple, split selves—woman, teacher, student, researcher, and mother.

A woman in India. That is what my mother, my sisters, my aunts, my grandmothers, my friends are, or have been for most of their lives. Women in America is what a few of them have become. A woman in India is something I have been my entire life, each day becoming ingrained deeper and deeper within me. A woman in the United States is something more indefinably complicated. A woman in India who becomes a woman in the United States is the most complicated of all. Where does she belong? What does she gain? What does she compromise? What does she call herself?

Disembarking from the plane in the United States I found myself pressing my nose to my wrist to remind myself, through the Indian musk I had used, of the comfortable territory I had left behind. Somehow the tandoori dinner, the kebabs, the rice pudding I had savored the night before amid the laughter of family and friends all blurred into a single fleeting second—hat *was* it? An emotion? A longing? A state of mind? A lifetime? Already a memory?—that seemed so distant and in excess of my grasp. Once outside the airport in the midwest, I did not know how to react, and this surprised me. I had to take responsibility for myself, to recognize where I fit into the scheme of things. In India, my place was marked before I was born—scripted into the role of playing daughter, sister, wife, mother, aunt, and grand-aunt. Here the uncertainty of my role was striking. What was it, even, to be a woman in the United States? Or in India for that matter?

The journey from India to the United States is unending. Upon arrival, the existence of space everywhere feels bizarre. In every direction the empty space stretches on and on . . . miles and miles of highway . . . so much breathing space, it all simply takes the breath away. The mechanistic order of things is frightening. We stop in the city, where everything follows a computerized agenda—signs, buildings, roads, sidewalks, even people. The city crowds are nothing like the sweaty moving jumbled throngs that made the Delhi streets swell with color, smells, vibrancy, noise, life. I feel uprooted. I already feel the permanence of my transition.

Over the next few years of transition, I incurred a huge debt to my students to whom I owe many moments of laughter, joy, sadness, frustration, anger, and kindness. I am indebted to those who won my heart and to those who challenged me. Often I struggled to connect with students. The odd thing is, in India I lived between the continuous tension of being the woman I was expected to be, however grudgingly I played the part, and the woman who was tarred with the brush of feminism and wanted to break out of the shackles of Indian tradition. Now as I stand in the classroom, my privilege, struggles, and tensions are all relative. I am convinced of the old feminist cliché—no single woman is liberated until all women are liberated. Yes, liberated from what? I wanted to create a just and safe world for all my students. I could not stop giving personal and educational advice to students on what they should or should not do, what they must never do, and what they can safely do. In that case, a student tells me, "Sharma, you may as well bubble wrap us."

How it all began: The first moment January 23, 2003

I am on the detention facility campus. The Midwest snow and slush is hostile. The facility even more so because cameras, intercoms, and locked doors greet me. The place is cold, damp, and depressing; the introductions are polite, distant, and tense. Again the open space is everywhere, yet everywhere it is invaded. It is my first day in the classroom. The room has security cameras, a guard, and a barred window. The walls are bare, and the classroom has no resources—no textbooks, no stationery, and no chalk. I am not nervous. I am simply blank, absorbing, soaking the alienation of it all. I am in a classroom with 16 students who are not allowed to keep a pencil or pen or speak to one another.

My training into being a teacher in detention begins the next week even though I spent some time each day in the classroom with students. I stare because I am not used to a security guard at the back of the room, who in turn has not stopped staring at me. I do not know who is more shocked! Days later, the security guard explained his shock had to do with an Indian woman speaking in English. What will I do without books, I wonder. And why are all the students sitting in the same position, hands flat on the desk, feet flat on the ground, eyes forward, looking trapped? I break the silence by talking about myself, my name, the flight, anything to break the ice. I look around, searching for what? My teacher-mode swings into action. I make eye contact with a student, thin, emaciated, and anorexic. There is another student asleep at the end of the room, lazy backbencher? I am going into full throttle teacher-mode; my teaching self is computing, placing students in slots, naming, labeling, restructuring, racing to be ahead of the teaching game.

A student in the front reaches out to touch my gold bangles and the security guard shatters her move lunging toward the student. I am shocked at the way he treats her and equally stunned when the silence is shattered into a million pieces as students let out a tsunami of profanities at the guard and all hell breaks loose in the room. I am already backed against the wall, and if I wanted to run from the building, where was I going to go? Home was an ocean or two away.

When we settled down, the Director of the facility joins the class, perhaps, to monitor the peace. The students want to know what my name means, why I am wearing "American clothes," and why I want to teach girls behind bars. In ten minutes I am exhausted. The intense emotional movement of the last few minutes is in stark contrast to my teaching in India, which operated within a culture of silence—students are silent while teachers lecture. It does not matter what is being taught—Homer, Yeats, Tagore, equations, trigonometry, specific gravity—students in India listen, memorize, test, and move to the next class. How was I going to sum up the will to teach this group of students who had just spent five minutes in silence, three minutes fighting the security guard, five minutes talking to me, and the last 20 minutes talking to each other about their sexual experiences?

Thereafter, the students discussed rape, prostitution, suicide, and STDs. All this interspersed with jargon from the criminal and the juvenile justice system—case manager, probation, sentence, and prison. The candor with which they spoke and the rawness of the sexual openness was something I never got used to. A student, Crystal, was telling another that she could not differentiate between a "date" and "rape," and it did not matter anymore when prostituting for a living. Crystal's conversation was the last thing I took away with me that first day; the violence of her sexual experiences would replay with a rising crescendo in my head, matched only by my increasing panic and helplessness. As a teacher I was unprepared. The next few days were the same, the daily seven to four routine was the same, alienation was everywhere, only students' stories changed. By the end of the first week, it felt like a long day's journey into Hades.

Even more troubling was the knowledge that I did not trust myself to make "wise" decisions as a teacher when my emotions conveyed the chaos and uncertainty. Effective teaching, masterful teaching, good teacher, best teacher, experienced teacher, holistic education, planned curriculum, professional development—who invents these terms? And for whom? What theories was I going to depend on? What teaching philosophy was I going to keep in mind?

Message in a bottle: The second moment July 4, 2003

Lisa is a problem for me, as I listen to her voice coming from the other end of the corridor—the yelling, screaming, the profanity—I wonder how long I can stand it. I am in the classroom waiting for the students to arrive. I listen to her voice, high strung, shrill, young, at 13 struggling to sound assertive and unafraid. Whatever prompts a promising life to turn into this unfathomable shriek I cannot bear to hear? Now in the classroom, Lisa is a problem for me because she is too young, too unschooled, and too unrestrained to remain in the classroom without a behavioral outburst. I also think of the odds stacked against her—Black, poor, raped, orphaned, and waging her own personal war against all odds. My problem is, I also feel drawn to Lisa because I cannot stand or understand her; I feel repelled because she pushes me away from her. In part, I have brought my problems with me—I am looking for the straightforward, obedient student I am familiar with, one who would take instructions, get the school work done, and be ready the next day. The shrieking has been replaced with Lisa's fragile body shaking violently with silent uncontrolled sobs. If there is anything more disturbing than a shrieking child, it is a child haunted by her own life experiences.

Fifteen minutes later, Lisa sits before me, calmly stringing beads to make a pair of earrings for herself. She has been working with a group of students who are making Indian jewelry as part of the summer 4 H youth development project. As the detention facility is opened all summer, teachers are encouraged to suspend regular teaching and engage students in creative projects from June to August. The facility suggested I run a poetry club as part of the 4 H project. Poetry? We write poetry every day in class, but of course I do not want to tell them that because then I have to answer questions from the Principal about why I am not following the lesson plan I submit each Monday. In effect, I am running a parallel curriculum here—one that I deceitfully submit to the Principal, and the other that we follow willy nilly according to the need for the day.

Halfway through the 4 H project, the facility administration realized we were using sharp objects banned inside the facility—needles, scissors, metal wire, and pliers. I had been approved for the project but left the list of required supplies unmentioned. I bought my own supplies in order to avoid questions. For a month, we made jewelry, and the students loved every minute of it. Many of the students long for jewelry but are not allowed to wear it in detention. I had stopped wearing jewelry because I felt guilty I was flaunting what students were not allowed to wear.

I watch Lisa, as she meticulously threads each colored bead; twirling, twisting, stringing. Like a surveillance camera, I am focused on her movements as she threads one bead, then another, closing the spaces between the beads. Every now and then a bead escapes her little nimble fingers or the wire entangles. Each time she struggles to disentangle, the wire gets more entangled and a small exasperated sigh escapes. It releases her concentrated tension. Then the process starts again, this tangling and unraveling. I want to hug her. I will not because I do not want to rupture the moment or break the tension. I want to capture this harmonious moment forever.

She is making her first earring and says she had never owned a trinket. I am surprised. Six months ago, a misshapen string of plastic beads hanging on a thin copper wire would be a piece of junk for the dustbin; today it feels like the most precious and sacred thread that has brought Lisa, problem Lisa, and me together in a shared, quiet moment. Lisa wraps something in a sheet of lined paper torn out of a notebook and hands it to me. I almost toss the crumpled ball of paper away but have learned the hard way from students never to discard any paper without reading. It is a mistake to rationalize all the time, I think; better to use the senses and let embodiment take over. I feel overwhelmed; wrapped inside the paper are Lisa's priceless earrings. The note reads, "To Miss Sharma, you are my message in a bottle." I could taste the salt of my own tears.

Lisa, unaware, returns to her desk and is absorbed in her bead work. But there is something that unsettles me each time I look at Lisa. Lisa is me . . . the rebellious nine-year old angry for the loss of my father. Angry that my mother wears white now because she is a widow in a male world where a woman's greatest honor comes from living in the shadow of her husband. I learned as early as nine (when my father died of a heart attack in the prime of his life) that in India the worst thing for a Hindu woman is to survive her husband. Hindu widows in India must wear white without any make-up or jewelry because a widow is always in mourning for her loss. My mother was 45. I learned that Hindu widows are dressed in white when they die and women are dressed in red bridal finery bedecked in jewels if they die before the husband. A woman in India. My mother, a widow in India. One day she wore so many shades of bright orange and red, it hurt the eye, jarred the senses. Cultured in a boarding school run by Caucasian Catholic nuns, St Joseph's Convent, I preferred sedate shades of lilac and blue, I told her. I told her too many shades of orange and red were claustrophobic.

My mother wore her bright oranges and reds together, anyway. Keep the white for the "convent," she told me. The next day, upon my father's death, my mother was condemned to wear white for the rest of her life. For the next 30 years, my mother was a symbol of mourning for the loss of her identity, her body, her spirit, her self. I never felt the loss of my father in the way I felt my mother's loss. My mother spent her years mourning the loss of her husband; I have spent years raging against the sentence of widowhood imposed on a woman in India.

In India, everything attached to the title "woman" had made it restrictive and crowding for me. As I watch Lisa, the claustrophobia of being a woman in India so lacking in the United States now seems to close in from the other side. Here, on the surface there is a thickness of absence. Yet, the social and academic pressures on Lisa are crowding. Her self-blaming is crowding. Who could Lisa depend upon as an orphan, when everyone was someone, and no one her family? What do I make of a culture in which pregnant mothers are fussed over, babies adored, yet children and youth are manipulated by school, society, and the justice system? Lisa's anger against her losses even beyond her child-like understanding has set my own ghosts in motion. Students give form to my ghosts, terrors, and my desires. Lisa has taught me how to interpret what I experience differently. What her world asks from me it also answers from within me.

Romeo and Juliet for You: The third moment
February 13, 2004

I remember my ninth grade English teacher in India. I was anointed into the special world of English literature—heroic, tragic, terrible, and mysterious—I was 13-years-old. Mrs Morrison was an English schoolteacher who had come all the way from Essex, London to teach English to us "heathens," as she lovingly called us! I remember the day she was reading from *Antigone,* Antigone's desperate and courageous response to give her brother a proper burial, denied by the king, her uncle. As Mrs Morrison read, I felt something obscure open up inside me—I recognized some unknown, some strange sense of rage against the lot of women, a frenzied silentless sobbing, a delirium of tears. I looked outside myself to keep my sanity, but outside the rain was swirling in a mad rage beating down everywhere. Or was it? I knew I was transported. I was enthralled by Antigone's unflinching courage. Now I am an English teacher.

Teaching *Romeo and Juliet* is a pleasure and a discovery for me. At the facility we started the spring semester reading Shakespeare's *Romeo and Juliet,* always a favorite with English teachers. The students started out with great expectations. And so did I. But I was not permitted to watch them practice as they "knew what we are doing." The students immersed themselves in reading and rehearsing Shakespeare. The day of the final presentation, I was eager, and nervous. The entire facility attended the play called "*Romeo and Juliet, For You!*" To my total surprise, there was neither a Romeo nor a Juliet in the play, let alone any of the other characters. I need not have worried if the students would keep the Montagues and the Capulets on the right side of the blood feud or keep the peace for two hours without running their own blood feud. Somewhere between Leonardo deCaprio as Romeo and the beat of *West Side Story,* that afternoon the detention facility watched a musical about the Crips and the Bloods—two of the deadliest gangs in the United States.

On stage was a cast of actors dressed in hooded sweatshirts and pants in red and blue to distinguish between the Crips and the Bloods. Each side wore a different set of bandannas and baseball caps in blue and red. The music played from a cassette player, and students choreographed—which I was beginning to understand, perhaps, appreciate somewhat—rap. Dancing, humping, grinding, gyrating, the Crips and Bloods dizzied across the makeshift stage. Students had produced and directed a remix of "gansta" music and enacted a story— supposedly *Romeo and Juliet* with a happy ending! In the last scene, the Crips and Bloods throw up their baseball caps and sweatshirts as a gesture of peace and reconciliation. While the students performed with wonderful aplomb, the students in the audience cheered and screamed with enthusiasm.

Shell-shocked, the adults in the audience sat on the bleachers. Gang talk is banned in juvenile and most adult prisons, as are gang signs and rap music. Throughout the performance, the students were passionate and did convey an immediate and intense sense of life and drama. Secretly, I was in awe, proud of a job well done! For me the play was daring, exuberant, and disturbing. While I watched the ravages of Shakespeare, I was hypnotized by the creative magic of the students. I was also conscious of the seismic vibrations building in the administrative office—wondering when I would be summoned to explain what had just happened on stage! I was walking the perilous line between collision and collusion.

My students had activated my secret world, my inner life where I craved for creative transformation of English literature. The play opened the students' world to me in a new way because they had shocked me awake, pried their world open, thus opening mine. Whoever said girls behind bars had ADHD, poor cognitive decision-making skills, and low IQ? Between the chanting and the dancing that was "*Romeo and Juliet For You!*" I was initiated into the sacred, embodied, forbidden world of students that felt deeper than any form of rational knowledge. I experienced that the best drama is subversive of all politics, in literature or in life. Students' creative energy enabled me to learn how to questions myself as an English teacher, and how to endure myself—to confront my own values. Students opened a new space that cleared the overcrowding in my head caused by literary giants long dead. This was my literary wide-awakening, Virginia Woolf style.

Yes, Mr Principal, in "real" school, teachers make a difference in students' lives. In a surreal one like detention, students make a difference in my life. I was not directly confronted about the "gansta" play, but the tension hung in the air, questioning my ability to teach like a "real" English teacher. How could I convince the world that my students are hard working? In detention, I was not focused on the war against poverty, prejudice, and illiteracy. The students were negotiating and resisting poverty, prejudice, and illiteracy. I was too busy fighting against my own upbringing, straining the limits of my values, questioning the received wisdom of my teaching. In this marginalized space, where everyone is on edge, I am learning to relinquish established patterns of teaching in exchange for the possibility of simply experiencing. Without these possibilities my story is incomplete.

Synthetic snow cones and spicy kebabs: The fourth moment June 21, 2005

It is the first day of summer, so I have brought a snow cone machine for the students to compensate for having to attend summer school while their friends were off for the summer. When the last taste of the snow cone slips away, I will bribe them with some other inexpensive treat. It is easy to please children in detention when the routine of surveillance takes away all forms of ownership leaving students with little more than memories and hope. I watch them linger long over their cones, the synthetic blue and red trickling all over their hands. Sam, a 14-year-old student, asks me, "Grandma, do you have snow cones in India?" and I tell her we use a different set of flavors. She hands me hers, saying "You have to taste the blueberry, you will love it." Sam, this is synthetic and carcinogenic and repulsive, I think. Of course, I do not say anything.

Sam is sensitive to my hesitation and asks, "Do you not eat American food?" Innocent question, and yet my mind starts intellectualizing every word. American food? The fat steaks and chocolate syrup, one heavily doused in oil, the other in sugar—the love of Americans—churns rudely in my stomach and my head. I take her precious cone, made even more precious in detention, not wanting to offend a generous, loving, young kid. Why was the cone so refreshing to her and not to me? Suddenly, I hated being a foreigner, hated the looks the other teachers were giving me. I hated the Indian taste buds for their repulsion of blue snow cones, their spicy kebab cravings. I should have savored this moment of trust and love from students that other teachers were working hard to attain. Instead, my self-consciousness hung in the air like stale, familiar perfume, while my repulsion simmered and pulsated inside me.

Sam and some of the other students have adopted me as their grandmother. It gives them the chance for personal contact, intimacy, and trust. I miss my children grown now, the closeness of family and friends, and the fulfillment that comes from feeling needed. We are both forced to invent relationships; our desires set the words in motion and a longing that things might be different. Even as Sam and the other students want to belong and have a home, build relationships, the metaphor of grandma conjures up contradictory images—could I fulfill the promise of safety and love, as well as erase the memory of their exclusion and neglect? Or am I blatantly using Sam's metaphor to fulfill my needs and tell stories about my life? I am guilty of repositioning and reinterpreting my story within hers.

Chain by chain: The fifth moment August 1, 2006

As I greet the students in the class, their faces bright with anticipation, a handful of students almost knock me over my own desk as they hug me, then grab me once again to make sure I am okay! For as long as I can remember, their histories have not changed, yet *we* have changed. There is total misalignment between the prescribed standardized curriculum and my teaching, but I do not feel any long lasting discomfort over it. I am not allowed more than 18 students; however, my class is overflowing, and some have to sit on the carpet. I look at the odd bunch ranging from 11 to 21. The facility has stopped questioning the students for coming to my class outside their schedule. The principal continues to make snide remarks about my teaching methods and professional expertise, suggesting I enroll in a course on "real" teaching and classroom management in graduate school. In my scheme of things, he does not exist and I just fall short of telling him so.

Today the students and I plan to crochet. A far cry from the English teacher I was who was once moved to tears by the reading of *Antigone*! We tell stories, yell across the room, quarrel with each other, share our secrets, and crochet chain by chain, link by link. Time flies and I am moved to tears again—today I have learned to crochet from my students. What I have recounted is a revelation conveying the memory of a magical teaching and learning moment of fulfillment. There is no representation quite like it, and its achieved happiness will save it from being replicated.

I am trying to educate students who I am told by the facility need it most desperately. I wonder now, though, what does this education really do? What should an education do for a young girl behind bars? My parents were educated; they had learned their values through Indian education. I am educated; I have learned my values from Western education. And then I left the country, because the values from Western education had become important to me. Where do the students I now teach go when the values from their education stop being valuable to them?

In a country with over a billion people and no space to stand, time and space in India were both rare. Here I have the time and space but have sacrificed the camaraderie of my life for the pursuit of personal goals. *Personal* goals. Goals I acquired through my western education. Goals that need time. Goals that need space. Which I found. I also found that the overcrowding in India is a protective blanket, stained, colorful, always there, passed through generational embodied knowledge among people milling all around—seeping through the layers of tradition—a closeness whose existence I felt without comprehending *how* it came to be. In the United States why is it that this reassuring intimacy I find in detention, among my students, but absent in the world outside? Perhaps because coming into a detention classroom is a chance to forget worldly pursuit.

Worldly pursuit. What does a young girl behind bars pursue? I look at Cassandra, the child, the woman, reading *Chicken Soup* something or the other, and I think, is there any room for pursuit in her life? She came into the world, abandoned on day one, tossed around like a rubber ball from foster care to foster care, school to school, facility to facility. Foster care is expensive, as is schooling and detention, and her life is needed, precious, worth far more locked up and inside detention than free on the outside. So she moves from school suspension, expulsion, detention, probation, and rehabilitation, living her daily routine always someone else's child, someone else's problem, someone else's case while her body weeps silently in more ways than one. Self-harming, raging, inflicting, acting, manipulating, dying. What will Cassandra pursue?

I have pursued what I am trained to pursue, rarely challenging my value system and beliefs. I see my own fulfillment on the terms I have been taught to measure myself by. How do I begin to look at pursuit and fulfillment from another lens? Now I look at Cassandra and feel the sterility of my own world. To me, pursuit lay in leaving India for life in the United States of America. My country—over a billion people and a rich cultural heritage—was crowded, too crowded for one woman to follow her quest. I boarded a plane in pursuit of space, time, and personal goals. I found and treasured space, time, and personal goals for what they allowed me to accomplish, who they allowed me to be; I hate them for what they took away from me. For, sometimes, when the pursuit is forgotten, I long to find myself again.

This is also a story of my erasure. An erasure of my history and ancestral memory. An erasure of experience, knowledge, and life. But there is another kind of erasure. The erasure of importance, of significance—a woman in India, a woman from India. Through their plays, stories, poems, and essays students give my memories significance. I remember who I am by remembering the places that have power and meaning in my life. But I fear I may lose this knowledge. So I lie to myself. I am dishonest in my refusal to take a look at the depth of my feelings, to pick up the fragments of my life and smooth the jagged edges. How am I to understand the sobbing body of Lisa or the marks on Cassandra's body—images of a world of despair if I know nothing of such pain? How am I to know what to do or teach? My shock, my outrage pales before students' lived experience.

The last day: The sixth moment March, 2009

I never kept count of the times I drove from home to the detention facility. In the years since the first day, it has been numerous, because the students were like a magnet whose insistent attraction pulled me to the facility more times than I needed to be there. Students activated something inside me, engaged me as deeply as possible, brought their own life into it, forced mine into theirs, now our present histories are seeped each in the other's body, the exchange of sisters, soul mates, children, mothers, the tenderness and the poignancy indestructible. As soon as I arrived home from school, I would start thinking about the next time I would return. The ability to return day upon day was a dense, comfortable joy.

But this time is different. After this trip there is no classroom to which to return. I have decided to leave my full-time teaching assignment and visit the facility once a week as a researcher to continue with the autobiographical writing project. Teaching in detention had taken me back into my history, to my past— and even, it seems, my childhood itself—that would soon no longer be mine. It was all too brief. It crept into my skin as I lived through it, and when it is gone I am left with emptiness. No one else knows what it feels like, even if they have their own experiences with the hidden places of the past. Who could have imagined there would be so much to reflect in detention, so many experiences that had remained unknown and unrecognized in teaching and learning? I needed the students to be there always, somehow, and not just in my heart. My future classrooms bear the imprint of all my detention students.

In the years I have spent sitting in this classroom, I have learned the more knowledge I have, the greater becomes the gap between academic knowledge I acquire and what I experience in my classroom. Watching the two ten year olds, Pat and Waker, I am amazed but afraid too, that my teacher training tells me what a young girl behind bars is, blithely ascribing the label of delinquency to the two ten year olds. Sitting by them, following them play Judge Judy a few inches away from my desk, the joy of performance glistening on their faces, I ask myself, What do I know about their world?—that Pat knows all about Judge Judy's court and nothing about Wordsworth, that Waker knows how to swim the entire stretch of a river—nothing about how to navigate an essay. Can I hold all this experience together and still pretend that I know what knowledge is important? Can I imagine Pat and Waker evolving into women I want them to be?

Firsthand knowledge of students in detention has been difficult for me; knowledge of students in detention is also outside the short-term demands of modernist schooling and teaching. Knowledge of students in detention teaches me of my own fallibility, and is an antithesis to what is considered as progress. In the past, I have sought to disregard knowledge when its sources lay outside my precious and expensive education. By silencing those with nonnormative lived experiences, I minimized the contradictions in my political or educational standing, and so felt safer. Now when I am by Pat and Waker, I am simply here. I watch them intently and feel myself part of their moment. I do not feel the need to explain the experience. I wonder sometimes, though, whether I am responding to the wrong question when it comes to asking, "What is a young girl behind bars?" Perhaps the issue is not whether I have the authority to ask the question, but whether I believe I have the authority to help shape and transform their world.

What being a teacher has come to mean to me, sitting my mornings in the classroom, hearing the call of Judge Judy through the laughter of Pat and Waker, so far removed from Tyler and Bobbitt, and even the NCLB Act, is this: *Listen to students, listen to what they have to say, pay attention to what they do not say.* I have rediscovered in students my own lived experience, the pharmakon to my teaching—the remedy that makes me is also the poison that threatens to break me.

Pat and Waker's life-stories tell me memories are fragile, beliefs are tenuous, contexts are temporary, knowledge is partial. Life-stories tell me nothing is stable—not Tyler, not Bobbitt, not Pinar, not Foucault. My students take the qualities that are supposed to render them delinquent and use them defiantly as well as strategically to transform my moral ground in every sense. My sojourn ends with a warm feeling washing over me, crying, smiling; it is time to stop. Time to begin a different journey, the old one stitched under the lining of the new, the texture brighter, perhaps, a little heavier.

New understandings: The seventh moment January, 2012

This book is about rereading the life-stories of girls behind bars. It is also a rereading of my own life-story through the life-stories of girls behind bars. I no longer teach at the facility; however, I call on students to testify about curriculum and teaching. I present precious moments from my experience at the facility without giving in to the impulse to theorize or instruct. The moments are interpretive, suggesting that something about my experience evades a full understanding, an indefinable element that illuminates and hides. This is the story of my initiation into education in detention, encounters with the other, responses to the volatile, experiences that invite, exalt, and disturb—the story of my transformation.

Time has passed. I cannot remember what I felt when I said my final goodbye, although I do remember how I felt when I returned to visit the facility in late 2009 to find that the facility was closing. This should be a moment of happiness—no child needs detention; however, it felt like an absence implanted in my autoethnographic story that made everything that had gone before it transitory and difficult to describe. Suddenly, the troubling stories were closed off to me, and that was more troubling and terrifying than students' stories had ever been. Indeed, the experience demonstrated how unstable and indeterminate life can be—here today, gone tomorrow now stands for an ominous hole that darkens my sense and my senses.

How do I deal with this absence of students in my experience? I am now left to deal with my own psychic fragments that make thinking about the experience impossible. There is no "I told you so" that "detention is impossible," just a sudden cleavage that dislocates feeling, memory, experience, who I am, destruction of time that is not on my terms. There were always dislocations and interruptions in detention further punctuated by unimaginable anguish, a quest, lives in transit. Is my loss a desire for the other? Yes, we do need each other, my students and I.

When I think of the magic of our secret classroom rituals and the hypnotic charm of students' eccentricities, I am drawn deeply toward my students. The refrains of their stories blend into mine, their emotional needs that match mine evoke an embodied closeness empowering the relationship among us. This physical absorption restructures my memory as an embodied space. The adult in me realizes that I need to be separate from students; the child wants to remain connected with students. As a teacher, I attempt to keep everything in the classroom calm on the outside while chaos breaks loose inside me. My body speaks in many registers of the profound disordering of my world. I remember the first day at the facility and the feeling of alienation. Yet, how can the crisscross of life histories bring us in such a synchrony of impassioned togetherness?

How can the passionate and the disturbing inhabit the same space and at the same time? Today I experience difference more fully, more deeply, and more reflectively. In a sense this story is a secret unfolding of the person, dare I say woman, behind the research. The nature of the experiences I write about has certainly affected the ways in which I write about them. Differences are felt, they are embodied and moral. My inability to resolve students' stories is also part of my story. Pat's story—Lisa's story, my story, all the other stories—cannot be told as one central story of education in detention; it is both the interruption and the counter story. Once a story is told, ways of reading it change. As students invite me into their lives, the thresholds I cross lead me relentlessly into my own.

I know the story is already slipping away from me, looking for a way to elude me once again. Writing reveals what I do not know about myself before I have written it. But some things I will never know in spite of the writing. If there is one thing I have experienced, it is not to underestimate the power of not knowing. When I decided to leave India, all I knew was that the decision felt amiss, like a story that does not make sense, that I would now stay away from home, that my children did not need me as they once did, and I was uncomfortable. Over the years, memory and experience have transformed what it means to be a woman in India. I have examined the word "woman" from so many angles that I have almost forgotten why I examine the word at all. My problem is, I cannot bear witness to my experience because it means letting go of the tradition, the beliefs, the knowledge that have proven deceptive anyway. Perhaps I have become an embittered feminist or a poststructural skeptic fighting against the impossibility of knowledge. Perhaps my ability to represent myself or anyone else is in jeopardy, my autoethnography is in crisis.

I needed—I still need—to make sense of my experiences and my memories, old and new. I acquired a brand new identity as a researcher, a new title to my old one, a teacher. I read about paradigm shifts, the call for self-reflexive scholarship, the turn to messy, vulnerable texts, and the loss of clarity, the stammering of not knowing. In detention I was already face to face with uncertainty, messiness, stammering; only now the capacity to intellectualize my experience and the words to articulate the condition of not knowing is acknowledged.

So now I am an autoethnographer and subject of my own research. There is a chasm between students' and my lived experiences and the stories I write about, and it troubles me. I am concerned that my stories threaten to falsify experience in my pursuit of academic knowledge. When I am telling stories of sadness and grief, my voice is not broken, the articulation itself is an insult. In fact, I have learned how to turn pain, mine and my students' pain, into knowledge. I am not afraid of the subjectivity in my stories or the vulnerability in their telling. What I am more afraid of is how I am able to compose stories, all the while insulating myself under ontologies, epistemologies, and methodologies that instead make me feel that if I really understood students' lives I would want to forget, not remember. Because what breaks my heart also chokes my voice. It does not matter what frame of reference I use, what methodology I hide under—I cannot write how I actually feel. In interpreting life stories, some things hold meaning for me alone and I keep them to myself. Some losses I can never recover, except in memory.

Why do I still persist? Maybe if I recover from my lived experience I will be able to write coolly, calmly, fully composed—an intellectual and a scholar, with work to do. But what of the work that needs to be messy, vulnerable, close to the bone? The old teacher in me says I have started my own vagina monologue, speculum in hand. The messy me I have turned into says that some stories I cannot tell any other way. Have I abandoned my Western education, my Indian tradition, my life-stories, my students' stories? How can I? They are saturated in my marrow, my veins—my body will always carry traces of all that has touched me, excited me, angered me, frustrated me, and escaped me. So I think of students in the middle of the night. I think of them when I am wide-awake. And if I have ever felt that for a long time someone or something was making its way toward me, my students have made me feel that way. Dearest Sam, Pat, Waker, Cassandra, and most of all, Lisa, I am the one who has found the message in the bottle—and the finder is the keeper for posterity.

Author's Notes

1. Pseudonyms have been used for all participants in this study.
2. For the purpose of this study, permission for the writing project was granted by the Director of the detention facility. Permission was also granted for using official documents such as the facility's handbook and official website, the author's journal and personal notes, and students' journals from 2003 onwards that were written before the research project started
3. The study was conducted with IRB approval.
4. Excerpts from Sharonika, Amanda, and Chantia's life stories have been published in 2010 in the journal, *Race, Ethnicity and Education* 13(3), 327–47, under the title "Contesting institutional discourse to create new possibilities for understanding lived experience: Life-stories of young women in detention, rehabilitation, and education."

List of References

Addams, J. (1925). *The Child, the Clinic and the Court*. New York: New Republic.

Alexander, B. K. (2005). "Performance ethnography." In N. K. Denzin and Y. S. Lincoln (eds), *The Sage Handbook of Qualitative Research* (pp. 411–41). Thousand Oaks, CA: Sage Publications.

Anderson, L. (2006). "Analytic autoethnography." *Journal of Contemporary Ethnography* 35(4), 373–95.

Apple, M. (2004). *Ideology and Curriculum*. New York: RoutledgeFalmer.

Arias, A. (2001). "Authoring ethnicized subjects: Rigoberta Menchu and the performative production of the subaltern self." *PMLA* 116(1), 75–88.

Arrigo, B. (1999). "Constitutive theory and the homeless identity: The discourse of a community deviant." In S. Henry and D. Milovanovic (eds), *Constitutive Criminology at Work: Applications to Crime and Justice* (pp. 67–86). Albany, NY: State University of New York Press.

Baker, B. (2001). *In Perpetual Motion: Theories of Power, Educational History, and the Child*. New York: Peter Lang.

— (2002). The hunt for disability: The new eugenics and the normalization of school children. *Teachers College Record*. Retrieved 23 January 2009. www.tcrecord.org/PrintContent.asp?ContentID=10895

Baker, D. B. and Maguire, C. P. (2005). "Mentoring in historical perspective." In D. L. DuBois and M. M. Karcher (eds), *Handbook of Youth Mentoring* (pp. 14–30). Thousand Oaks, CA: Sage Publications.

Baudrillard, J. (1983). *Simulations*. (P. Foss, P. Patton, and P. Beitchman, Trans.). New York: Semiotext (e).

Behar, R. (1997). *The Vulnerable Observer: Anthropology that Breaks Your Heart*. Boston: Beacon Press.

Blechman, E. A. and Bopp, J. M. (2005). "Juvenile offenders." In D. L. Dubois and M. J. Karcher (eds), *Handbook of Youth Mentoring* (pp. 454–66). Thousand Oaks, CA: Sage Publications.

Bochner, A. P. and Ellis, C. S. (2002). *Ethnographically Speaking: Autoethnography, Literature and Aesthetics*. Walnut Creek California: Altmira Press.

Braidotti, R. (1993). "Embodiment, sexual difference, and the nomadic subject." *Hypatia* 8(1), 1–13.

Brereton, B. (1998). "Gendered testimonies: Autobiographies, diaries and letters by women as sources for Caribbean history." *Feminist Review* 59, 23–7.

Britzman, D. (1989). "Who has the floor? Curriculum teaching and the English student teacher's search for voice." *Curriculum Inquiry* 19, 143–62.

— (1995). "Is there a queer pedagogy? Or, stop reading straight." *Educational Theory* 45(2), 151–65.

— (1998). *Lost Subjects, Contested Objects: Toward a Psychoanalytic Inquiry of Learning.* Albany, NY: State University of New York Press.

— (2000). "'The question of belief': Writing poststructural ethnography." In E. A. St. Pierre and W. S. Pillow (eds), *Working the Ruins: Feminist Poststructural Theory and Methods in Education* (pp. 27–40). New York: Routledge.

— (2003). *After-Education: Anna Freud, Melanie Klein, and Psychoanalytic Histories of Learning.* Albany, NY: State University of New York.

— (2009). *The Very Thought of Education: Psychoanalysis and the Impossible Professions.* Albany, NY: State University of New York Press.

Brunson, R. K. and Miller, J. (2001). "Girls and gangs." In C. M. Renzetti and L. Goodstein (eds), *Women, Crime, and Criminal Justice: Original Feminist Readings* (pp. 44–59). New York: Oxford University Press.

Burnett, J. H. (1969). "Ceremony, rites, and economy in the student system of an American high school." *Human Organization* 28(1), 1–9.

Butler, J. (1990). *Gender Trouble.* New York: Routledge.

— (1992). "Contingent foundations: Feminism and the question of 'post-modernism.'" In J. Butler and J. W. Scott (eds), *Feminists Theorize the Political* (pp. 3–21). New York: Routledge.

— (1997). *Excitable Speech: A Politics of the Performative.* New York: Routledge.

— (2005). *Giving an Account of Oneself.* New York: Fordham University Press.

Chang, H. (2008). *Autoethnography as Method.* Walnut Creek, CA: Left Coast Press.

Chesney-Lind, M. (2001). "'Out of sight, out of mind': Girls in the juvenile justice system." In C. M. Renzetti and L. Goodstein (eds), *Women, Crime, and Criminal Justice: Original Feminist Readings* (pp. 27–43). New York: Oxford University Press.

Coulter, E. (1913). *The Children in the Shadow.* New York: McBride, Nast.

Crenshaw, K. (2001) "Race reform and retrenchment: Transformation and legitimation in antidiscrimination law." In K. Crenshaw, K. Thomas, and G. Peller (eds), *Critical Race Theory: The Key Writings that Formed the Movement* (pp. 103–26). New York: New Press.

Cussick, P. A. (1973). *Inside High School: The Student's World.* New York: Holt, Rinehart and Winston.

Cusset, F. (2008). *French Theory: How Foucault, Derrida, Deleuze, and Co. Transformed the Intellectual Life of the United States* (J. Port, Trans.). Minneapolis: University of Minnesota Press.

Daniels, H. (2007). *The Cambridge Companion to Vygotsky.* Cambridge: Cambridge University Press.

Delamont, S. (2009). "The only honest thing: Autoethnography, reflexivity and small crises in fieldwork." *Ethnography and Education* 4(1), 51–63.

Deleuze, G. (1977). "Anti-Oedipus," trans. Janis Forman. *Semiotext (e)* 2(3), 77–85.

— (1990). *The Logic of Sense* (M. Lester and C. Stivale, Trans.). New York: Columbia University Press.

— (1994). *Difference and Repetition* (P. Patton, Trans.). New York: Columbia University Press.

Denzin, N. K. (2006). "Analytic autoethnography, or déjà vu all over again." *Journal of Contemporary Ethnography* 35(4), 419–28.

Denzin, N. K., Lincoln, Y. S., and Smith, L. T. (eds) (2005). "Introduction." *The Sage Handbook of Qualitative Research* (pp. 1–32). Thousand Oaks, CA: Sage Publications.

Derrida, J. (1970). "Structure, sign and play in the discourse of the human sciences" (R. Macksey, Trans.). In R. Macksey and E. Donato (eds), *The Sructuralist Controversy: The Languages of Criticism and the Sciences of Man* (pp. 247–72). Baltimore: Johns Hopkins University Press.

— (1972). *The Other Heading: Reflections on Today's Europe* (P. Brault and M. B. Naas, Trans.). Bloomington: Indiana University Press.

— (1978). *Writing and Difference* (A. Bass, Trans.). Chicago: University of Chicago Press.

— (1981a). *Positions* (A. Bass, Trans.). Chicago: University of Chicago Press.

— (1981b). *The Law of Genre* (A. Ronell, Trans.). In W. J. T. Mitchell (ed.), *On Narrative* (pp. 51–77). Chicago: University of Chicago Press.

— (1982). *Margins of Philosophy* (A. Bass, Trans.). Chicago: University of Chicago Press.

— (1987). *The Truth in Painting* (Geoff Bennington, Trans.). Chicago: University of Chicago Press.

— (1988). *Limited Inc* (G. Graff, ed., J. Mehlman and S. Weber, Trans.). Evanston, IL: Northwestern University Press.

— (1992). "Force of law: The 'mystical foundation of authority.'" In D. Cornell, M. Rosenfeld, and D. G. Carlson (eds), *Deconstruction and the Possibility of Justice* (pp. 3–67). New York: Routledge.

— (1994). *Specters of Marx, the State of the Debt, the Work of Mourning, & the New International,* (Peggy Kamuf, Trans.). New York: Routledge.

— (1995). "'Eating well' or the calculation of the subject." In E. Weber (ed.), *Points . . . Interviews, 1974–1994* (P. Kamuf et al., Trans.) (pp. 255–87). Stanford, CA: Stanford University Press.

— (2001). "Deconstructions: The im-possible" (H. Tomlinsonn, Trans.). In S. Lotringer and S. Cohen (eds), *French Theory in America* (pp. 13–31). New York: Routledge.

Derrida, J. and Ronell, A. (1980). "The law of genre." *Critical Inquiry* 7(1), 55–81.

Dubois, D. L. and Karcher, M. J. (2005). "Youth mentoring: Theory, research, and practice." In D. L. Dubois and M. J. Karcher (eds), *Handbook of Youth Mentoring* (pp. 2–11). Thousand Oaks, CA: Sage Publications.

Dyson, M. (2007). "My story in a profession of stories: Auto ethnography – an empowering methodology for educators." *Australian Journal of Teacher Education* 32(1), 36–48.

Ellingson, L. and Ellis, C. (2008). "Autoethnography as constructivist project." In
J. A. Holstein and J. F. Gubrium (eds), *Handbook of Contructivist Research*
(pp. 445–66). New York: Guiford Press.

Ellis, C. (2004). *The Ethnographic I: A Methodological Novel about Autoethnography.*
Walnut Creek, CA: AltaMira Press.

— (2007). "Telling secrets, revealing lives: Relational ethics in research with intimate
others." *Qualitative Inquiry* 13(1), 3–29.

— (2009). "Telling tales on neighbors: Ethics in two voices." *International Review of
Qualitative Research* 2(1), 3–28.

Ellis, C. and Bochner, A. P. (2000). "Autoethnography, personal narrative, reflexivity." In
Norman K. Denzin and Yvonna S. Lincoln (eds), *Handbook of Qualitative Research*
(2nd edn, pp.733–68). Thousand Oaks, CA: Sage Publications.

— (2006). "Analyzing analytic autoethnography: An autopsy." *Journal of Contemporary
Ethnography* 35(4), 429–49.

Emmanuel, S. M. and Gould, P. (eds) (2002). *Modern Philosophy – from Descartes to
Nietzsche: An Anthology.* Malden, MA: Blackwell.

Feld, B. C. (1999). *Bad Kids.* New York: Oxford University Press.

Felman, S. (1982). "Psychoanalysis and education: Teaching terminable and
interminable." *Yale French Studies* 63, 21–44.

— (2000). "In an era of testimony: Claude Lanzmann's Shoah." *Yale French Studies,*
No. 97: 50 Years of Yale French Studies: A commemorative anthology, Part 2:
1980–1998, 103–50.

Felman, S. and Laub, D. M. D. (1992). *Testimony: Crises of Witnessing in Literature,
Psychoanalysis, and History.* New York: Routledge.

Fine, M. and McClelland, S. I. (2006). "Sexuality education and desire: Still missing after
all these years." *Harvard Educational Review* 76(3), 297–338.

Firth, R. (1957). *Man and Culture: An Evaluation of the Work of Bronislow Malinowski.*
London: Routledge and Kegan Paul.

Foucault, M. (1965). *Madness and Civilization: A History of Insanity in the Age of
Reason.* New York: Random House.

— (1972a). *Archaeology of Knowledge* (Alan Sheridan, Trans.). New York: Pantheon.

— (1972b). *Power/Knowledge: Selected Interviews and Other Writings* (C. Gordon, ed.).
New York: Pantheon Books.

— (1973). *The Birth of the Clinic: An Archeology of Medical Perception.* New York:
Vintage Books.

— (1977). *Discipline and Punish.* New York: Vintage Books.

— (1978). *The History of Sexuality: An Introduction.* New York: Vintage Books.

— (1984a). "What is enlightenment?" In P. Rabinow (ed.), *The Foucault Reader*
(pp. 32–50). New York: Pantheon.

— (1984b). "Nietzsche, genealogy, history." In P. Rabinow (ed.), *The Foucault Reader*
(pp. 76–100). New York: Pantheon.

— (1990). *Politics, Philosophy, Culture: Interviews and other Writings, 1977–1984.*
     New York: Routledge.

Galton, F. (1881). *Inquiries into Human Faculty and its Development.* London:
     Everyman's Library.

Gilmore, L. (1994). *Autobiographics: A Feminist Theory of Women's Self- Representation.*
     Ithaca, NY: Cornell University Press.

— (2001) *The Limits of Autobiography: Trauma and Testimony.* Ithaca, NY: Cornell
     University Press.

Goodall, H. L. (2000). *Writing the New Ethnography.* Walnut Creek, CA: AltaMira.

— (2003). "What is interpretive ethnography? An eclectic's tale." In R. P. Clair (ed.),
     Expressions of Ethnography: Novel Approaches to Qualitative Methods (pp. 55–63).
     Albany: State University of New York Press.

Goodson, I. F. (2003). *Professional Knowledge, Professional Lives.* Maidenhead, England:
     Open University Press.

Goodstein, L. (2001). "Introduction: Women, crime, and criminal justice – An overview."
     In C. M. Renzetti and L. Goodstein (eds), *Women, Crime, and Criminal Justice:
     Original Feminist Readings* (pp. 1–12). New York: Oxford University Press.

Gould, E. R. L. (1895). "The statistical study of hereditary criminality." Proceedings of
     the National Conference of Charities and Correction (PNCCC) in The ANNALS of
     the American Academy of Political and Social Science 5(5), 134–43.

Greene, M. (2000). *Releasing the Imagination.* San Francisco: Jossey-Bass.

Grumet, M. (1980). "Autobiography and reconceptualization." *Journal of Curriculum
     Theorizing* 2, 155–8.

— (1988). *Bitter Milk: Women and Teaching.* Amherst, MA: University of Massachusetts
     Press.

— (2006). "Where does the world go when schooling is about schooling?" *Journal of
     Curriculum Theory* 2(3), 47–54.

Hekman, S. (1991). "Reconstituting the subject: Feminism, modernism, and
     postmodernism." *Hypatia* 6(2), 44–63.

Herman, J. L. (1992). *Trauma and Recovery.* New York: Basic Books.

Holt, N. L. (2003). "Representation, legitimation, and autoethnography: An autoethnographic
     writing story." *International Journal of Qualitative Methods* 2(1), 18–28.

hooks, bell. (1998). *Teaching to Transgress: Education as the Practice of Freedom.*
     New York: Routledge.

Humphreys, M. (2005). "Getting personal: Reflexivity and autoethnograhic vignettes."
     Qualitative Inquiry 11, 840–60.

Jones, S. H. (2005a). "(M)othering loss: Telling adoption stories, telling performativity."
     Text and Performance Quarterly 25(2), 113–35.

— (2005b). "Autoethnography: Making the personal political." In Norman K. Denzin
     and Yvonna S. Lincoln (eds), *Handbook of Qualitative Research* (pp. 763–91).
     Thousand Oaks, CA: Sage Publications.

Kennedy, B. M. (2000). *Deleuze and Cinema: The Aesthetics of Sensation*. Edinburgh: Edinburgh University Press.

Kerlin, I. N. (1890). "The moral imbecile." Proceedings of the National Conference of Charities and Correction (PNCCC) in The ANNALS of the American Academy of Political and Social Science 1(2), 244–50.

King, A. R. (1967). *The School at Mopass: A Problem of Identity*. New York: Holt, Rinehart and Winston.

Krisberg, B. (2005). *Juvenile Justice*. New York: Sage Publications.

Kristeva, J. (1980). *Desire in Language* (L. Roudiez, Trans.). New York: Columbia University Press.

— (1984). *Revolution in Poetic Language* (M. Waller, Trans.). New York: Columbia University Press.

— (1987). *In the Beginning was Love: Psychoanalysis and Faith* (A. Goldhammer, Trans.). New York: Columbia University Press.

Lacan, J. (1977). *The Four Fundamental Concepts of Psychoanalysis*. London: Hogarth Press.

Ladson-Billings, G. (1997). "For colored girls who have considered suicide when the academy's not enough: Reflections of an African American woman scholar." In A. Newmann and P. L. Lather (1992). Critical frames in educational research: Feminist and post-structural perspectives. *Theory into Practice* 31(2), 87–99.

Lather, P. (1992). "Critical frames in educational research: Feminist and post-structural perspectives." *Theory into Practice* 31(2), (Spring), 87–99.

— (1996). "Troubling clarity: The politics of accessible language." *Harvard Educational Review* 66(3), 525–45.

— (2000a). "Reading the image of Rigoberta Menchú: Undecidability and language lessons." *Qualitative Studies in Education* 13(2), 153–62.

— (2000b). "Drawing the line at angels: Working the ruins of feminist ethnography." In E. A. St. Pierre and W. S. Pillow (eds), *Working the Ruins: Feminist Poststructural Theory and Methods in Education* (pp. 284–311). New York: Routledge.

— (2001). "Postbook: Working the ruins of feminist ethnography." *Signs: Journal of Women in Culture and Society* 27(1), 199–227.

— (2004). "This is your father's paradigm: Government intrusion and the case of qualitative research in education." *Qualitative Inquiry* 10(1), 15–34.

Lather, P. and Smithies, C. (1997). *Troubling the Angels: Women Living with HIV/AIDS*. Boulder, CO: Westview Press.

Lombroso, C. (1893). *Crime, its Causes and Remedies* (H. P. Horton, Trans.). Boston: Little, Brown.

Lorde, A. (1984). *Sister Outsider: Essays and Speeches*. Berkeley, CA: Crossing Press.

Lyotard, J.-F. (1984). *The Postmodern Condition: A Report on Knowledge* (G. Bennington and B. Maussumi, Trans.). Minneapolis: University of Minnesota Press.

Malinowski, B. (1922). *Argonauts of the Western Pacific, an Account of Native Enterprise and Adventure in the Archipelagoes of Melanesian New Guinea*. London: George Routledge & Sons, Ltd. and New York: E. P. Dutton & Co.

Maréchal, G. (2010). "Autoethnography." In A. J. Mills, G. Durepos, and E. Wiebe (eds), *Encyclopedia of Case Study Research* (Vol. 2, pp. 43–5). Thousand Oaks, CA: Sage Publications.

McKay, N. Y. (1998). "The narrative self: Race, politics, and culture in Black American women's autobiography." In S. Smith and J. Watson (eds), *Women, Autobiography, Theory: A Reader* (pp. 96–107). Madison, WI: University of Wisconsin Press.

McNay, L. (1991). "The Foucauldian body and the exclusion of experience." *Hypatia* 6(3), 125–39.

Mead, M. (1928). *Coming of Age in Samoa: A Psychological Study of the Primitive Youth for Western Civilization*. New York: William Morrow and Company.

Meiners, E. (2007). *Right to be Hostile: Schools, Prisons, and the Making of Public Enemies*. New York: Routledge.

Miller, J. L. (2005). *Sounds of Silence Breaking: Women, Autobiography, Curriculum*. New York: Peter Lang.

Muncey, T. (2010). *Creating Autoethnographies*. Los Angeles: Sage Publications.

Newburn, T. and Shiner, M. (2005). *Dealing with Disaffection: Young People, Mentoring and Social Inclusion*. Portland, OR: Willan.

Nietzsche, F. (1967). *The Will to Power*. New York: Vintage Books.

— (2003). *Genealogy of Morals* (H. B. Samuel, Trans.). Mineola, NY: Dover.

Niranjana, T. (1992). *Siting Translation: History, Post-structuralism, and the Colonial Context*. Berkeley, CA: University of California Press.

No Child Left Behind Act (2001). Executive Summary. United States Department of Education. Retrieved 12January 2009, from www.ed.gov/nclb/overview/ intro/ execsumm.pdf

Okley, J. (1992). "Anthropology and autobiography: Participatory experience and embodied knowledge." In J. Okley and H. Callaway (eds), *Anthropology and Autobiography* (pp. 1–28). London: Routledge.

Olney, J. (1980). "Autobiography and the cultural moment." In *Autobiography: Essays theoretical and critical* (pp. 3–27). Princeton, NJ: Princeton University Press.

Peters, M. (ed.) (1998). *Naming the Multiple: Poststructuralism and Education*. Westport, CT: Bergin and Garvey.

— (2001). *Poststructuralism, Marxism, and Neoliberalism: Between Theory and Politics*. Lanham, MD: Rowman and Littlefield.

Piaget, J. (1947). *Psychology of Intelligence*. (M. Percy and D. E. Berlyne, Trans.). London: Routledge.

Pinar, W. F. (ed.) (1998). *Curriculum: Toward New Identities*. New York: Garland.

— (2000). *Curriculum Studies: The Reconceptualization*. Troy, NY: Educator's International Press.

— (2004). *What is Curriculum Theory?* Mahwah, NJ: Lawrence Erlbaum Associates.

Pinar, W. F. and Grumet, M. (1976). *Toward a Poor Curriculum*. Dubuque, IA: Kendall Hunt.

Pinar, W. F., Reynolds, W. M., Slattery, P., and Taubman, P. M. (eds) (2004). *Understanding Curriculum: An Introduction to the Study of Historical and Contemporary Curriculum Discourses*. New York: Peter Lang.

Platt, A. M. (1969). *The Child Savers: The Invention of Delinquency*. Chicago: University of Chicago Press.

Reed-Danahay, D. E. (1997). *Introduction. Auto/Ethnography: Rewriting the Self and the Social*. Reed-Danahay (ed.) (pp. 1–17). Oxford: Berg.

Rhodes, L. A. (2001). "Toward an anthropology of prisons." *Annual Review of Anthropology* 30, 65–83.

Richardson, L. (2000). "Evaluating ethnography." *Qualitative Inquiry* 6(2), 253–55.

— (2007). "Writing: A method of inquiry." In N. K. Denzin and Y. S. Lincoln (eds), *Handbook of Qualitative Research* (2nd edn, pp. 923–48). Thousand Oaks, CA: Sage Publications.

Rosenfeld, G. (1971). "*Shut those Thick Lips!*": *A Study of Slum School Failure*. New York: Holt, Rinehart and Winston.

Russell, B. (1945). *A History of Western Philosophy*. New York: Simon and Schuster.

Said, E. (1978). *Orientalism*. New York: Vintage.

Sanchez, L. (1999). "Sex, law, and the paradox of agency and resistance in the everyday practices of women in the 'Evergreen' sex trade." In S. Henry and D. Milovanovic (eds), *Constitutive Criminology at Work: Applications to Crime and Justice* (pp. 39–66). Albany, NY: State University of New York Press.

Saukko, P. (2003) *Doing Research in Cultural Studies*. Thousand Oaks: Sage Publications.

Saussure, F. de. (1959*). Course in General Linguistics* (C. Bally and A. Sechehaye, eds, W. Baskin, Trans.). New York: Philosophical Library.

Scheper-Hughes, N. (1992). *Death Without Weeping*. Berkeley:University of California Press.

Scheurich, J. J., and Foley, D. E. (2000). "Comments from the editors." *Qualitative Studies in Education* 13(2), 101–2.

Schrift, A. D. (2006). *Twentieth-Century French Philosophy: Key Themes and Thinkers*. Oxford, UK: Blackwell.

Sharma, S. (2010). "Contesting institutional discourse to create new possibilities for understanding lived experience: Life-stories of young women behind bars, rehabilitation, and education." *Race, Ethnicity and Education* 13(3), 327–47.

Slattery, P. (2006). *Curriculum Development in the Postmodern Era* (2nd edn). New York: Routledge.

Smith, L. M. and Geoffrey, W. (1968). *The Complexities of an Urban Classroom*. New York: Holt, Rinehart and Winston.

Smith, L. T. (1999). *Decolonizing Methodologies: Research and Indigenous Peoples*. Dunedin, NZ: University of Otaga Press.

Smith, S. (1994). "Identity's body." In K. Ashley, L. Gilmore, and G. Peters (eds), *Autobiography and Postmodernism* (pp. 266–92). Amherst, MA: University of Massachusetts Press.

Smith, S. and Watson, J. (1998). "Introduction: Situating subjectivity in women's autobiographical practices." In S. Smith and J. Watson (eds), *Women, Autobiography, Theory: A Reader* (pp. 3–56). Madison, WI: University of Wisconsin Press.

Snyder, H. N. and Sickmund, M. (2006). Juvenile Offenders and Victims: 2006 National Report. Office of Juvenile Justice and Delinquency Prevention (OJJDP). Office of Justice Program. U.S. Department of Justice. (also available online at www.ncjrs.gov/pdffiles1/ojjdp/221338. pdf)

Spivak, G. C. (1987). *In Other Worlds: Essays in Cultural Politics*. New York: Routledge.

— (2000). "Diasporas old and new: Women in the transnational world." In P. P. Trifonas (ed.), *Revolutionary Pedagogies: Cultural Politics, Instituting Education, and the Discourse of Theory* (pp. 3–29). New York: RoutledgeFalmer.

Spry, T. (2001). "Performing autoethnography: An embodied methodological praxis." *Qualitative Inquiry* 7(6), 706–32.

— (2011). *Body, Paper, Stage*. Walnut Street, CA: Left Coast Press.

St. Pierre, E. A. and Pillow, W. S. (2000). "Introduction: Inquiry among the ruins." In E. A. St. Pierre and W. S. Pillow (eds), *Working the Ruins: Feminist Poststructural Theory and Methods in Education* (pp. 1–24). New York: Routledge.

Stullken, E. H. (1956). "Misconceptions about juvenile delinquency." *The Journal of Criminal Law, Criminology, and Police Science* 46(6), March–April, 833–42.

Wang, H. and Yu, T. (2006). "Beyond promise: Autobiography and multicultural education." *Multicultural Education* 13(4), 29–35.

Winfield, A. G. (2007). *Eugenics and Education in America: Institutionalized Racism and the Implications of History, Ideology, and Memory*. New York: Peter Lang.

Wolcott, H. (1967). *A Kwakuitl Village and School*. New York: Holt, Rinehart and Winston.

Wyatt, J. (2008). "No longer loss: Autoethnographic stammering." *Qualitative Inquiry* 14(6), 955–67.

Zimmerman, M. (2000/2001). "Testimony, Menchu, me and you." *The Journal of the Midwest Modern Language Association* 33(3), 4–10.

Index

lived experience 23, 71, 84–8, 90–6, 98–9,
    102–4, 107, 109, 119–21, 124–30,
    132–3, 155–62, 164–6, 186–7,
    189–91

marginalization 21, 60, 79, 93, 100, 119,
    149, 160, 168
medical 32–3, 35, 39–40, 48–50, 61, 67,
    73–4, 77–8, 99
Meiners, E. 2, 20, 49, 157, 198
memory 92, 110, 117–18, 120–1, 124–5,
    128, 149, 166, 175, 183–4, 187–90,
    200
methodologies 22, 71, 82–4, 87, 93–4, 96,
    98, 100, 102, 155, 163, 190, 194
methods 50, 61, 82, 84–7, 91–2, 106,
    159–60, 163, 167, 172, 193, 197, 200
modernist subject 24, 54, 56–64, 67–8,
    70, 79

Nietzsche, F. 54, 57–8, 75, 195, 198
normalization ix, 33, 35, 39, 47, 74–5, 77,
    160, 167, 192
norms 6–8, 17–18, 49, 54, 56–7, 67, 75–6,
    91–2, 99, 125, 129, 132–3, 136–7,
    144, 161

objects 2, 6, 28, 33, 35–6, 40–2, 48, 51–2,
    57–8, 70, 73–4, 132–3, 145, 163,
    167–9
objects of discourse 25, 50, 155–6
Office of Juvenile Detention and
    Delinquency Prevention
    (OJDDP) 2
ontology 58, 67, 132, 190
opposition 10, 14, 25, 31, 56, 58, 62, 84,
    124, 144, 156
origins 29–30, 34–5, 41–2, 51, 72, 82, 91,
    114

Pat 186–7, 190
performativity 68–9, 133–8, 141–2, 147,
    151–2, 168, 173
philosophy 20, 43–4, 54, 59–63, 65–8, 70,
    79, 128, 131, 153, 160, 162–4, 166,
    171, 194
Piaget, J. 7, 199
Pinar, W. 19, 21, 47, 65, 85–6, 106, 187, 199

Pinar's autobiographical theory 104,
    106–7, 169
PNCCC (Proceedings of the National
    Conference of Charities and
    Correction) 39, 41, 196–7
policies 3, 5, 14, 16, 24, 29, 34, 47, 51–2, 55,
    80, 82, 107, 156, 160–1
politics of difference 88, 159
politics of identity 85–6, 89–90, 127, 160
portrait 134–5, 139–40, 142–3, 145–6,
    148–9, 151
possibility vii, x, 7, 23, 28–9, 33–4, 41–2, 47,
    62, 64, 68–9, 71, 135–6, 165–6, 172–3
poststructuralism 59, 64, 70, 90–1, 103,
    127, 198
power 38, 43, 48, 50–1, 53–4, 59–64,
    66–70, 72–3, 76, 100–1, 119–21, 127,
    137–8, 143, 164–5
practices 18–20, 22–5, 28–9, 33–6, 42–8,
    55–6, 61–3, 65–7, 81–2, 96, 102,
    127–8, 156, 159–62, 169–73
prisons vii–x, 4, 8, 27, 30, 36, 46, 61, 67,
    128, 141, 146, 165, 178, 198–9
privilege 20, 23–4, 30, 38, 44, 61, 64, 86,
    88, 93, 100, 115, 121, 153, 172
problem 31, 36, 38, 46, 48–9, 118, 135, 168,
    171, 178, 185, 189, 197
project, writing 104–5, 108, 111, 117, 122,
    130–2, 142, 144, 186, 191
psychoanalysis 64, 193, 195, 197

qualitative inquiry 195–7, 199–200
qualitative methodology v, 24, 81, 83, 85,
    87, 89, 91, 93, 95, 97, 99, 101
qualitative research methodology 80, 82,
    91, 97, 101

race xi, 59, 65, 85, 90–1, 93–5, 100–1, 134,
    157–9, 191, 198–9
rationality 7, 9, 19–21, 42, 44, 56–9, 68, 72,
    113, 156, 166
reclaiming education i, 2, 22, 25–6, 103,
    106–7, 125, 161
reform, educational 8, 66
reformers, educational 25, 155–6, 159, 174
rehabilitation 7–8, 15, 17, 19–22, 33–4,
    44–5, 47–51, 53, 55, 73–4, 80, 103–4,
    120, 156–8, 168–70